The Historical Roots of Corruption

Why does corruption persist over long periods of time? Why is it so difficult to eliminate? Suggesting that corruption is deeply rooted in the underlying social and historical political structures of a country, Eric M. Uslaner observes that there is a powerful statistical relationship between levels of mass education in 1870 and corruption levels in 2010 across 78 countries. He argues that an early introduction of universal education is shown to be linked to levels of economic equality and to efforts to increase state capacity. Societies with more equal education gave citizens more opportunities and power for opposing corruption, whilst the need for increased state capacity was a strong motivation for the introduction of universal education in many countries. Evidence for this argument is presented from statistical models; case studies from Northern and Southern Europe, Asia, Africa, Latin America, the United States, Canada, Australia, and New Zealand; as well as a discussions of how some countries escaped the "trap" of corruption.

ERIC M. USLANER is Professor of Government and Politics at the University of Maryland, College Park. He is the author of nine books, including *The Moral Foundations of Trust* (2002); *Corruption, Inequality, and the Rule of Law* (2010); *Segregation and Mistrust* (2012); and the editor of *The Oxford Handbook of Social and Political Trust* (2018).

T0372706

The Historical Roots of Corruption

Mass Education, Economic Inequality, and State Capacity

ERIC M. USLANER
University of Maryland, College Park

CAMBRIDGE
UNIVERSITY PRESS

University Printing House, Cambridge CB2 8BS, United Kingdom

One Liberty Plaza, 20th Floor, New York, NY 10006, USA

477 Williamstown Road, Port Melbourne, VIC 3207, Australia

4843/24, 2nd Floor, Ansari Road, Daryaganj, Delhi - 110002, India

79 Anson Road, #06-04/06, Singapore 079906

Cambridge University Press is part of the University of Cambridge.

It furthers the University's mission by disseminating knowledge in the pursuit of education, learning and research at the highest international levels of excellence.

www.cambridge.org
Information on this title: www.cambridge.org/9781108416481
DOI: 10.1017/9781108241281

© Eric M. Uslaner 2017

First published 2017

Printed in the United Kingdom by Clays, St Ives plc

A catalogue record for this publication is available from the British Library

ISBN 978-1-108-41648-1 Hardback
ISBN 978-1-108-40390-0 Paperback

Contents

Figures

Tables

Preface

This project stemmed from ideas I developed in my 2008 book, *Corruption, Inequality, and the Rule of Law* (Cambridge University Press). I formulated the idea of an "inequality trap" (see Chapter 1 here) to explain why institutional reforms do not "cure" corruption, but public policies that lead to universal social welfare programs do, an idea that my colleague and friend Bo Rothstein had developed. We developed this argument in a 2005 article for *World Politics* ("All for All: Equality, Corruption, and Social Trust"). The universal social welfare program that we believe is most important and that I discuss in my 2008 book is mass education. Education frees ordinary people form depending upon corrupt leaders and instills in them feelings of civic pride and national unity – all of which lead to less corruption.

All I had in my 2008 book were some anecdotes about the impact of education in the United States. So the link between education and corruption remained hypothetical. In 2011 I came upon a paper through the Social Science Research Network by Christian Morrison and Fabrice Murtin, "A Century of Education" (originally written in 2008) with estimates of primary, secondary, and tertiary education across what are now 78 countries. There was a link to their data set, now expanded to include estimates from 1870 to 2010. I first plotted the 1870 school enrollment data (the earliest year) to levels of corruption in 2010 from Transparency International. The result was an $R^2 = .699$, and using more recent education data did not improve the fit.

The questions that gripped me were: How do we account for the effect of education on corruption 140 years later? And why does this effect persist over time? I sent the initial graph (see Figures 2.2–2.4 in Chapter 2) to Bo Rothstein with the puzzle of why this persists over time. He responded that the answer lay within the development of a strong state that could compete with other institutions (notably religious). So we set out to work together on this book and the explanation involved state power but quickly included economic inequality (which had been the subject of our earlier work). We developed the framework together and in 2012 published an article in *Comparative Politics*. Since then Rothstein departed from Göteborg, Sweden to take on a position at the University of Oxford – and that has occupied him fully. So he withdrew from this joint project, other than reading it and giving me suggestions, but leaving the bulk of the work to me. There are sections of Chapters 1, 3, and 6 that are his work, but I have redone most of them to fit my larger argument. He will agree with most of my argument, but not all of it so his culpability is limited.

So apart from my wife, who had to tolerate my moods when things were not always going smoothly and the long hours it takes to write a book, my greatest debt is to Bo. That said, others were of great help. Ewout Frankema, Claudia Goldin, Phil Keeefer, and Frederick Solt (in alphabetical order) helped by providing data. We received useful comments (also listed alphabetically) from Isabella Alcaniz, Christian Bjørnskov, Ernesto Calvo, Peter Thisted Dinesen, Sergio Espuelas, Jacob Gerner Hariri, Ira Katznelson, Phil Keefer, Robert Klitgaard, Alex Lascaux, John McCauley, Fabrice Murtin, J Katarina Ott, Aleksandar Stulhofer, Jong-sung You, Christian Welzel, Bob Woodberry, and especially David Sartorius (who taught me much of what I know about education in Latin America).

I am grateful to Sofia Jansson for excellent assistance on the section on religion and education for Bo Rothstein and David Sartorius for very helpful comments on early education in Latin America. I also thank Isabella Alcaniz, Christian Bjørnskov, Ernesto Calvo, Michelle D'Arcy, Peter Thisted Dinesen, Robert Klitgaard, Alex Lascaux, John McCauley, Jacob Garner Haririri, Alina Mungiu-Pippidi, Fabrice Murtin, Katarina Ott, and Aleksandar Stulhofer, Christian Welzel, and Jong-sung You for helpful comments. Several University of Maryland undergraduates gave of themselves with help in understanding early education policies across the world: Samantha Ammons, Marianela L. Boso, Carolina Corbett, Shreya Khadke, and especially YiJie Tan.

I also benefited greatly from audiences at universities where I presented this work. They include (those marked by an asterisk were keynote speeches):

- Fifth Laboratory for Comparative Social Research Workshop, "Social and Cultural Changes in Cross-national Perspective:

Subjective Well-being, Trust, Social capital and Values," Higher School of Economics, Moscow, April 6–10, 2015.

- Conference on Education and Global Cities; Horizons for Contemporary University, Higher School of Economics, St. Petersburg, Russia, May 21, 2016.
- Hans Dieter Klingemann Lecture, University of Lueneberg, Germany, June 13, 2016.
- Summer Academy on "Path Dependencies in Economic and Social Development," Institute for East and Southeast European Studies, Akademie für Politische Bildung, June 15, 2006.
- Martin Paldam Workshop, Aarhus University (Denmark), September 25, 2012.
- Department of Economics, Ben Gurion University of the Negev, Beersheva, Israel, January 10, 2013.
- Instituto Tecnologico Autonomo de Mexico, Mexico City, February 19, 2015.
- Seinan University, Fukukoa, Japan, March 19, 2015.
- American Political Science Association Annual Meeting, San Francisco, August 31–September 3, 2016.
- School of Business, Department of Economics and Finance, Queensland Institute of Technology, Brisbane, Australia, July 14, 2016.
- Conference on Understanding Governance Virtuous Circles: Who Succeeded and Why, European Research Centre for Anti-Corruption and State Building, Berlin, Germany, July 8–12, 2015.
- Department of Political Science and Government, Aarhus University (Denmark), October 5, 2015.
- Department of Political Science, University of Copenhagen, October 7, 2015.
- International Congress on Applied Sciences Social Capital ICAS 2015, Konya University, Turkey, October 23–24, 2015 (Member of Scientific Committee for the Conference).

I am particularly grateful to Benno Torgler of the Queensland University of Technology; Christian Welzel, Alina Mungiu-Pippidi of the Hertie School of Government, Berlin; Eduard Ponarin of the Laboratory of Comparative Social Research at the Higher School of Economics, Moscow; Kim Mannemar Sonderskov of Aarhus University; and Peter Thisted Dinesen of the University of Copenhagen for arranging trips to Australia, Germany, Russia, and Denmark to present my work.

I have received strong support over the years from the Department of Government and Politics at the University of Maryland, College Park and especially from my department chairs, Mark Lichbach and Irwin Morris. John Haslam has been greatly supportive as editor at Cambridge University Press.

But the real support lies at home, where I am fortunate to have a son who is sometimes cynical, but always very bright and very humorous. After four years of a very demanding academic regimen at Colorado College, Avery better appreciates academic arguments and makes some strong ones himself. And I am more than fortunate to have in my life Debbie, my loving wife. She never doubted me or the worth of this project because she is a superb exemplar of why honesty in public and private life is so critical.

1 | *The Theoretical Framework*

Corruption is widespread in Greece. The widely recognized malfeasance is objectionable not just because it flaunts norms of honesty, but because it exacerbates inequality. As the American journalists Donadio and Alderman (2012) write:

Greece's economic troubles are often attributed to a public sector packed full of redundant workers, a lavish pension system and uncompetitive industries hampered by overpaid workers with lifetime employment guarantees. Often overlooked, however, is the role played by a handful of wealthy families, politicians and the news media – often owned by the magnates – that make up the Greek power structure. In a country crushed by years of austerity and 25 percent unemployment, average Greeks are growing increasingly resentful of an oligarchy that, critics say, presides over an opaque, closed economy that is at the root of many of the country's problems and operates with virtual impunity. Several dozen powerful families control critical sectors, including banking, shipping and construction, and can usually count on the political class to look out for their interests, sometimes by passing legislation tailored to their specific needs. The result, analysts say, is a lack of competition that undermines the economy by allowing the magnates to run cartels and enrich themselves through crony capitalism.

Corruption and its roots in inequality are not a new concern in Greece. Aristotle (1962, Book III, 1279a, 114; Book V, 1308b, 228) worried about this linkage in 350 BCE, 2,400 years earlier:

... when the One, or the Few, or the Many, rule with a view to the common interest, the constitutions under which they do so must necessarily be right constitutions. On the other hand the constitutions directed to the personal interest of the One, or the Few, or the Masses, must necessarily be perversions ... The masses are not so greatly offended at being excluded from office ... what really annoys them is to think that those who have the enjoyment of office are embezzling public funds.

1

Corruption persists over long periods of time (though not necessarily two dozen centuries). Corruption is not easy to eliminate. Systemic corruption is deeply rooted in the underlying social and historical political structure.

A country's history shapes the conditions for honesty in government: economic equality and a state that is strong enough to provide services to its citizens.[1] The most important service a state can provide is education. *Countries with higher levels of education in the past have less corruption today.*

Why education? Education promotes economic equality. The linkage between equality and lower levels of corruption is well established (cf. Uslaner, 2008; You, 2015; see below). And education promotes the civic values that underlie "good government" – or honesty in government. Education provides the foundation for ordinary people to take part in their governments – and to take power away from corrupt leaders.

Education empowers people to make their own way in the world without having to rely upon clientelistic leaders for their livelihood. When people depend upon "patrons" for their well-being, their welfare, even their sustenance, is tied to their loyalty. They may "tolerate" corruption by these leaders, either because these "big men" defend them against others who might exploit them even more or because ordinary people do not have alternative sources of income. The patron–client relationship is founded on inequality.

Education also promotes loyalty to the state rather than to local (or tribal) leaders. When governments provide services such as education, people will associate benefits with the state and will be more likely to have a broad identity with their fellow citizens (Darden, 2013; Peterson, 2016; Uslaner, 2002, 208). This broader identity is the foundation of generalized trust – trust in people we don't know who may not be like us. Higher levels of trust are strongly linked to lower corruption (Uslaner, 2008, chs. 2, 3). A common identity, like trust, is only possible where there is greater equality (Uslaner, 2002, chs. 2, 4, 6, 7). The strong aggregate relationship between trust and mean school years in 1870 ($r^2 = .462$) suggests that education is part of the "inequality trap," perhaps even a surrogate measure for trust.

I am not alone in arguing that education is critical for good governance. Aristotle argued: "All who have meditated on the art of governing mankind have been convinced that the fate of empires depends on the education of youth"[2] and (Aristotle, 1962, V, 1309b, 233):

The greatest...of all the means...for ensuring the stability of constitutions...is the education of citizens in the spirit of the constitution. There is no profit in the best of laws, even when they are sanctioned by general civic consent, if the citizens themselves have not been attuned, by the force of habit and the influence of teaching, to the right constitutional temper...

The larger story is that the effects of education levels in the past have effects that persist over time. "Path dependence" is the argument that the present – and the future – look a lot like the past (North, 1990). Once a country's trajectory is set, it is difficult to change. Countries with high levels of education in 1870 (when the available data begin) have the highest levels 140 years later.

Education leads to greater equality but it is the most equal societies that are most likely to provide universal education. Governments are most likely to provide education where there is public demand – where resources are more equal – and where the state has sufficient resources and power to provide widespread public education. These conditions were found mostly in Protestant Western European countries – and in some former colonies with large European populations. In colonies where most of the population was indigenous, the colonial powers provided few benefits such as education. This was also the case in other less developed countries with high levels of inequality, where education was provided largely by religious authorities or by local elites – and also in Catholic countries, where the church feared that educated people might challenge its authority.

Countries with high levels of education in the late nineteenth century – where there are the first cross-national measurements – not only were more equal then, but continued to have more equitable distributions of wealth a century and a half later. They also had less corruption and this "virtuous" cycle persists over long periods of time.

I first show (Chapter 2) that the mean number of years of schooling in 1870 is strongly related to the level of corruption across 78 countries in 2010. Historical levels of education remain tightly connected to contemporary corruption even controlling for current levels of education and historical income levels.

Where inequality was high – and especially where colonial powers exploited the local population and did not live among them – unequal distributions of wealth persist over long periods of time. And this was fertile ground for dishonest governance well years later. Providing education is a policy choice – and "bad" decisions on social welfare can be reversed. They are easier to change than political institution or a country's biological or technological legacy. Policies may not change readily, but they are not set in stone.

I do not try to resolve the debate as to what corruption means. There are many definitions of corruption, from Mungiu-Pippidi's (2006) "ethical universalism" to Rothstein's (2011) "impartiality" in the exercise of public power (Rothstein 2011). No single definition can cover what everyone means by corruption – and what constitutes corruption is often disputed. Are campaign contributions "corruption"? And where does one draw the line between private and public corruption? It is more straightforward to compare relative levels of corruption among countries than to engage in definitional disputes as to what corruption "means." The measure I use for corruption, the Transparency International Corruption Perceptions Index, has considerable face validity – the countries ranking as honest or dishonest on this index reflect what most people would see as honest/dishonest in governance. While some have criticized this measure, other researchers have responded with a spirited defense of related measures (Kaufmann, Kraay, and Mastruzzi, 2007).

A Cure for Corruption?

Much of the literature on malfeasance in public life is focused on ways to reduce corruption in the short term. Some of this literature comes from anti-corruption agencies such as Transparency International or the Mo Ibrahmin Foundation or from economic institutions such as the World Bank or the European Bank for Reconstruction and Development.[3] Banks make loans and want to get repaid. Anti-corruption agencies and other research organizations also have stakes in immediate results, since their *raison d'être* is to reduce misbehavior in public life. Pessimism is not a message that will lead financial institutions to invest even more funds in borrowers who may not repay their debts. Nor will research shops or other non-governmental organizations find it easy to stay in business without remedies.

Academics gain visibility by promoting ready solutions: Michael Johnston (2015, ch. 3) suggests that incremental reforms – notably by improving benchmarks for performance and enhancing the delivery of basic services – are small steps to "make haste slowly." "Visible improvement in the effectiveness and fairness of just one or two of these key services can drive a process of institution-and-trust building" (Johnston, 2015, 64). Olken and Pande (2012) review a range of short-term fixes including audits of government programs, greater transparency of government procedures, and more competition among bureaucrats for the provision of services.

Yet "corruption has outlived all predictions of its demise. Indeed, it appears to be thriving" (Keefe, 2015). While some countries seem to have been able to carry out substantial reductions of corruption, perceived levels of corruption remain high throughout much of the world. In the 2010 Corruption Perceptions Index from Transparency International (TI), measuring elites' evaluations of the honesty (or dishonesty) of political and economic institutions in their countries, 131 of the 178 nations fell below the midpoint on the 10 points of the index, with higher scores representing low corruption. Only 23 nations had scores (7 or higher) indicating that their governments are basically honest. In the Global Corruption Barometer for 2013, public opinion surveys in 107 countries conducted by TI, a majority did not see corruption as a major problem in only one country (Denmark).

While Olken and Pande (2012) find that some interventions led to short-term declines in corruption, the longer-term effects of such reforms are often illusory: " . . . corrupt officials are resilient: over time, they adapt to changes in their environments, in some cases offsetting anti-corruption policies with new avenues for seeking out rents." Johnston (2015, 60–61, italics in original) admits, "Where trust is weak, anti-corruption efforts are likely to have little credibility at the outset, and may appear to be – indeed may *be* – just another way for a political faction to gain or keep the upper hand." So the most prominent proposals for reducing corruption – harsh penalties for officials who are "on the take," the establishment of anti-corruption commissions, and public campaigns against corruption – are all likely to have minimal effects.

I am pessimistic about finding "quick fixes" to the problem of corruption. Corruption persists over time. Its roots lie in a nation's history. My argument is in line with a growing body of historical institutionalism arguing that conditions ranging from institutions to natural resources can have long-term effects on economic prosperity as well as governance. The legacy of the past has strong effects on the present, according to this framework. It is difficult for countries to change, but it is not impossible. When countries do fight corruption – successfully, they almost always combine this campaign with a program of economic reform. And such reforms put education policy at their center. Large-scale economic reform and the development of universal education is a much more demanding task than the structural reforms that anti-corruption agencies and some scholars propose.

The Roots of Corruption

My account follows an argument that I made in an earlier book. There I argue (Uslaner, 2008, ch. 2) that corruption is part of an "inequality trap," where inequality, mistrust, and corruption are mutually reinforcing. My model is:

inequality— > low trust— > corruption— > more inequality

The poor become trapped as clients to their patrons in corrupt societies. The well-off "redistribute" society's resources to themselves and entrench themselves in power by controlling all of society's institutions (Glaeser, Scheinkman, and Shleifer, 2003, 200–201). The poor who depend upon powerful leaders for their livelihood – and for justice – have almost no opportunity to challenge the balance of power (Scott, 1972, 149). Corruption stems from inequality and reinforces it.

Glaeser, Scheinkman, and Schleifer (2003, 200; see also You, 2005, 45–46) argue:

... inequality is detrimental to the security of property rights, and therefore to growth, because it enables the rich to subvert the political, regulatory, and legal institutions of society for their own benefit. If one person is sufficiently richer than another, and courts are corruptible, then the legal system will favor the rich, not the just. Likewise, if political and regulatory institutions can be moved by wealth or influence, they will favor the established, not the efficient. This in turn leads the initially well situated to pursue socially harmful acts, recognizing that the legal, political, and regulatory systems will not hold them accountable. Inequality can encourage institutional subversion in two distinct ways. First, the havenots can redistribute from the haves through violence, the political process, or other means. Such Robin Hood redistribution jeopardizes property rights, and deters investment by the rich.

Similarly, You and Kaghram (2005, 138) argue: "The rich, as interest groups, firms, or individuals may use bribery or connections to influence law-implementing processes (*bureaucratic corruption*) and to buy favorable interpretations of the law (*judicial corruption*)."

Inequality breeds corruption by: (1) leading ordinary citizens to see the system as stacked against them (Uslaner, 2002, 181–183); (2) creating a sense of dependency of ordinary citizens and a sense of pessimism for the future, which in turn undermines the moral dictates of treating your neighbors honestly; and (3) distorting the key institutions of fairness in society, the courts, which ordinary citizens see as their protectors against evildoers, especially those with more influence than they have (see also Glaeser, Scheinkman, and Schleifer, 2003; and You and Khagram, 2005).

Corruption and inequality wreak havoc with our moral sense. Della Porta and Vannucci (1999, 146) argue that pervasive corruption makes people less willing to condemn it as immoral. As corruption becomes widespread, it becomes deeply entrenched in a society (Mauro, 2002, 16). In an unequal world, people of the dominant group may not see cheating those with fewer resources as immoral (Gambetta, 1993; Mauro, 1998, 12; Scott, 1972, 12) and about evading taxes (Mauro, 2002, 343; Oswiak, 2003, 73; Uslaner, 2006). People at the bottom of the economic ladder will have little choice but to play the same game even as they may resent the advantages of the well-off (Gambetta, 2002, 55).

Corruption leads to lower levels of generalized trust – the belief that "most people can be trusted." This linkage is strong – but it holds only for "grand corruption," malfeasance that involves large stakes and high-level officeholders. Grand corruption leads to less trust in others (notably to people who are different from yourself) because it leads to inequality. And inequality is the strongest determinant of trust – across countries without a legacy of Communism, over time in the United States, and across the American states (Uslaner, 2002, chs. 6, 7; Uslaner and Brown, 2005). Petty corruption – small payments to bureaucrats, police officers, doctors – for routine services do not lead to a loss of trust in others. These small payments do not enrich anyone and hence do not destroy the social fabric.

Inequality leads to more corruption (either directly or indirectly through trust – and education). But corruption also results in more inequality. The three components of the inequality trap are all *sticky* – they do not change much over time. The r^2 between the 2004 Transparency International estimates of corruption and the historical estimates for 1980–1985 across 52 countries is .742. Using the V-DEM estimates of corruption (Coppedge *et al.*, 2015), the r^2 for this measure in 1900 and the TI index in 2010 is .704 for non-colonies (see Chapter 6). For 2010, the r^2 is .740 for 39 countries in both data sets. Just as corruption is "sticky," inequality and trust do not change much over time, either. The r^2 for the most commonly used measures of economic inequality (Deininger and Squire, 1996) between 1980 and 1990 is substantial at .676 for a sample of 42 countries. A newer measure of inequality (Solt, 2009) also shows substantial continuity: The r^2 for net inequality in 1981 and 2008 is .582 for 34 countries.

The r^2 between generalized trust, as measured in the 1981, 1990–1995 World Values Surveys across between 1980 and the 1990s is .81 for the 22 nations included in both waves – the r^2 between generalized trust in 1990 and 1995 is also robust (.851, N = 28). The stickiness of corruption, inequality, and trust are the heart of the inequality trap. *Inequality, low trust, and corruption are all sticky because they form a vicious cycle.* Each persists over time and it is difficult to break the chain.

In addition to the "inequality trap" there may also exist a parallel problem that can be called the "corruption trap." Countries that start out with a high level of corruption will not be able to raise taxes for launching social and educations programs for alleviating poverty because corruption results in a high level of distrust in the ability of the state to: (a) collect taxes in a fair and efficient manner; and (b) implement the programs in a competent and fair manner. Even people with a preference for more economic equality will refrain from supporting higher levels of public spending (and higher taxes) if they perceive that corruption is high and competence low in the public administration that is supposed to implement the reforms (Svallfors 2013; Rothstein, Samanni and Teorell 2012). People distrust a state with high levels of corruption because it is not able to deliver services and so they will not support higher taxes. Yet the government cannot deliver better services and increase the competence of the civil service until it has more economic resources. The mutual distrust between citizens and the state that is the effect of systemic corruption creates an effective "social trap" (Rothstein 2005)

Rothstein and Uslaner (2005, 43) argued that universal social welfare programs are the key to building both trust and better governance. Universal programs provide benefits to people regardless of their economic (or social) circumstances. While "means-tested programs exacerbate class and often racial divisions within a society – and thus lead to less generalized trust and more in-group trust. By contrast, universalistic programs enhance social solidarity and the perception of a shared fate among citizens. Education opens up opportunities for greater equality.

In American big cities in the early twentieth century, political bosses provided immigrants with the needs of daily life: jobs, loans, rent money, contributions of food or fuel to tide them over . . . " (Cornwell, 1964, 30). Free public education liberated their children from submission to political bosses. Especially the free education at the City University of New York created a new professional class who did not need the "benefits" of the political regime – and founded a reform movement to fight the bosses and establish clean government (Uslaner, 2008, 236–241). Education became a major tool in the fight against corruption in the United States. It also was a key element in the development of universal social welfare programs in the Nordic countries, where it has been a central focus of programs designed to promote equality (Knudsen, 1995).

Education also has a more direct payoff. Countries with higher levels of education fare better in long-term economic growth (Glaeser *et al.*, 2004; Gylfason and Zoega, 2003) and to more wealth (Glaeser, Scheinkman, and Shleifer, 2003). Gylfason and Zoega (2002, 24) report that a 1 percent increase in public expenditure on education reduces the Gini index by 2.3 points across 74 countries from 1980 to 1997.

The Industrial Revolution took hold in nations that had the greatest levels of increase in book production – and this led to faster growth (Baten and van Zanden, 2008, 232–233; Easterlin, 1981, 14; Glaeser *et al.*, 2004, 285; Goldin and Katz, 1999, 699). Mass education developed as institutions for economic opportunity for the mass public. In the United States, local governments sought to fulfill the demands of the manufacturing sector for managers with training in "accounting, typing, shorthand, and algebra" and blue collar workers "trained in mathematics, chemistry, and electricity" (Galor, Moav, and Vollrath, 2009, 165).

The mean education level across countries has increased markedly (by sixfold) from 1870 to 2010. Yet the past has a heavy hand: The countries with the highest levels of education at the start of the series were also those at the top 140 years later ($r^2 = .576$). And those countries that departed most from this linear relationship were the countries with the highest levels of education in 1870. While education may be the way to break out of the "inequality trap," the high correlation over time between levels of education across countries indicates that it is not easy to break out of the trap. Mean school year attainment, I shall argue, is strongly related to economic inequality in the late nineteenth century. The 1870 educational attainment measure is just as strongly related to contemporary post-redistribution inequality.[4]

Corruption and Education

Darden (2013) and Uslaner (2002) argue that universal education creates strong social bonds among different groups in a society. In turn, this makes cleavages based upon clientelism and corruption less likely. The introduction of free universal education should lead to a "virtuous cycle" of widespread education and increased socio-economic equality. High levels of inequality enable the elite to undermine the legal and political institutions and use them for their own benefit. If inequality is high, the economic elite is likely to pursue socially harmful policies, since the legal, political, and regulatory systems will not hold them accountable (Dutta and Mishra, 2013; Glaeser *et al.*, 2004, 200; You, 2008).

Access to education provided more people with the skills to find gainful employment so they did not have to rely on corrupt, or clientelistic, structures of power (Goldin and Katz, 2008, 29, 133; Uslaner, 2008, 239–241). Over time, the educational inequalities between the rich and the poor in countries that established universal education were sharply reduced, though not eliminated (Morrison and Murtin, 2010). Literacy had direct economic payoffs. Countries with higher levels of book production in the early nineteenth century were more likely to industrialize and to have greater levels of economic growth by the twentieth century (Baten and van Zanden, 2008, 233).

More widespread education was critical for increasing gender equality. Nineteenth century school enrollments were highest where girls had access to education, notably the United States and lowest when girls were excluded (Goldin and Katz, 2008, 21, 133; Benavot and Riddle, 1988, 201). Gender equality is strongly related to lower levels of corruption (Wängnerud 2012, Grimes and Wängnerud 2010).

Some have argued that a free press with a broad circulation is important for curbing corruption (Adserà, Boix, and Payne, 2003; Brunetti and Weder, 2003). The effectiveness of a vigilant press for curbing corruption depends on widespread literacy. If most people cannot read, there will be fewer newspapers sold and the popular knowledge about corruption and the demand for accountability and "clean government" will be lower.

The framework I employ derives from my work with Rothstein: Reforms such as free universal education is an important *signal* from the state to its citizens, sending a message that the state serves more than the particularistic interests of the economic and political elite. The introduction of free universal education implies that the state is also an operation built on universal principles promoting a "common good." Mungiu-Pippidi (2006) conceptualize such policies as a change from corrupt particularism to ethical universalism – what North *et al.* (2009) call the transition of the state from a "limited access order" to an "open access order." However, the frameworks of Mungiu-Pippi and North *et al.* lack an operational device that explains what type of institutional change will a society on the path away to universalism/open access order. The introduction of universal education can serve as such a device.

Alternative Explanations for Corruption

The major alternative explanations I consider are historical institutionalism and factor endowments. Adherents to historical institutionalism and factor endowments don't focus on governance (or corruption). Instead their argument is that the past shapes the level of economic development centuries later.

Spolaore and Wacziarg (2013, 1, 31) summarize the case for historical institutionalism:

The fortunes of nations are notoriously persistent through time, and much of the variation in economic performance is rooted in deep history . . . the past history of populations is a much stronger predictor of current economic outcomes than the past history of given geographical locations . . . Europeans who settled in the New World brought with them the whole panoply of vertically transmitted traits – institutions, human capital, norms, values, preferences. This vector of vertical traits was by definition easier to transmit to the descendents of Europeans than it was to convey to colonized populations . . .

Good institutions in the past lead to stronger economic performance in the future.

Acemoglu and Robinson are the most prominent exponents of historical institutionalism. They argue (2012, 43):

. . . while economic institutions are critical for determining whether a country is poor or prosperous, it is politics and political institutions that determine what economic institutions a country has. Ultimately the good economic institutions of the United States resulted from the political institutions that gradually emerged after 1619.

Democratic institutions, Acemoglu and Robinson argue, provided countries with greater political equality. And this equality led to political and social stability that led countries, especially former colonies, to have stronger economic growth and stability. Democratic institutions were much more likely to occur in countries with a legacy of British colonialism rather than Spanish rule (Acemoglu and Robinson, 2012, 18–19, 27).

Democratic institutions and property rights protections derived from their British colonial power account for the contemporary prosperity of the United States, Australia, and New Zealand. The extractive states in Africa and in other colonies transferred resources to the "metropole" (where colonial authorities lived and exported them). Such arrangements "were detrimental to investment and economic progress" (Acemoglu, Johnson, and Robinson, 2001, 1395). Treisman (2007) and You and Khagram (2005) have argued that *contemporaneous* democracy leads to less corruption, although Rothstein (2011, 105) and Uslaner (2008, ch. 2) find less support for this argument.

A different, and more compelling argument, is that the nature of the party system can shape government performance. Cruz and Keefer (2010, 9) distinguish between clientelistic (or particularistic) and programmatic political parties – a distinction made earlier about American parties by Fenton (1966) and Mayhew (1986). Programmatic parties focus on issues and "a public administration that is less permeable to ad hoc deviations from public policies," rather than providing particularistic benefits to people. They argue that parties emphasizing "broad-based benefits" can be held accountable by voters – and that they will lead to better overall institutional performance (Cruz and Keefer, 2010, 9, 11). Fenton's distinction is between job-oriented (particularistic) and issue-oriented parties, while Mayhew establishes a scale of "traditional party organizations" in the American states. Strong parties focus on patronage and are most likely to occur in states with high levels of corruption (Uslaner, 2008, 227–228).

One might expect that programmatic parties would lead to lower levels of corruption. I caution that this distinction is not strictly institutional. Particularistic or programmatic parties can exist in any institutional setting – and Mayhew's "traditional" parties share the same institutional structure across the American states as do his weak parties. The programmatic–particularistic distinction is more about the *quality* of institutions rather than simple institutional design. The provision of basic services impartially is the foundation of Rothstein's (2011, 12–17) concept of high-quality institutions. So I expect that programmatic parties would be associated with lower levels of corruption. I find support for this across the American states, but not cross-nationally.

What distinguishes my account from the other historical accounts is agency. The decision of a state to invest in public education for its citizens is a political act, whether it occurs by government actors making that choice in independent governing bodies in the nineteenth century or colonial powers deciding whether to fund schools at all for the indigenous populations. State funding of education reflects both responses to demands from the governed *and* the capacity of the state to enact programs that provide for the public good. In Europe, from the sixteenth to nineteenth century, education was largely the province of churches and other private agencies. Relatively few young people were educated and the Parliament actually blocked local governments from raising revenue to fund schools. Education was to remain the province of a small elite. Only one European country enacted universal public education in the early nineteenth century: Prussia (Lindert, 2004, vol. 1, 19, 102, 113–119). The Scandinavian countries were early adopters of universal education in the second half of the nineteenth century. Outside of Europe, the leader in universal education was the United States.

A second account in historical institutionalism is Comin *et al.*'s (2012) argument that ancient technology led to greater prosperity in

2002. They construct measures of technology as far back as 1000 BC as well as 0 AD and 1500 AD for military, industrial, agricultural, transportation, and communication technologies, as well as a composite measure they call "sectoral" technology. They find no effect of technologies in 1000 BC or 0 AD on current levels of income, but significant effects for technology adoption in 1500 AD. Early adoption of technology is a strong predictor of both current levels of scientific development and on prosperity. Their account is at least partially consistent with mine. The measure of communication technology in 1500 AD includes using movable block printing, woodblock printing, and the use of both books and paper. These are clearly measures of literacy and should be related to later levels of schooling. Military technology is measured by having a standing army, warfare capable ships, and artilleries involving teams of soldiers (among other factors) – which required coordination and a knowledge base. So early technology should have effects on education, if not corruption, almost four centuries later. In Chapter 2 I find that none of their measures affects contemporary corruption. There are moderately high correlations between military and sectoral technology in 1500 AD and especially communication technology in 1500 AD (which is closest to literacy) on mean school years in 1870.

What distinguishes my account from the other historical accounts is agency. The decision of a state to invest in public education for its citizens is a political act, whether it occurs by government actors making that choice in independent governing bodies in the nineteenth century or colonial powers deciding whether to fund schools at all for the indigenous populations. State funding of education reflects both responses to demands from the governed *and* the capacity of the state to enact programs that provide for the public good.

In Europe, from the sixteenth to the nineteenth century, education was largely the province of churches and other private agencies. Relatively few young people were educated and the Parliament actually blocked local governments from raising revenue to fund schools. Education was to remain the province of a small elite. Only one European country enacted universal public education in the early nineteenth century: Prussia (Lindert, 2004, vol. 1, 19, 102, 113–119). The Scandinavian countries were early adopters of universal education in the second half of the nineteenth century.

Outside of Europe, the leader in universal education was the United States. The level of school attendance in the United States, as across nations, varied by how equal farm ownership was – and by the share of slaves in a state's population, two measures of inequality (Chapter 5). Where education was far from universal – in Africa – the *increase* in mean school years from 1870 (under colonial rule) to 2010 (under independence) reflected earlier levels of slave exports to the West, what I view as a long-term indicator of inequality (Chapter 4).

The logic behind factor endowments is deterministic. In countries with temperate climates, farmers grew crops such as wheat and corn and had domesticated farm animals – on arable land (McCord and Sachs, 2013, 19). Crops such as wheat and corn (maize) could be grown by family farmers and wealth would be widely distributed. In turn, this led to greater social and economic equality. Countries with tropical climates were more suitable to crops such as tobacco and cotton, which could not be grown on small independent farms. Tobacco and cotton were grown on plantations and harvested by slaves or (especially in Latin America) by indigenous peoples (Frankema, 2010, 420; Hibbs and Olsson, 2004). In "sugar colonies" such as Barbados, Cuba, and Brazil – countries with more tropical climates – " . . . economies came to be dominated by large slave plantations and their populations by slaves of African descent. Plantations were part of a highly unequal economy. So were the copper mines in tropical areas, where miners were largely indigenous and indentured, leading to high levels of inequality (Engerman and Sokoloff, 2002, 12–13; Frankema, 2010, 420).

Areas with temperate climates developed more equal and productive economies. The world was divided into the wealthy countries with moderate temperatures and independent farmers and poor countries where a small number of plantation and mine owners ruled over native populations (Angeles, 2007, 1173). Where malaria was prevalent, it led to lower GDP per capita and lower foreign investment (Carstensen and Gundlach, 2006, 314–316). Sachs and Malaney (2002, 681) argue that "malaria and poverty are intimately related" and that average growth rates in countries with high malaria rates are six times lower than in other countries. A country's "factor endowments" determined its economic future. Easterly and Levine (2012, 14, 20) argue that high rates of malaria led to lower levels of European settlement, which in turn was associated with lower levels of current income across nations.

Engerman and Sokoloff (n.d., 6, 13) argue: " . . . economies came to be dominated by large slave plantations and their populations by slaves of African descent. The overwhelming fraction of the

populations that came to be black and slave in such colonies, as well
as the greater efficiency of the very large plantations, made their distributions of wealth and human capital extremely unequal. Even among
the free population, such economies exhibited greater inequality than
those on the North American mainland ... heterogeneity made it more
difficult for communities to reach consensus on public projects. Where
the wealthy enjoyed disproportionate political power, they were able
to procure schooling services for their own children and to resist being
taxed to underwrite or subsidize services to others. Although the children of the elite may have been well schooled in such polities, few were
so fortunate. No society realized high levels of literacy without public
schools."

Temperate climates also had more domestic plants and animals.
But this led to the spread of diseases such as measles, tuberculosis,
influenza, and smallpox. Many settlers died but eventually they developed resistance – but the native populations didn't and were decimated
in many places. Where European settlers constituted larger shares of
the population, they prospered and the distribution of incomes was
more equal (Engerman and Sokoloff, 2002, 8, 9; Nunn, 2009, 87;
Welzel, 2013, 123–124).

Olsson and Hibbs (2005, 917. 923, 933) describe how climate
shaped early economic development:

domesticated plants gave a reliable source of food with high nutritional
value that could feed a much greater population per unit area than hunting-
gathering. Domesticated animals gave meat, milk, fertilization, wool, leather,
and were subsequently used for transport, plowing, and warfare. The close
physical proximity of man and animal also eventually gave agriculturists
a high resistance to animal-related germs such as those causing smallpox,
measles, and tuberculosis. All these advantages gradually made organized
food production the dominant way of living in all of Eurasia where expanding agricultural communities swept away most of the remaining hunter-
gatherers.

The path to what is usually referred to as "civilization" was now open. In
densely populated towns and cities, a non-producing class emerged which
was able to dominate the rest of the population by gaining control of the agricultural surplus ... The establishment of a non-food sector in settled communities, whose members lived on the agricultural surplus, was nonetheless
one of the most fundamental societal changes in human history that ini-
tiated a process of endogenous technological change. In this sector were

the kings, the warriors, the bureaucrats, the priests, and the specialized craftsmen. Their activities were a prerequisite for the gradual evolution of civilization. These elites coordinated labor and allocated resources. In doing so they also invented written language, mathematics, science, law and institutions for social control and governance. New knowledge was created more systematically. Old knowledge began to be recorded and codified . . . **geography and biogeography are able to account for between 40% and 50% of the variance in 1997 log incomes per capita.**

People in the Northern hemisphere had a climate that gave them advantages in future economic development. Where climates were temperate, European settlers in colonies in Latin America, Africa, and Asia settled in large numbers. Where climates were tropical, only a handful of settlers Americas largely settled in countries with temperate climates and exploited slaves and native populations.

Engerman and Sokoloff (2002, 8) argued:

Since their factor endowments were far more hospitable to the cultivation of grains than sugar (or other crops that were grown on large slave plantations during this era), these colonies absorbed relatively more Europeans than African slaves, and their populations were accordingly disproportionately made up of whites . . . Of particular significance for generating extreme inequality were, first, the suitability of the climate and soils for the cultivation of sugar and other highly valued commodities that embodied economies of production in the use of slaves and, second, the presence of large concentrations of Native Americans. Both of these conditions encouraged the evolution of societies in which a relatively small elite of European descent could hold a highly disproportionate share of the wealth, human capital, and political power and establish economic and political dominance over the mass of the population.

Historical institutionalists also highlight the importance of resources in the settlement of colonies. Acemoglu, Johnson, and Robinson (2002, 1264, 1266, emphasis added) argue:

colonization introduced relatively better institutions in previously sparsely settled and less prosperous areas: while in a number of colonies such as the United States, Canada, Australia, New Zealand, Hong Kong, and Singapore, Europeans established institutions of private property, in many others they set up or took over already existing extractive institutions in order to directly extract resources, to develop plantation and mining networks, or to collect taxes. Notice that what is important for my story is not the "plunder" or the direct extraction of resources by the European powers, but the long-run consequences of the institutions that they set up to support extraction... the main objective of the Spanish and Portuguese colonization was to obtain silver, gold, and other valuables from America, and throughout they monopolized military power to enable the extraction of these resources. The mining network set up for this reason was based on forced labor and the oppression of the native population... **when a large number of Europeans settled, the lower strata of the settlers demanded rights and protection similar to, or even better than, those in the home country.**

I draw attention to these arguments about European settlers because my analysis (Chapter 2) indicates that the European share of a country's population is the strongest factor shaping the level of education in a less developed country (especially colonies) in 1870. Which explanation, if either, accounts for this strong linkage between education and the European share of the population?

The factor endowment account stresses the connections between European settlement and greater economic equality. But the factor endowment explanation is too deterministic. Geography may give some countries early advantages, but it is *not* destiny. Acemoglu and Robinson (2012, 49) argue persuasively that " ... the geography hypothesis cannot explain differences between the north and south of Nogales (Texas and Mexico), or North and South Korea, or those between East and West Germany before the fall of the Berlin Wall" (cf. Lindert, 2008, 367). In Chapter 2 I report that malaria susceptibility was the most important aspect of factor endowments shaping European settlements, but also that malaria's effect on mean school years increased dramatically over time *even as malaria susceptibility itself became geographically isolated (to Africa).*

Wright (2003, 536, 548) argues that slavery in the United States was not simply a response to a farm economy based upon crops such as tobacco, sugar, and cotton. Slavery was also widespread in the Valley of Virginia, where the major crop was wheat. "[S]lavery as an institutional and organizational form was fully compatible with a wide range of farm products and work routines. [T]he decision to abolish slavery was fundamentally political, not the inevitable consequence of profit calculations or an inherent logic of economic evolution." Even with slavery, colonial Americans – and even free citizens in the South – had relatively equal incomes – more so than today and more so than West Europeans (Lindert and Williamson, 2011, 23).[5]

Factor endowments do not seem to be a principal reason for why some countries adopted widespread education and others did not (see Chapter 2). But neither did "good institutions." Democratic governments were not significantly more likely to provide education (Chapter 2, cf. Murtin and Wacziag, 2010, 21). Instead, good institutions seemed to stem from more widespread education (Murtin and Wacziag, 2010, 16–17). Using an earlier and smaller data set on historical levels of education,[6] Glaeser *et al.* (2004, 296) report that "[t]he data show ... no effect of initial political institutions, no matter how measured, on the growth of human capital [education] ... Initial levels of schooling are a strong predictor of improving institutional outcomes over the next five years ... "

The expansion of education went hand in hand with land reform in Japan, South Korea, Russia, and Taiwan (Galor, Moav, and Vollrath, 2009, 162; You, 2015, ch. 4). Prior to the development of mass public education, schooling was largely the province of churches or other private sources. Protestantism fostered early education. Martin Luther, the sixteenth-century Protestant theologian who broke with the Catholic Church, advocated individual reading of the Bible – which required literacy – as a way of forging a direct connection with God (Ferguson, 2011, 263). Catholics were more worried that literacy might lead to challenges to church authority. The Catholic Church actively discouraged literacy, promoted burning books, and sent scientists to prison (Young, 2009, 15).

Luther advocated not just basic literacy, but other skills that "functioned as human capital in the economic sphere" (Becker and Woessmann, 2009, 581). Using historical data on Switzerland (from 1870), Boppart. Falkinger, and Grossman (2014, 875) showed that literate Protestants also were more proficient in mathematics and other subjects – so that they were better prepared for the economic marketplace. The church and the state were both partners and competitors in providing education. Woodberry (2012) argues that "conversionary Protestants" – missionaries – were central to the development of mass education throughout the world. Missionaries were not always welcome (see Chapter 3 and Ferguson, 2011, 263). The church and state were often competitors for providing education (Ansell and Lindvall, 2013). Through public education the nation-state, be it democratic or not, consolidated its power as the reigning secular authority (Meyer, Ramirez, and Soysal, 1992, 131).

Literacy (education), on this account, not only made people able to read the Bible. It also led to the development of other skills that helped people get ahead on their own. It did more than lead people to teach personal morality. The message of the Protestant Reformation was *reading* about both the "common good" and the evils of corruption in the Catholic Church (Dittmar and Meisenzhal, 2016, 2–3). Luther's initial "published" theses in 1517 focused on "church corruption, [specifically] the Catholic church's practice of selling indulgences which were believed to secure the release of dead relatives from purgatory in the afterlife" (Dittmar and Seabold, 2015, 7).

The provision of widespread education was not foreordained either by geography or institutions. It was a political choice that depended upon the resources of the lower classes. Lindert (2004, vol. 1, 115–123) trace the development of widespread public education in both Prussia and America to pressure from below. Cinnirella and Hornung (2011, 1, 8, 16) summarized this argument: "The delay in the expansion of formal education is caused by large landowners who oppose educational reforms to reduce the mobility of the rural labor force . . . Literacy was seen as a potential weapon which might be used by peasants to appeal to royal courts in order to reduce their servile duties" and in areas with more concentrated landownership there was considerably less enrollment in public education. In the Protestant Reformation, pressure for reform came from *below*: " . . . the city Reformations were citizens' movements that emerged without initial support from oligarchic city governments or territorial lords . . . The constituency for reform came from citizens who were excluded from political power by oligarchic elites, typically lesser merchants and guild members" and "[t]he most fundamental provisions established compulsory public schooling" (Dittmar and Meisenzahl, 2016, 7, 9). The demand for schools arose from demonstrations, often violent, from middle-class "burghers" who demanded – and ultimately won – schools for their children (Schilling, 1983, 448–451).

Public education was a state response to popular demands – even in the absence of democratic government. Greater economic equality first empowered the mass public to demand public education. Second, where there was more equality (America), the economic interests of the masses and the elites were not necessarily in conflict. Where colonial powers ruled over indigenous peoples, there were few bonds of common interest. Colonial powers had little interest in providing education to people of different backgrounds (see Chapter 4). There was less hesitation to educating young people of their own heritage – and in most cases, funding came from local authorities, not the colonial power. Education was a policy choice, not a response to environmental conditions or a result of democratic institutions.

The Plan of the Book

My focus is the connection between contemporary corruption and both historical and contemporary educational levels. In Chapter 2 I formulate statistical models predicting corruption from historical and contemporary education levels. I also examine the impact of other historical factors – institutions, technology, and factor endowments. I find that most other factors are either not significant or matter far less than historical levels of education.

I also find that changes in levels of education *do* shape contemporary corruption, but they are far less powerful factors than the 1870 measures. And it matters far more than historical institutions, technical capacities, early state formation, or factor endowments. There is strong support for the argument that history matters. And agency matters as well.

Different forces shape how widespread mass public education was in 1870. For the more developed countries, the key factors are the level of equality (as measured by the percentage of farms run by families in 1868) and the Protestant share of the population. For the less developed countries – including colonies and former colonies – one variable dominates: the share of a country's population in 1900 of European background. Europeans were better situated to demand the provision of public education. Indigenous groups had less political clout – and the colonial powers were more likely to exploit them than to provide any basic services. Independent countries that were less developed generally lacked the resources to invest in education. Schooling was provided by missionaries – who were not always welcomed as representatives of "alien" religions and who generally did not have sufficient resources to teach more than a small share of the young people.

I spend most of the book describing the forces leading to the provision – or lack of it – for public education. In Chapter 3 I focus on the developed states of Europe, in Chapter 4 I consider Latin America, Asia, Africa, and some parts of Europe (not the most heavily developed states). The early leader in universal education was the United States and I tell the American story in Chapter 5 (including the Wisconsin Idea). More for the United States than for any other country, there are historical data – on schooling, as well as for inequality and even corruption. So I exploit this rich data set to examine these linkages over time and across the American states. The availability of state-level education and inequality measures for the late nineteenth century and contemporary corruption estimates permits me to estimate similar models for the American states that I do in the cross-national analysis in Chapter 2. And the results are reassuring: The same factors shaping corruption across nations also do so for explaining malfeasance in the American states.

My account thus places less emphasis on political institutions than do most others. The main unit analysis in almost all studies is the nation-state and the particular institutions associated with it. Yet there are variations in both education and corruption within nation-states, as in the north–south division in Italy (Chapter 3) and the American states (Chapter 5). In each of these cases, there are variations within the same basic institutional structure of the state – and these cannot be explained simply by formal institutions. Regional variations are important in both Italy and the United States, and likely elsewhere, even as different regions work under the same formal institutions of government.

I do not claim that universal education is a "mono-causal" factor underlying corruption. Other variables matter, as I show in Chapter 2. However, universal education, both historically and over time, is consistently related to corruption. When I seek explanations for how some countries reduced corruption, there is generally a clear relationship to the development of universal education. No other "cure" for corruption seems to have such strong effects. While the cost for this cure may be very expensive, it is doable, certainly more feasible than changing a country's factor endowments or its political history (cf. Rothstein, 2017). Expanding educational opportunities may not even be the most important factor in a reform movement. In many countries it was either part of a religious (Protestant) Reformation (see Chapter 3) or part of a broader campaign to reduce inequality (see Chapter 6).

Notes

1 This framework draws on earlier work on corruption by myself (Uslaner, 2008) and Bo Rothstein (2011). We developed much of the argument together but the work is mostly mine: Portions of this chapter and the final chapter and some of Chapter 3 are his work, but the overall argument was developed together.

2 The source is reportedly a largely lost manuscript, "A Treatise on Education," https://answers.yahoo.com/question/index?qid=20090912151751AAFoQP5.

3 See the sites at www.transparency.org, www.moibrahimfoundation.org, www.worldbank.org, and www.ebrd.org.

4 The measure of mean school years I employ from Morrison and Murtin (2009) – see www.fabricemurtin.com – is correlated with our nineteenth-century measure of inequality – percent farms run by families – at $r = .756$ (N = 35) and with Solt's (2009) post-redistribution Gini index for 49 countries in 2004 at $r = .773$.

5 The correlation between the measure of school attendance in 1870 employed in Chapter 5 and alternative measures of a state's population enslaved is just -35.

6 The education data Glaeser *et al.* (2004) use come from Lindert (2004), vol. 2. This data set covers only 20 countries for 1880 and 30 for 1890. The correlations with the Morrison and Murtin data are .857 for 1880 and .855 for 1890.

2 | *The Quantitative Evidence*

In Western countries, citizens see the state as the provider of basic services, to deliver them fairly and competently, and to be held accountable if it fails to do so. In many other parts of the world, people are more likely to see the state as an adversary and its leaders as grabbing as much of the public purse as they can and expecting loyalty in return for any benefits they provide. In the modern welfare state, the public will not tolerate widespread dishonesty by public officials. Elsewhere, leaders will be reluctant to provide services that would undermine their authority.

For much of human history, the state was not the "friend" of the citizen. Even in the nineteenth century, when the seeds of the welfare state took root, most of today's countries were colonies of Western powers. With only a handful of exceptions, the Western "masters" exploited people in the colonies for their resources and saw little obligation to provide any services in return. The legacy of colonialism has led to persistent inequality and poverty even after the countries achieved independence. Local leaders could be as unresponsive as the colonial masters – and had little interest in reducing inequality. The quality of service delivery remained very low – and corruption remained endemic. Under both colonial rule and independence, under rule by the colonial powers and under governance by indigenous leaders, under an authoritarian regime and under democratic government with periodic elections, ordinary people had few resources and the elite – including public officials – were wealthy and in control of the resources of the state.

The resource that is most important for the development of an independent public is education. Hospitals, roads, and electricity are all important services that the state delivers to the people. But education stands out as distinctive. It empowers people to challenge authority in at least two ways (as I argued in Chapter 1):

- More highly educated people are more likely to participate in politics and, even in authoritarian regimes, are more likely to challenge authorities; and, even more critically,
- More highly educated people will be less dependent upon corrupt leaders for their livelihoods so they have fewer reasons to be loyal to corrupt leaders.

Corrupt leaders have little reason to provide their publics with widespread public education. Education is the most expensive social service. Not everyone uses the hospital. You only have to build a road once. And there are economies of scale in providing electricity to large numbers of people. But education is a continuing expense. Schooling for a population of young people is very expensive. Since education is a key factor in reducing inequality and increasing a country's wealth, nations face an "inequality trap" in which corruption and inequality persist over long periods of time.

I provide the quantitative evidence linking corruption with historical levels of education in this chapter. Our story is that history matters – but also that history is not destiny. Historical levels of education shape contemporary corruption, but *changes* in mean school years also lead to less corruption, even if not as strongly. Democratic institutions – in either the nineteenth century or today – matter much less, if at all, for corruption. There is at best mixed support for longer-term determinants such as factor endowments and historical technology. Providing education to large numbers of students is a policy choice that is shaped by historical forces, not fully determined by them. And this means that corruption can also be reduced – and I shall show that there have been anti-corruption programs – often successful – that are explicitly linked to providing social welfare, and notably education–to the public.

Historical levels of education have the strongest effect on reducing corruption: No other factor is nearly as important. In turn, mean school years in 1870 for the more developed countries are largely determined by the level of equality in a country (as measured by the percent of farms owned by families) and the Protestant share of a country's population. Protestant countries did have greater levels of schooling in the nineteenth century, for the most part. However, this is only a rough estimate of a population's demand for education. As I show in Chapter 3, Catholic countries that took schooling out of the hands of the state did achieve high levels of education, so the Protestant share of the population is an indirect measure. For other countries, especially present and former colonies, the share of the population of European stock accounts for almost all of the variation in levels of education. Colonial powers exploited indigenous populations but provided benefits to colonists who looked like them.

Persistence

Corruption is widespread throughout the world. In the 78 countries I examine in this chapter, 41 percent have scores of 3 or lower on Transparency International's 10-point scale for 2010 (where higher scores indicate less dishonesty). Almost two-thirds have scores below the midpoint of 5, while just 10 countries (11.5 percent) have scores of 8 or more, indicating very low levels of corruption. All of the most honest countries are in Northern Europe (except for Canada and Australia). Almost all of the countries scoring 3 or lower are in Africa, Latin America, the Middle East, or South Asia (see Figure 2.1).

Corruption persists because poor people in highly unequal societies depend upon corrupt patrons for their livelihood. They do not have sufficient education to make their own way in the world – or the education system does not provide access to jobs that pay well enough to make people independent of political leaders. The 31 countries in which people averaged seven years or fewer of education are *all* in Africa, South Asia, the Middle East, and Latin America (except for Turkey). The 20 countries with the lowest mean level of education are all in Africa (except India and Bangladesh). There is thus a strong overlap between lower levels of education and greater corruption and the maps look very similar (see Figure 2.2 for mean levels of education across the world).

I cannot trace past levels of corruption, but data from Morrison and Murtin (in press) let us examine historical education patterns. Their data set begins in 1870 and I argue that: (1) countries with the greatest levels of education in 1870 have the most educated publics 140 years later; and (2) historical levels of education are strongly related to contemporary corruption. In line with historical institutionalism in both economics and political science, I argue that there is a strong "path dependence" in levels of education. Mean levels of education in 1870 are very similar to those of 2010. The 14 countries with the highest levels of education (mean school years) in 1870 are all in northern

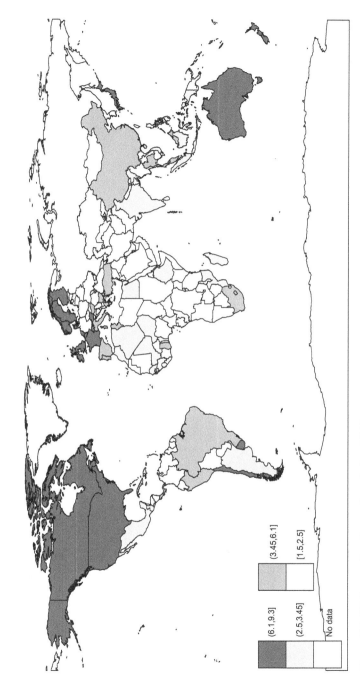

World Map TI Corruption Perceptions Index 2010

[6.1,9.3]

[3.45,6.1]

(2.5,3.45]

[1.5,2.5]

No data

Figure 2.1 TI Corruption Perceptions Index, 2010

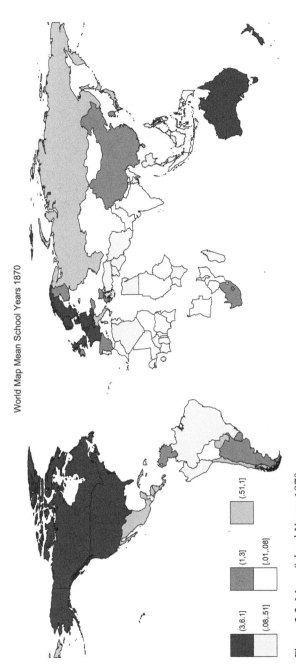

World Map Mean School Years 1870

[3,6.1]   [1,3]   (.51,1]

(.08,.51]   [.01,.08]

Figure 2.2 Mean School Years, 1870

Europe or North America. The 20 countries in which people averaged less than 0.1 year of schooling in 1870 were all in Africa (14) or South Asia (6) – see Figure 2.2.

I first examine the roots of contemporary corruption by analyzing the linkages with measures of educational attainment, inequality, and democratization in the nineteenth century Our measure of corruption is the widely used Corruption Perceptions Index (CPI) of Transparency International for 2010, which is based on expert surveys.[1] There is no direct measure of corruption, so I rely upon a measure of perceived corruption. Corrupt acts are almost always hidden. If you are behaving honestly in either the public or the private sector, you will rarely have a need to hide your actions. When you flout the law or norms of acceptable behavior, in almost all cases you don't want others to know. The most corrupt countries have the lowest scores on the 10-point scale. The CPI is not without critics: Abramo (2005), among others, argues that the index is not strongly correlated with peoples' actual experiences with corruption. However, this is not what the index is supposed to measure. The CPI is an estimate of elite corruption (also known as "grand corruption") rather than the "petty corruption" involving small payments to public officials for routine services as well as to doctors, to the police (to escape traffic fines), and even to university professors (for better grades). Ordinary people pay these small bribes, not the large payments that the CPI taps (see Kaufmann, Kraay, and Mastruzzi, 2007, for a defense of a similar measure from the World Bank).

I use new data sets on historical levels of education developed by Morrison and Murtin (in press) and on historical income levels by Bourginon and Morrison as well as existing data on democratization, percent family farms, and percent Protestant.[2] The year 1870 is the earliest date for which data about mean levels of schooling are available for a reasonably large set of countries (n = 78). Benavot and Riddle (1988) and Lindert (2004, vol. 1, 91–93) also have estimated education levels for the late nineteenth century for smaller samples. I present graphs of the Morrison-Murtin data compared to these alternative measures in Figure 2.3. The fit with the Benavot-Riddle estimates is extremely strong ($r^2 = .87$, with Australia being the only outlier of the 40 countries). The fit with the Lindert data is slightly weaker ($r^2 = .73$ for 30 countries) but the data are less directly comparable: The Lindert measure is the number of students enrolled in school of young people

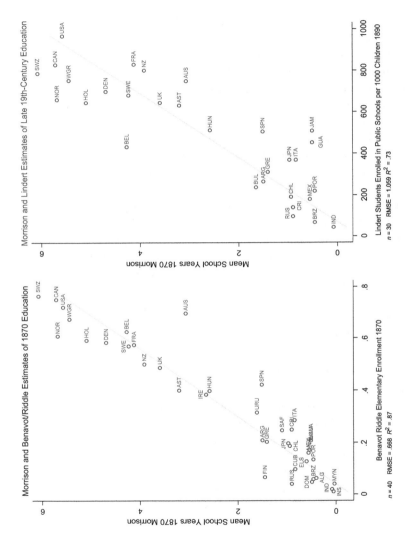

Figure 2.3 Morrison-Murtin Mean School Years, 1870, Compared to Benavot-Riddle and Lindert Estimates

5–14 years old – so it is not quite the same measure as the number of school years.

Some measures – gross national product per capita, the level of democracy, and family farm percentage – are only available for a small number of countries. So I estimate ordinary least squares regressions for equations in which I include these measures. I estimate models for corruption and for mean school years separately and then an instrumental variable regression for corruption. The exogenous variables predicting levels of education are colonial status and European share of the population.

More highly corrupt countries are also less likely to invest in higher education (Uslaner, 2008, 74–79). Investigating this is outside our agenda – and data. It makes no sense to "predict" 1870 education levels from contemporary corruption perceptions and there are insufficient measures of corruption for the nineteenth century.

The central result is the strong correlation between the mean number of years of schooling in a country in 1870 and its level of corruption in 2010 (see Figure 2.4). Moving from the fewest years levels of education (.01 for four African nations) to the most (6.07 in Switzerland) leads to an increase in the CPI of 7.0, which is the difference between Angola, the fourth most corrupt country, and Canada, the fifth least corrupt nation. The relationship is very strong ($r^2 = .699$). The level of education in 1870 shapes corruption far more than does GNP per capita in the same year.

The mean number of school years and wealth are strongly related ($r^2 = .604$, $N = 46$), but one is not a proxy for the other. In the regression the most educated country in 1870 is 4.5 units less corrupt than the least corrupt country, while the wealthiest state is 2.5 units less corrupt than the poorest (see Table 2.1).

Is it all about long-term effects? Mostly, though not completely. Countries with high levels of education in 2010 also had more educated publics 140 years ago ($r^2 = .578$). Sixteen of the countries with the greatest increase in mean school years were in the 20 most educated countries in 1870; 17 of the 20 countries with the smallest growth in education were among the least educated third in 1870.

The regression predicting 2010 levels of corruption from both 1870 education levels and changes in schooling over 140 years shows that both are significant (details available upon request). The impact of historical levels of education is 2.5 times that of change in education

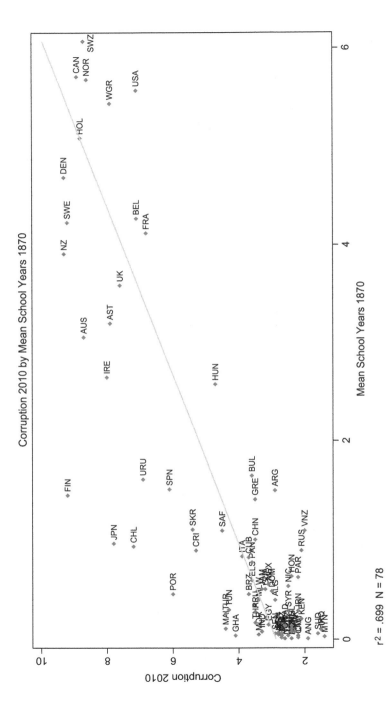

Corruption 2010 by Mean School Years 1870

$r^2 = .699$ N = 78

Figure 2.4 Corruption 2010 by Mean School Years, 1870

Table 2.1 *Regression of 2010 Corruption by 1870 Mean School Years and GNP Per Capita*

Variable	Coefficient	Standard error	t ratio
Mean School Years 1870	.738**	.174	4.22
Gross National Product Per Capita 1870	001*	.0004	2.07
Constant	2.710**	.422	6.42

Notes: $R^2 = .677$; R.M.S.E. $= 1.433$; N $= 46$. ** $p < .01$; * $p < .05$.

(6.36 units of the CPI corruption index compared to 2.71; t ratios of 12.23 and 3.88, respectively; N $= 78$, $R^2 = .750$). There is evidence of a catch-up effect. Countries with the fewest years of schooling in 1870 (less than two) had stronger growth in education levels – but, even here, the countries that were at the "top of the bottom" experienced the greatest growth rates in schooling ($r^2 = .376$). But history matters: The simple correlation between contemporary corruption and levels of education in 1870 is higher ($r = .836$) than between corruption and contemporary mean school years ($r = .760$).

I reestimate this model including the Polity IV measure of democracy in 1870. The sample size is reduced to 40 countries ($R^2 = .734$). The coefficient for democracy is insignificant; going from the least to the most democratic nation increases transparency by a mere .27 points on the 10-point scale, compared to 5.95 and 2.96 for mean level of education and education change. This is not an issue of collinearity. The correlation between mean school years and democracy in 1870 is just .435 and the simple r between democracy in 1870 and corruption in 2010 is only .421. The small effect may reflect the fact that there were few democratic regimes in the latter part of the nineteenth century. Green (1990, 31f) provides qualitative support: "One of the great ironies of educational history is that the more 'democratic' nineteenth-century powers like France, England and the USA, ..., were forced to look to the autocratic German states for examples of educational reforms to adopt at home."

I argued in Chapter 1 that generalized trust is a key factor shaping corruption. I do not include it in our estimations here because: (1) it is highly correlated with most of our independent variables, notably mean school years in 1870 ($r = .680$), the European share of population (r = .580), colonial status (r = −.541), the net Gini index (r = −.679), and the Protestant share of the population (r = .642) using Uslaner's (2008, 51–53) indicator. There are insufficient observations from the nineteenth century to establish a causal order – and it is implausible that levels of education in 1870 were "caused" by aggregate trust in the late twentieth century. The estimation of the instrumental variable regression below yields an insignificant estimate for generalized trust and depressed coefficients and significance levels for other variables. I acknowledge the role of trust in reducing corruption, but I do not examine it here.

The model is limited in the number of contemporaneous institutional variables I consider. I thus estimated 24 other models using a set of variables that Treisman (2007) considers to be institutional.

The logic behind these predictors is:

- Institutionalists would expect democratic regimes (years of consecutive democracy, always a democracy) to have lower levels of corruption and thus positive coefficients.
- As above, media usage (newspaper readership, newspapers per capita, television sets per capita) should lead to less corruption – and thus positive coefficients.
- Parliamentary systems should have less corruption than Presidential systems because the latter put too much power in a single actor (Treisman, 2007, 22).
- Plurality electoral systems should lead to less corruption compared to proportional representation because there is a more direct linkage between officeholders and voters (Persson, Tabellini and Trebbi, 2003).
- Closed list electoral systems should have less corruption than open list regimes. In closed list systems "voters cannot choose their preferred candidate, an individual's chance of re-election depends on his rank on the list, not his individual performance. If lists are drawn up by party leaders...the ranking is likely to reflect criteria unrelated to competence in providing benefits to voters, such as party loyalty, or effort within the party (rather than in office)" (Persson, Tabellini and Trebbi, 2003, 961). Open list systems with proportional representation should be especially prone to higher levels of corruption. Mixed systems should rank in between these two alternatives.

- Federal systems, especially where larger shares of a country's budget are spent at subnational levels, should have lower levels of corruption (Fisman and Gatti, 2002) since there will be more checks on corrupt leaders.
- Countries with greater reliance on trade will be less corrupt, since their economies will be more intertwined with those of other countries – which may have less corruption themselves. The earlier a country opened its markets, the lower its level of corruption should be as well.
- Countries rich in natural resources should have higher levels of corruption. Natural resources, such as oil or minerals, are easy to steal (Leite and Weidmann, 1999; Sachs and Warner, 1997).
- Countries with specific procedures for evicting non-paying tenants or for handling bad checks should have *more* corruption since these regulations are indications of a weak judicial system (Treisman, 2007, 26). Where procedures make it easier to start a business, corruption should be lower (Treisman, 2007, 27).
- As I argued in Chapter 1, Gender equality – in both the workforce and government – is strongly related to lower levels of corruption (Wängnerud 2012, Grimes and Wängnerud 2010).

I test these arguments in Table 2.2, including each in a model with mean school years for 1870, mean school year change 1870–2010, Solt's index of net inequality (2009), and GNP per capita for 2000. My own expectations are modest. The rationale for many of these measures does not appear to be strong. And some measures, such as years of consecutive democracy and "always a democracy," may be too broad: For countries with 40 or more years of consecutive democracy, this indicator may hide other changes embedded in a simple count.

Newspaper readership matters, but television sets per 1,000 people doesn't, so it is not clear that there are media effects. Some electoral system variables are significant: Plurality electoral systems lead to more corruption. But most others are not. Stronger laws for evicting non-payment of rent and for bounced checks seemingly lead to more corruption – which may indicate that punitive legal systems are found where dishonesty is otherwise high. Overall the results are mixed. None of the institutional variables have effects that are comparable to mean school years and GNP per capita. The impacts are closer to mean school year change.

Table 2.2 *Effects of Institutional Variables from Treisman Data Set on 2010 Corruption*

Variable	Coefficient	S.E.	t ratio	N
Years of consecutive democracy	.026***	.009.	2.89	68
Always democracy	.1.004**	.456	2.20	68
Newspaper readership per capita	.005**	.002	2.27	41
Television sets per 1000 people (1997)	.002	.002	.99	42
Newspapers per capita 1998	.005***	.002	2.76	66
Parliamentary system	.335*	.220	1.52	68
District magnitude 2000	.006	.006	.93	66
Plurality electoral system 2000	−.407*	.319	−1.28	64
Proportional representation 2000	.228	.348	.66	63
Mixed electoral system 2000	−.189	.328	−.88	63
Electoral system closed list 2000	−.050	.499	−.10	46
Electoral system open list 2000	−.887*	.689	−1.29	32
Open list with proportional representation	.188	.507	.37	43
Federal system (Elazar defined)	−.619+	.366	−1.69	68
Subnational share revenue 1995–2000	−.010	.017	−.58	35
Imports as share of GDP 2000	.001	.008	.07	68
Year country opened to trade	−.028+	.014	−2.08	67
Fuel exports percent manufacturing exports 1995	−.025**	.015	−1.71	40
Total fuel exports 2000	−.013**	.007	−.231	67
Eviction index non-paying tenant	−.405**	.191	−2.12	53
Procedures for bounced checks	−.415**	.179	−2.32	53
Ease of starting business	−1.108***	.387	−2.86	55
Percent women in government	.043***	.014	3.03	61
Female workforce	.014	.012	1.18	68

Notes: * p < .10; ** p < .05; *** p < .01; + not in predicted direction.
All models include mean school years 1870, mean school years change 1870–2010, Solt's index of net inequality (2009), and GNP per capita 2000.

The Roots of Education Levels

To account for the development of education across nations, I consider the effects of equality, democratization, colonial history, Protestant population, and European background. I use Vanhanen's (1997, 48) estimates of the percent of family farms in a country in 1868, the share of all farms that are owned and operated by small farmers (with no

Table 2.3 *Regression for Mean School Years, 1870*

	Coefficient	Standard error	t ratio
Protestant % 1980	.025**	.009	2.90
European share 1900	.016**	.006	2.56
Family farm % 1868	.039**	.013	2.90
Democracy Polity IV	.065	.102	.63
Colony (present or former)	−.061	.435	−.14
Constant	−.540	.836	−.65

Notes: $R^2 = .798$; R.M.S.E. $= .960$; $N = 35$; ** $p < .01$.

more than four employees), as our indicator of equality. Boix (2008, 207) argues: "The percentage of family farms captures the degree of concentration and therefore inequality in the ownership of land." Easterly (2006, 15) holds that "...the family farm measure from earlier dates since 1858 is a good predictor of inequality today" (cf. Rueschemeyer, Stephens, and Stephens, 1992, 139–140; Frankema, 2010, 118; Galor, Moav, and Vollrath, 2009, 144). Galor, Moav, and Vollrath (2009, 143, 162) show that inequality in the ownership of land led to lower levels of education – and income.

I report the regressions for all countries, independent nations, and (former) colonies in Tables 2.3 and 2.4. For the contemporary or former colonies in 1870,[3] the mean level of education was .42, less than half a year of schooling, compared to 2.88 for the developed and independent nations. The publics in only five Western countries

Table 2.4 *Regression for Mean School Years 1870 by State Status*

	Independent states		Colonies/former colonies	
	b	S.E.	b	S.E.
Protestant % 1980	.023*	.011	−.088	.071
European share 1900	.013	.009	.023***	.007
Family farm % 1868	.044**	.019	.034*	.016
Democracy Polity IV	.118	.147	−.074	.092
Constant	−.934	1.186	.648	.585

Notes: Independent States: $R^2 = .737$; R.M.S.E. $= 1.239$; $N = 21$; Colonies: $R^2 = .656$; R.M.S.E. $= .279$ $N = 14$; *** $p < .0001$; ** $p < .01$; * $p < .05$.

(Portugal, Italy, Japan, Greece, and Finland, in descending order) had average schooling less than half a year in 1870, while only two (former) colonies (Argentina and Uruguay) had publics with that much education.

The major powers ruling colonies in the sample were Great Britain (19 countries) and France (9). The British and French did little to provide education for their colonies, which had .17 and .11 school years each in 1870. The data set includes a diverse set of independent nations, with some countries (Bulgaria and Hungary) having education levels just below levels in Western Europe, and others (China, Japan, Russia, and South Korea) with schooling comparable to many former Spanish colonies, and a third group (Iran, Thailand, Turkey) in the bottom third of nations. The ten independent nations averaged 1.2 years of education in 1870, still well below levels in Western Europe and the four English-speaking countries outside Europe (3.68) but greater than the former colonies of Britain (.99), and Spain/Portugal (.66).

These estimations are based upon *very* small samples (35 overall, 21 independent countries, and 14 colonies), largely because family farm percentage is only available for these 35 countries. So I urge caution in interpreting them. However, the story they tell confirms our expectations.

There are two critical differences below between current or former colonies and independent states. First, the Protestant share of the population led to higher levels of education *only for independent states*. Second, the European population share is the most important factor shaping education levels in 1870 in colonies but is insignificant in independent states. The bivariate correlations for larger sample sizes confirm these estimates. The Protestant share is strongly related to 1870 education levels for independent states ($r = .733, N = 27$) but not for colonies ($r = .182, N = 51$). Education and the European share are strongly linked in present and former colonies ($N = 49, r = .857$).

Higher levels of democracy do not matter in either colonies or independent states. Land inequality is significant in both, but more in independent states, largely because there was less variance in both land inequality and mean school years for colonies.

Countries with a larger share of European stock also were more equal ($r^2 = .235$). Our story of state capacity in Northern Europe above fits the story of equality as well. While Prussia had relatively low levels of land and income inequality (see above), Britain had a highly

Table 2.5 *Instrumental Variable Regression of Corruption Perceptions, 2010*

Variable	Coefficient	Standard error	t ratio
First stage: Estimation of mean school years			
European population share	.020****	.005	4.09
Protestant population share	.023****	.006	4.18
Colonial status	−1.286****	.372	−3.46
Mean School Year Change 1870–2010	−.111	.058	−1.91
Press Freedom	−.004	.010	−.43
GNP per capita PPP (× 10000)	−.003	−.004	−.87
Democracy Polity IV	−.013	.066	−.20
Net Gini 2004 Solt	.002	.018	.11
Constant	5.225***	1.212	4.31
Second stage: Estimation of corruption			
Mean School Years 1870	.760***	.144	5.26
Mean School Year Change 1870–2010 Press Freedom	.211***	.063	3.35
Press Freedom	−.040***	.012	−3.34
GNP per capita PPP (× 10000)	.066	.042	1.58
Democracy Polity IV	−.091	.075	−1.22
Net Gini 2004 Solt	−.026	.020	−1.31
Constant	5.225***	1.212	4.31

Notes: $R^2 = .813$; R.M.S.E. = 1.02; N = 67; **** $p < .0001$.

unequal distribution of land: Only 5 percent of farms were owned by individual families in 1868, a level comparable to most Latin American countries and far lower than their former colonies in North America, where 60 percent of farms in the United States and 63 percent in Canada were family owned (ranking only behind Norway). Inequality was lower when the Protestant share of populations was greater ($r^2 = .410$). The factors shaping the provision of education – and ultimately low corruption – were part of a larger syndrome.

Putting It Together

I estimate an instrumental variable model for contemporary corruption with mean levels of education in 1870 endogenous (see Table 2.5). The instruments for mean education levels are the Protestant share of the population, the European share, and colonial status. All are significant at p < .01.[4] The model includes the instrument for mean school years, mean school year change, gross national product per capita adjusted for purchasing power parity (for 2000 from the Penn World Tables), the Polity IV democracy index, Solt's net Gini index, and Freedom House's Press Freedom index for 2002 (from Daniel Treisman's Decentralization data set).[5]

In the regression for 67 countries, wealth and inequality are barely significant (at p < .10). Democracy is not. What matters most are historical levels of education and to a lesser extent change in education levels.

The estimated effect of the mean school year instrument on corruption perceptions in 2010 is 13.7, which is greater than the full range of the CPI. For the mean school year measure without instrumentation, the estimated effect is 4.6, which amounts to the difference between Denmark (the least corrupt country) and Hungary. For mean school year change, the effect is half as great (2.3). But press freedom may not be a simple institutional solution to corruption. Färdigh (2013) shows that press freedom reduces corruption *only* in "well-established electoral democracies." So the belief that you can engineer lower corruption may be misplaced. Freedom of the press is strongly related to historical levels of education (r = −.648 and −.807 with the instrument). Press freedom can help combat corruption, but the power of the press depends upon a literate public.

These results extend Glaeser *et al.* (2004), but differ from those of Acemoglu and Robinson (2012, 18–19, 27), who argue that English colonial rule led to better contemporary outcomes than did Spanish colonization. Spanish rule was more based on "looting, and gold and silver lust," while English colonies were less extractive. This dichotomy is too simplistic. Nor does the Protestant–Catholic religious distinction matter in the colonies. Spanish and English colonies with large European populations had high levels of education, while territories with few colonials (including English dependencies in Africa and Asia) lagged behind. Nor is there evidence that democracy led either to greater education in the 1870s or to less corruption today.

Does the nature of the party system matter? I estimated instrumental variable models using the Cruz-Keefer measure of programmatic parties and also Kitschelt's measure of programmatic parties from his database on the Democratic Accountability and Linkages Project.[6]

Table 2.6 *Instrumental Variable Regression of Corruption Perceptions 2010 with Programmatic Party Measure*

Variable	Coefficient	Standard error	t ratio
First stage: Estimation of mean school years			
European population share	.004	.006	.80
Mean School Year Change 1870–2010	− .231	.088	− 2.63
GNP per capita PPP (× 10000)	.001	.0003	4.07
Net Gini 2004 Solt	− .027	.022	− 1.22
Protestant share population	.022****	.006	3.90
Former colony	− .952***	.381	− 2.50
Programmatic party (Cruz-Keefer)	.489	.694	.70
Constant	2.727**	1.168	2.34
Second stage: Estimation of Corruption			
Mean School Years 1870	1.054***	.322	3.27
Mean School Year Change 1870–2010	.308**	.146	2.11
GNP per capita PPP (× 10000)	− .00006	.0005	− .11
Net Gini 2004 Solt	− .009	.035	− .27
Programmatic party (Cruz-Keefer)	.752	1.022	.74
Constant	.728	1.912	.38

Notes: R^2 = .710; R.M.S.E. = 1.29; N = 43; **** $p < .0001$; *** $p < .10$; ** $p < .05$.

The models include the European share of population in 1900, the Protestant share of the population, the net Gini index for 2004, and colonial status (now in the past) for the mean school years model and mean school years change, the net Gini index for 2004, GNP per capita in 1870, and the measures of programmatic party in the respective corruption models. Since parties only matter in democracies, I do not include the indicator for democratic government. I show only the estimation for the Cruz-Keefer measure in Table 2.6, but the impact of Kitschelt's indicator is virtually identical. The brief story is: There are moderate to strong zero-order correlations between the programmatic party measures and both corruption and mean school years ($r = .558$ and $.624$, respectively. for the Cruz-Keefer measure and $.668$ and $.662$ for the Kitschelt indicator). In the two-stage model, however, neither measure of programmatic parties is a significant predictor of either mean school years in 1870 or corruption in 2010.

Alternative Explanations

I consider two alternative accounts of corruption (and mean school years): factor endowments and historical levels of technology. First, I consider factor endowments and estimate an instrumental variable regression for both mean school years and corruption (see Table 2.7). The model includes several measures of factor endowments as well as the other factors I employed in earlier estimations. For mean school years I include the European share of the population, the Protestant share, and a dummy for former colonies. For corruption, I include the instrument for mean school years in 1870 as well as mean school year change 1870–2010, press freedom, GNP per capita PPP, the historical measure of democracy, and the net Gini index for 2004. The factor endowment variables I include are malaria susceptibility (Sachs, 1999), plants and animals "suited for domestication" 12,000 years ago (Hibbs and Olsson, 2004, 3716), arable land and temperate climate (McCord and Sachs, 2013, 6, 19), arable land, and mineral wealth. I include malaria susceptibility only in the equation for mean school years. I expect the impact of all factor endowment variables to lead to positive effects for both outcomes: mean school years in 1870 and corruption in 2010. The exception is malaria susceptibility, which should lead to more corruption.[7]

The results are not encouraging for an explanation based upon factor endowments. Only a temperate climate and malaria susceptibility are significant in the education equation – and neither has anywhere the explanatory power of colonial status or the Protestant share of a country's population. In the corruption equation, only domesticable large animals is significant. Perennial wide grasses and plants and arable land are incorrectly signed.

The most striking finding is that malaria susceptibility has a negative powerful effect on mean school years – consistent with the argument of Sachs and Malaney (2002) and Sachs's (2012, 5) claim that malaria is "a *cause* of poverty" (italics in original).

Do factor endowments have long-lasting effects? Geographic conditions set thousands of years ago shape current economic outcomes. Hibbs and Olsson (2004, 3715) argue that "biogeographic initial conditions 12,000 years ago, just before the origins of agriculture" are "more nearly ultimate sources of contemporary prosperity." The malaria measure is contemporary, but its effects are *not* constant over

Table 2.7 *Instrumental Variable Estimation of Corruption 2010 with Factor Endowments*

Variable	Coefficient	Standard error	t ratio
First stage: Estimation of mean school years, 1870			
European share of population	.012**	.007	1.84
Protestant share population	.024****	.005	4.61
Malaria susceptiblility	− 1.388***	.447	− 3.11
Temperate climate	.304**	.163	1.84
Domesticable large animals historical	− .101	.085	− 1.19
Perennial wild grasses/plants historical	− .018	.022	− .82
Arable land	− .008	.009	− .89
Mineral rich	.113	.401	.28
Press freedom	− .001	.010	− .13
Democracy Polity IV	− .014	.069	− .21
GNP per capita PPP (× 10000)	− .000003	− .00004	− .76
Net Gini Solt 2004	− .056***	.022	− 2.48
Mean school year change 1870 2010	− .193	.070	− 2.77
Present/former colony	− 1.470****	.369	− 3.98
Constant	5.660****	1.311	4.32
Second stage: Estimation of Corruption 2010			
Mean School Years 1870	.819****	.139	5.89
Mean School Year Change 1870 2010	.085	.075	1.13
Press Freedom	.042	.011	3.74
GNP per capita PPP (× 10000)	.0006**	.0004	2.08
Democracy Polity IV	− .084	.072	− 1.17
Net Gini 2004 Solt	− .036*	.024	− 1.52
Temperate climate	.163	.189	.86
Domesticable large animals historical	.181**	.082	2.20
Perennial wild grasses/plants historical	− .055+	.021	− 2.57
Arable land	− .030+	.011	− 2.74
Mineral rich	.535	.444	1.21
Constant	6.700****	1.273	5.26

Notes: * $p < .10$; ** $p < .05$; *** $p < .01$; **** $p < .001$; + not in predicted direction; N = 67.

Story: Factor endowments, notably malaria exposure and climate, shaped European settlement. To a moderate degree, they also shaped mean school years, but colonial status and inequality and Prot share were more important. Much less important today for corruption.

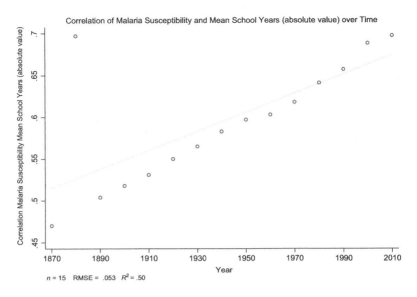

Figure 2.5 Correlation of Malaria Susceptiblity with School Years Over Time

time. The correlation of malaria susceptibility with a country's mean school years has increased dramatically over time (Figure 2.5). The correlation rises from just above .5 in 1870 to .7 in 2010. And the trend is sharply linear, the r^2 is .5; without the strong outlier of 1880, the r^2 increases to .99. This suggests that malaria susceptibility is not simply a "factor endowment" of geography.

What happened? About 90 percent of malaria cases occur in sub-Saharan Africa (Hamoudi and Sachs, 1999, 2). Mean school years in 1870 were also much lower in Africa than elsewhere (.16 compared to 1.58 in the rest of the sample). By 2010 the difference between education in Africa and other countries had expanded to 4.13 and 9.24 (Africa versus other countries). The correlation between mean school years and a dummy variable for Africa increased from −.356 to −.661. Even supposedly biological or biogeographical effects are not necessarily fixed over time. The upshot of Figure 2.4 is that malaria susceptibility had more of a negative effect in 2010 than it did in 1870. Since the malaria data are all from the late twentieth century, the pattern in Figure 2.4 may understate the changing relationship between malaria and bad outcomes.

Table 2.8 *Effects of Factor Endowments on European Settlements for Colonies/Former Colonies, 1900*

Variable	Coefficient	S.E.	t ratio
Malaria susceptibility	− 26.665****	7.677	− 3.47
Domesticable large animals historical	.378	1.933	.20
Perennial wild grasses/plants historical	− .576	.626	− .92
Temperate climate	4.750	4.834	.98
Arable land	− .581+	.296	− 1.96
Mineral rich	− 3.697	8.920	− .41
Constant	30.671****	8.482	3.62

Notes: * p < .10; ** p < .05; *** p < .01; + not in predicted direction; R^2 = .410; R.M.S.E. = 17.957; N = 42.

In the nineteenth century malaria was much more widespread. Since the 1940s, with the development of DDT to destroy the mosquitoes carrying the disease, infection rates fell almost everywhere except in Africa (Hamoudi and Sachs, 1999, 16; Hay *et al.*, 2004, 3). Mortality rates remained high in Africa largely because of climatic conditions and the type of mosquito (Sachs, 2012, 4–5). However, there are political issues as well: Hay *et al.* (2004, 4) point to "the complete disregard of sub-Saharan Africa in the 'global' eradication efforts." The larger story is that malaria led to greater poverty – and thus fewer resources for countries to invest in education in Africa. Historical data on malaria deaths, were they available, should point to an even greater correspondence between mean school years and the disease over time as African malaria rates remained high and education rates low.

There is support for the claim of Easterly and Levine (2012, 14, 20) that malaria susceptibility led to lower levels of European settlement in present and former colonies. I present a regression for European settlements in these countries in Table 2.8. Malaria susceptibility is the *only* indicator of factor endowment that is significant in predicting where Europeans settled. I expect positive coefficients for domesticated animals, perennial wild grasses, temperate climate, and arable land and a negative coefficient for mineral richness. But none of these coefficients is significant and the coefficient for arable lands has the wrong sign. While malaria susceptibility may have shaped European settlement patterns, it did *not* have an independent effect on education levels in 1870 (in an instrumental variable regression available upon request) over and above its impact on settlement patterns.

These findings are consistent with other critiques of factor endowments. Williamson (2015, 12) is critical of geography as destiny:

...Mexico, Bolivia and Colombia all had less inequality in 1820 than did the Netherlands, the United Kingdom and France, or even Portugal and Spain. It is not true that pre-industrial Latin America was more unequal than preindustrial northwest Europe. Nor were incomes more unequal in Latin America than the United States. In 1860, and just before the Civil War, the Gini measuring United States income inequality among all household (including slaves) was 0.51, while the Gini among all free households was 0.47...In 1870, and after a massive redistribution of southern incomes induced by slave emancipation, the Gini for all households was still 0.51 (e.g. the inequality rise up North matched the fall down South...)

Lindert (2008, 367) writes:

...comparing Russia with Western Europe has suggested that political forces were much more important than factor endowments in shaping the institutions that produced inequality and slow growth. If land abundance and labor scarcity led to the attraction of immigrants with better offers to ordinary folk, how are can one explain the fact that the expansion of Russia kept leading to greater oppression and relative stagnation over the centuries up to 1861?...Factor endowments were very similar in Colombia, Costa Rica, El Salvador, and Guatemala when they achieved independence. All four had land well- suited for coffee, and had broadly similar land areas per capita. Yet Costa Rica and Colombia developed much broader education, stronger urban development, relatively more independent free- holders, less income inequality, and higher gross domestic product (GDP) per capita than did El Salvador or Guatemala

Acemoglu and Robinson (2012, 49–50) argue that " . . . there is no simple or enduring connection between climate or geography and economic success," pointing to the "recent rapid economic advance of countries such as Singapore, Malaysia, and Botswana..." While my approach is different from theirs, I agree that Singapore and Botswana dramatically reduced corruption through expanded social programs, especially focused on education (Uslaner, 2008, ch. 7).

Are there stronger effects for historical technology? I present 18 regressions in Table 2.9 similar to those in Table 2.2. The dependent variable is the 2010 CPI index and the regressions include mean school

Table 2.9 *The Effects of Historical Technology Measures on Corruption,*
2010

Variable	Coefficient	S.E.	t ratio	N
Sectoral technology 1000 BC	− .620	.672	− .92	66
Sectoral technology 0 AD	1.150	.964	1.19	76
Sectoral technology 1500 AD	.616	.879	.70	73
Military technology 1000 BC	− .236	.570	− .41	66
Military technology 0 AD	.861	.806	1.07	76
Military technology 1500 AD	.378	.628	.60	73
Industrial technology 1000 BC	− .587	.641	− .92	66
Industrial technology 0 AD	2.862	2.516	1.14	76
Industrial technology 1500 AD	.208	.771	.27	73
Agricultural technology 1000 BC	.077	.609	.13	76
Agricultural technology 0 AD	2.058	2.618	.79	76
Agricultural technology 1500 AD	− .459	.724	− .63	73
Transportation technology 1000 BC	− .212	.415	− .51	66
Transportation technology 0 AD	.108	.309	.64	76
Transportation technology 1500 AD	.180	.524	.34	73
Communication technology 1000 BC	− .511	.434	− 1.19	66
Communication technology 0 AD	.161	.287	.56	76
Communication technology 1500 AD	.385	.399	.97	73

Entries are the coefficients, standard errors, and t ratios for regressions with the 2010
Corruption Perceptions Index as the dependent variable and including mean school
years 1870 and changes in mean school years 1870–2010 as predictors.

years in 1870 and mean school year change 1870–2010. The measures
of technology are for the military, industry, agriculture, transportation,
and communication for 1000 BC, 0 AD, and 1500 AD – as well as
composite indices ("sectoral technology") for each time period. These
measures are adjusted for migration patterns so that borders reflect
contemporary populations rather than historical distributions. Comin
et al. do not find any effects prior to 1500 AD. But my findings are
more striking: None of 18 coefficients for technology come anywhere
close to significance. Early technology did not shape current levels of
corruption.

The results are somewhat more positive for nineteenth-century education. I present simple correlations between the technology indicators
and mean school years in 1870 in Table 2.9. Only three correlations are

Table 2.10 *Correlations of Historical Technology Measures with Mean School Years, 1870*

Variable	Correlation
Sectoral technology 1000 BC	.185
Sectoral technology 0 AD	.372
Sectoral technology 1500 AD	.559
Military technology 1000 BC	.250
Military technology 0 AD	.114
Military technology 1500 AD	.574
Industrial technology 1000 BC	.402
Industrial technology 0 AD	.053
Industrial technology 1500 AD	.434
Agricultural technology 1000 BC	.102
Agricultural technology 0 AD	−.023
Agricultural technology 1500 AD	.140
Transportation technology 1000 BC	.240
Transportation technology 0 AD	.373
Transportation technology 1500 AD	.204
Communication technology 1000 BC	−.185
Communication technology 0 AD	.347
Communication technology 1500 AD	.640

.5 or higher: for the overall index, military technology, and communication technology for 1500 AD. The highest correlation is for communication technology (.640) – and this makes sense since this measure includes indicators of literacy. Contemporary education seems to have a longer legacy.

Why the Legacy of the Past Matters

The past matters simply because it has a big effect on the present. Patterns of income and income inequality do *not* change dramatically over time.

In Figure 2.6, I plot GDP per capita in 2010 (from the Penn World Tables) against the same measure for 1870 (provided by Petersen). The two measures are highly correlated ($r^2 = .68$). Countries that were wealthy in 1870 were also wealthy 140 years later. Japan and South

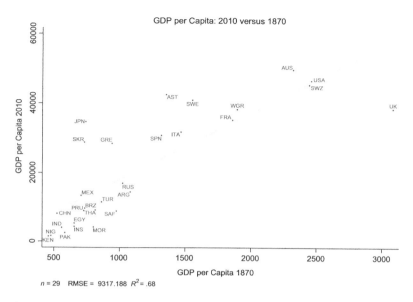

Figure 2.6 GDP Per Capita in 1870 and 2010

Korea stand out with greater income in 2010 than in the past – and they also show strong increases in the mean level of education (see Chapter 6).

Education levels also are consistent over time. I present a lowess plot of the 2010 and 1870 data in Figure 2.7. The relationship is curvilinear, with the sharpest increases for countries with low levels – but not the lowest – of schooling in 1870 ($r^2 = .58$ linear, .70 quadratic). The rank-order correlation is .85.

Mean school levels are also strongly related to the level of inequality in education in a country (van Zanden *et al.*, 2011).[8] The r^2 between mean school years in 1870 and the level of educational inequality across 24 countries in 1890 (the first year where there are measures for more than 20 countries) is .66, .75 without the United States (which was to become one of the most equal countries in the distribution of education in the world in the early twentieth century). The connection between levels of schooling and educational inequality persists over long periods (from 1870–2010). The r^2 between mean school years in 1870 and educational inequality in 2010 is .46, .52 if I exclude the most unequal distributions (see Figure 2.8). The level of education in

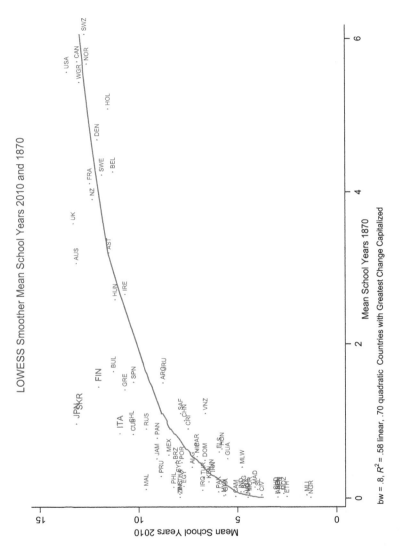

LOWESS Smoother Mean School Years 2010 and 1870

bw = .8, R^2 = .58 linear, .70 quadratic Countries with Greatest Change Capitalized

Mean School Years 1870

Mean School Years 2010

Figure 2.7 Lowess Smoother Mean School Years, 1870 and 2010

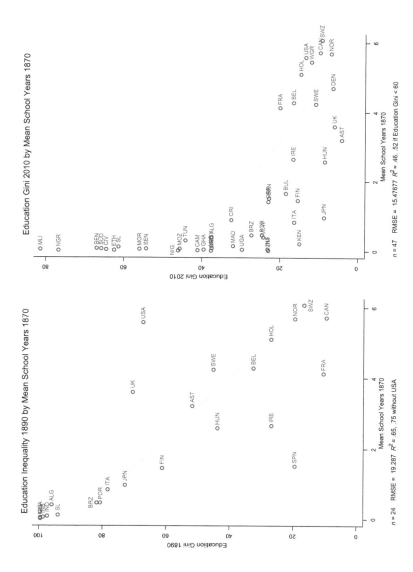

Figure 2.8 Levels of Education and Educational Inequality, 1870–1890–2010

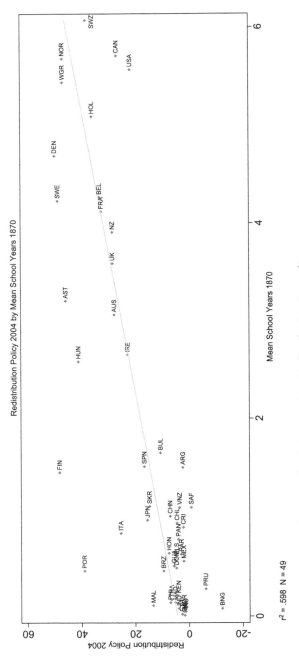

Figure 2.9 The Legacy of Mean School Years on Post-Redistribution Inequality

World Map Mean School Year Change 1870-2010

Figure 2.10 Mean School Year Change 1870–2010

1870 is strongly related to schooling inequality both 140 years ago and today.

Why is there so much persistence over time in levels of education and in national wealth? I shall not try to explain the wealth of nations, but offer one graph that shows why there is what I have called the "inequality trap." In Figure 2.9, I plot mean school years in 1870 against Solt's (2009) measure of post-redistribution inequality across 49 countries. The relationship is strong: $r^2 = .598$. More education does lead to greater equality (Rothstein and Uslaner, 2005). Yet more equal societies in the late nineteenth century were more likely to have higher mean levels of schooling. A simple instrumental variable regression (not shown) provides support for a path from nineteenth-century equality to higher levels of education to greater post-redistribution equality in the twentieth century. Most likely, there is a "virtuous circle" of equality and education (culminating in less corruption).

All is not lost for those countries that did not start out with high levels of education. Some countries have caught up – and some even have used education as a strategy to reduce corruption (see Chapter 6). While the countries with high levels of education in 1870 also had more students in school almost a century and a half later, other countries can – and have – increased their levels of education. The graph of mean school year change from 1870 to 2010 (Figure 2.10) looks somewhat different from the map of mean school years (Figure 2.3). The correlation between change and the initial measure is just .347. It is difficult for countries to catch up but it has happened. Before I get to the success stories, I must look at the history: the independent countries in Chapter 3, most colonies and former colonies in Chapter 4, and the United States in Chapter 5.

Notes

1 Other measures would not change the results. different expert-based measures of "good governance" correlate at a 0.9 level (Holmberg *et. al.* (2009). The expert-based measures correlate with measures from surveys of citizens at an almost equally high level (Bechert and Quandt 2009, Svallfors 2012).

2 The Morrison-Murtin data set is available at www.fabricemurtin.com/ and the Bourginon-Morrison economic data are available at www .delta.ens.fr/XIX/#1870. Since many of the countries in the Transparency International data were not in existence in 1870, I matched the

regional/colonial codes in these data sets to contemporary nations. This increased the sample size of the Morrison-Murtin data set from 74 to 78 (see the Appendix for a list of countries and their levels of education in 1870). Glaeser *et al.* (2004) use Lindert's measure of education for 1900; it covers fewer countries. The correlation between the two data sets is very high (.86 and .96 for the 1870 and 1900 Morrison-Murtin data, N = 30). Other data sets are Vanhanen (1997) for percent family farms and democratization (available at www.fsd.uta.fi/english/data/catalogue/FSD1216/) and You and Khagram (2005) for 1980 percent Protestant, provided by Jong-sun You. I also estimated models with both Vanhanen's measure of democratization and with the Polity IV historical measure of democracy (Marshall and Jaggers, 2010, available at www.systemicpeace.org/polity/polity4.htm). The results were similar using Vanhanen's measure.

3 Forty-nine of 57 countries were colonies or former colonies. The exceptions are Bulgaria, China, Iran, Hungary, (South) Korea, Thailand, Russia, and Turkey.

4 The weak and underidentification tests can be rejected at conventional levels.

5 Available at www.sscnet.ucla.edu/polisci/faculty/treisman/Pages/unpublishedpapers.html\. The highest scores are for the countries that have the most regulation is on the media, as well as the greatest number of political and economic pressures on the media (www.freedomhouse.org/report-types/freedom-press#.U81AbvldXh4).

6 I am grateful to Philip Keefer for providing the data and the Stata code to recreate his measure. The Kitschelt Democratic Accountability and Linkages Project can be found at http://sites.duke.edu/democracylinkage/ for both a description of the project and data as well as data downloads.

7 I am grateful to Michael Bang Petersen for providing these data.

8 The data can be found at www.clio-infra.eu/content/about-clio-infra Jan Luiten van Zanden.

3 | *Education in Developed Europe*

Universal education began in Europe – first in Prussia and then spread throughout Northern Europe. In this chapter I tell the story of the development of education in the more developed nations of Europe (I leave discussions of Bulgaria and Hungary to the next chapter).

Schooling was more widespread in Northern Europe. The European advantage over the rest of the world was substantial. Most of the "rest of the world" was less developed and had been colonized by Britain, France, and Spain. The colonial powers invested little in the indigenous peoples they ruled. They provided education mostly to their own citizens – at home or in colonies where they constituted a substantial share of the population.

Education was most widespread in Europe where:

- there was greater equality. I showed in Chapter 2 that economic equality was a critical factor shaping the provision of education in the more developed countries. The family farm percentage averaged 29 percent in Europe, compared to 15 percent elsewhere. Where there was greater equality, there were more demands – from below – for the provision of schools, even without democratic government.
- the country was predominantly Protestant. Protestant churches advocated education so that ordinary people could read the Bible. Reading the Bible empowered the individual. Literacy led to learning other skills so that people would be the masters of their own fates. Protestantism, Luther argued, offered a message of honesty that stood in contrast to the hierarchical and corrupt Catholic Church. Protestant churches usually worked with the state to support the development of literacy. Often churches accepted the state demand for the complete separation of religion and secular education.

Southern Europe was (and is) predominantly Catholic. The Catholic Church did *not* advocate widespread education. It feared that ordinary people reading the Bible would form their own interpretations and challenge the Church orthodoxy. In Catholic countries, schools were often run by the Church – or at least the Church set the curriculum. Universal schooling was not the norm in Catholic countries – and girls were mostly excluded.

Where the Protestant and Catholic population shares were relatively equal, the competition for advantage in education led to greater mean levels of schooling than we find in countries dominated by either form of Christianity. Competition fostered greater provision of education – and the two countries with the most even divisions – Switzerland and the Netherlands – ranked first and fourth in Europe in mean school years. Competition among religions led each Church to refrain from attempting to impose its doctrine on schools in Switzerland. In the Netherlands the two major churches were given effective domination of primary education in the nineteenth century, leading to segregated schools. With Catholics and Calvinists (Protestants) taking full control of schools for their children, religious antagonisms were reduced and each school system could flourish (Lijphart, 1968, 118).

At least two Catholic countries (Belgium and France) challenged church authority and required that schools have complete separation of church and state (on Belgium, see Spain Exchange Country Guide, n.d.).

Northern Europeans had two advantages over their Southern Europeans. First, there was more pressure from below in Northern Europe – land ownership was more equal and ordinary people pressured the state for greater benefits. Second, Northern European states were generally stronger than those in the South. In the North, the secular state worked with the Protestant church to provide education to the citizenry. In the South, the Catholic Church was an alternative source of power. The Catholic Church controlled the schools in most Southern European countries.

Northern Europe largely led the way, although not every Protestant country in the North had widespread education. Finland was the laggard in Northern Europe – and, perhaps surprisingly, so was the United Kingdom. Ironically, as the colonial powers largely outpaced their colonies in education, Britain surpassed most in Asia and Africa, but lagged behind the United States, Canada, Australia, and New Zealand (see Chapter 5).

The descriptive statistics show how sharp the Northern European advantage was in 1870. For the nine countries in the data set in

Northern Europe, the average level of education was 4.5 years. Excluding Finland and the United Kingdom, the average rises to 5.1 years. For Southern Europe (six countries), the mean is 2.1, still considerably higher than the average of .47 for the 59 other countries in the data set excluding the United States, Canada, Australia, and New Zealand. Northern Europe (outside of Finland and the United Kingdom) had an average of more than twice as much as Southern Europe and almost 11 times as great as the other countries in the data set.

Why was Northern Europe so advantaged? The most important part of the story is equality. The two most equal countries in the South – Austria and France – also had the highest level of education. The correlation between equality and education levels is .79, though with only five cases one should not make too much of this measure.

Hierarchy in Catholic countries flourishes where there is greater economic inequality: The correlation between the share of family farms in 1868 with contemporaneous measures of the share of Catholics in a country is strong: the correlation for various estimates are all similar, at .65. Protestant Europe had an average of 33 percent family farms compared to 29 percent in Southern Europe.

The confluence of forces gave a distinct advantage to Northern Europe. The payoff was immediate: The V-DEM corruption estimate for Northern Europe in 1900 was .055, compared to .333 for Southern Europe, and .51 for other countries (outside the United States, Canada, Australia, and New Zealand). In Protestant Europe, an average of 33 percent of farms were owned by families in 1868, compared to 23 percent in Catholic Europe. The outliers in Catholic Europe were France (29 percent) and Austria (35 percent), where the state intervened to wrest control of the schools from the Church. The major outlier in Protestant Europe was England, as I discuss below. For mean school years, the average for Protestant Europe was 4.5, 4.9 without the outlier of Finland. For Catholic Europe the mean is 2.13. Outside Europe, the mean is just .73.

I move to a discussion of nineteenth-century schooling in Europe. I begin with Protestant Europe: Germany, the Nordic countries, and England. Next I consider the mixed states: Switzerland and the Netherlands. Finally, I consider Catholic Europe – the countries that best fit my explanation: Italy, Spain, and Portugal, as well as the two great exceptions, France and Belgium and a "partial" exception (Ireland).

Religion, Colonialism, and Equality

In Western Europe, North America, Australia, and New Zealand, the movement for widespread education had an important ally in expanding education: Protestant churches wanted people to be educated so that they could read the Bible. In contrast, the Catholic Church generally feared that literacy might challenge its authority (Woodberry, 2011). Education empowered people not just to read the Bible, but to excel in other areas of learning. Protestant countries, largely because of their higher levels of education, had lower levels of land inequality than did Catholic countries in the nineteenth century (Frankema, 2010, 426).

More inclusive (that is, universal) education in the latter part of the nineteenth century was more likely to be found where governments, rather than private groups (most notably missionaries), took responsibility for funding and organizing schools – and in countries where there was a greater degree of economic equality. Outside the West, most countries in the late nineteenth century were either colonies or former colonies. The Protestant churches in Western countries supported public education more than the Catholic churches did. Before the twentieth century regions with more Protestant individuals within the same European countries did have higher literacy rates, especially among non-elites and women than their catholic counterparts (Woodberry 2011). In Europe, the type of religion was more important than economic prosperity. Scandinavia, lowland Scotland, and Iceland were all very poor and yet had broad-based literacy. What they had in common was the Protestant religion that resulted in both religiously financed literacy campaigns and support for public education through the state.

The Catholic Church invested in education only where it faced competition (such as in Ireland, North America, and in the British colonies) or where facing a secularizing state such as France. However, where competition for the souls was lacking, education was not a priority area for the Catholic Church as the cases of Italy, Spain, and Portugal clearly show. The Church often provided education to young people, but not as extensively as Protestant churches and mostly as an alternative to state-run schooling. At times, the Catholic Church also feared literacy as this was seen as a means to a Protestant reformation (Gill, 1998). Gill also argues that Protestantism more often stresses a personal relationship to God, while the Catholic religion sees that this rather is done by priestly meditation. Protestantism also implied that everyone would need direct access to the word of God in the form of being able to read the Bible in their own language (Woodberry, 2012).

Western Europe: Mass Education and the Need for State-Building

In Prussia, Denmark, France, and Sweden, the introduction of universal education reforms was a response to a sense of national crisis seen to stem from a fragmented social order (Boli, 1989, 218; Weber, 1976). The new systems of mass education that arose in Denmark, France, Prussia, and Sweden were built on principles that citizenship should be based on universality and egalitarianism: One of the most striking aspect of the universalism" of the law that established free mass education in Sweden in 1842 was that boys and girls would be treated equally in the new system and that they were to be thought together (Boli, 1989, 34, 232).

Can particular historical cases of the development of mass education be traced to contemporary levels of corruption? Today's Germany has a comparatively low level of corruption while Italy is the opposite case. Can this huge difference in levels of corruption between Germany and Italy be traced back to variations in efforts in mass education during the second half of the nineteenth century? The answer seems to be yes.

In 1806 Prussia became the first country to introduce universal mass education, almost a hundred years before England did. In 1870, Prussia ranked third in mean school years, behind Switzerland (6.07) and Norway (5.68).

Green (1990) argues that sociological theories such as the importance of urbanization, working-life conditions, and changing family structures cannot explain why France and Prussia (and Denmark and Sweden) developed universal mass schooling well before England. Green (1990), as well as Boli (1989) and Weber (1976), point to the political elite's perceived need for state-building and national unity as the main driving force. Prussia, Sweden, and France developed universal mass education as a mean for creating "new citizens" with a strong national identity which, in its turn, was seen as needed for effective state-building as a whole. But his argument neglects pressures from below.

Prussia was widely concerned to be an unequal society, at least in part because social classes had unequal representation in the legislature (Lindert, 2004, 114). No data are available on land inequality for Prussia in van Hanen's family farm data. However, Grant (2005, 46, 307, 327–329) argues: " . . . in Germany in 1895 over 86% of land was owner-occupied" and " . . . the overall level of inequality in Prussia in the period appears to have been relatively low for a country going through the disruptions of industrialization."

Ramirez and Boli (1987) argue that nation building was the primary reason Prussia introduced mass education. Schooling was a mean "to construct a unified national polity, where individuals would identify themselves with the nation." Sponsoring mass schooling was a strategy for the state to avoid losing power in the interstate system by using it as the means of "national revitalization." Prussia was a "state without a nation" while a strong central bureaucracy was in place. Its polity was dominated by local interests. Frederick II wrote the famous directive "General Regulations for Village Schools" (Ramirez and Boli 1987). Through state-directed education, " . . . all children were taught to identify with the state and its goals and purposes rather than with local polities (estates, peasant communities, regions, etc.).

In 1806 Napoleon triumphed over Prussia. The humiliation the Treaty of Tilsit provoked the Germans towards patriotism which would be fostered by mass education. According to the lectures of Fichte " . . . universal, state-directed, compulsory education would teach all Germans to be good Germans and would prepare them to play whatever role – military, economic, political – fell to them in helping the state reassert Prussian power." A bureau of education was established, ten years later a department of education was created. Between the years 1817–1825, a state administration of education was established, and taxes were imposed in order to finance the school system (Ramirez and Boli, 1987; cf. Green, 1990).

Wilhelm originally hoped that structural reforms would lead to a sense of patriotism among the Prussian public, but ultimately Baron Karl von Stein, who was put in charge of reforming state institutions, realized that they would not succeed "due to the insufficient level of education" (Aghion, Perrson, and Rouzet, 2012, 4). The rate of illiteracy among men fell from 17 percent in 1801 to three percent between 1837 and 1841 (Aghion, Perrson, and Rouzet, 2012, 7).

Not all agreed that the development of mass education in Prussia was driven by exclusively by the King and his minister. The provision of schooling reflected political demands from the middle class against the governing elites. The Prussian nobility was opposed to earlier efforts to expand education. When Prussia first introduced compulsory schooling in 1763, the Junkers (noblemen) feared that educated peasants would rebel and seek redress from the courts to seek fewer duties (Cinnirella and Hornung, 2011, 8, 9). The demand for education came from the rising middle class (the "burghers") who protested the elite domination of local councils and forced, through violence and with the support of the lower classes, new representation on the councils. These "reformed" bodies were responsive to the rising middle class rather than to the elites (Schilling, 1983). The demands for universal education came from below, not just from above.

The social reforms of the Reformation, Dittmar and Meisenzahl (2016, 2, 9–10) argued, "were citizens' movements that emerged without initial support from oligarchic city governments or territorial lords ... The constituency for reform came from citizens who were excluded from political power by oligarchic elites, typically lesser merchants and guild members ... The most fundamental provisions established compulsory public schooling. The educational provisions aimed to make the Reformation irreversible – by producing high-quality public servants to staff expanding Protestant church and state bureaucracies and by producing disciplined Protestant subjects." And it was Luther who emphasized the importance of the state, not the Church or parents, in providing these services (Strauss, 1988, 192).

The early adopters of universal education were mostly Protestant European states: Norway (5.68 mean school years in 1870), Denmark (4.69), Sweden (4.23), and the Netherlands (5.09). In England and the Nordic countries the church became an official part of the state. This made it easier for these states to use the schools that were run by the local parishes or were heavily influenced by the clergy as instrument for state-building, not least by influencing the content in disciplines such as history and literature (Weber, 1976, ch. 18; Tingsten, 1969). While the clergy ran the schools, the financing came from the state (or was mandated for the local municipalities by law). Universal mass education in Denmark, France, Prussia, and Sweden during the nineteenth century was not a mere extension of earlier forms of church-dominated education (Boli, 1989, 209–212; Weber, 1976, 362–364; and Green, 1990). Instead, as Green (1990, 29) argues:

What characterized the national education system was its "universality," and its orientation towards the secular needs of the state and civil society. As a signal of "universalism" and "open access," free mass education was introduced several decades before universal welfare state programs such as public pensions or health insurance.

The underlying mechanism behind Weber's Protestant ethic, Becker and Woessmann (2009) argue, is not the religious message of hard work, but the greater literacy where Protestantism was dominant.

The church played a central role in the development of mass education in Norway. While most of the population was illiterate at the outset of the eighteenth century, mandatory elementary schooling for seven years – free to everyone – was adopted in 1736 (*Oslo Times*, n.d.). Norway had the most equal land distribution in the entire van Hanen database (64 percent of all farms were owned by families).

Norway was a poor agrarian society. It faced widespread emigration as prices for agricultural (and manufactured) products fell dramatically. The provision of universal education was a response to public demands for new skills that would let them earn a living without emigrating (University of Chicago Chronicle, 1997).

Denmark and Sweden were both relatively equal in the late nineteenth century. In each, 35 percent of farms were family owned. Denmark also had a long tradition of social equality, which more recently (in the 1930s) was "codified" in a series of commandments about proper behavior toward one's fellow citizens, Jante Law (after a small town in Denmark renamed "Jante" by the author Sandemose). Among the ten prescriptions of Jante Law were: You shall not believe that you are any wiser than we are, know more than we do, and are more important than we are, (Booth, 2015, 81–83). Danes have long believed that education is a basic right. Frederick VI abolished serfdom at the beginning of the nineteenth century and one of his first reforms was to require that all children had to take examinations certifying that they had basic competence in subjects covered in schools (Hald, 1857). What spurred the development of mass education in Denmark? Denmark was under constant threat from Prussia and Sweden, having lost a third or the country to Russia in 1809. In the mid-nineteenth century, it managed to curb systemic corruption to gain the support of its citizens (Frisk Jensen, 2008; Rothstein, 2011, ch. 8) and mass education was the tool to promote good government.

Sweden did not have a feudalistic economy – but it was a poor country. Yet it was among the more equal in Europe (and the world) and adopted a Church Law aimed at raising literacy rates in 1686 (Baten and Luiten van Zanden, 2008). Compulsory elementary education was enacted in 1842. Sweden stood out in establishing co-educational primary schools (Garrouste, 2010, 33). In Sweden, national unity was also the purpose for mass education, according to the authors, even though the clergy and aristocracy tried to stop this fearing that education in Sweden could make people rebellious. However, the clergy had before the nineteenth century proposed education for the purpose religious instruction.

As in Prussia, the aristocracy and the clergy had opposed universal education, worrying that an educated peasantry would be rebellious. Yet the clergy had earlier supported education to give people instruction in religion (Johansson, 2009; Ramirez and Boli [1987]). The responsibility for literacy had rested with parents prior to the nineteenth century (Johansson, 2009).

Lindmark (2009, 102) argues that the Lutheran Church is the origin of the universalist model of the Nordic welfare system. In Lutheran doctrine, daily labor is considered a divine calling. Universalism in Sweden originated from "the mission of the Lutheran state church: to bring the divine word to everyone" (Lindmark, 2009, 102, citing Johansson [2009]). Nordic universalism stresses the equality of people and the right of each person to benefits, especially education, from the state (Rothstein and Uslaner, 2005).

Initially, mass education through the Church stressed reading, but in 1842 writing skills were added to the curriculum as part of a larger program of elementary school reforms. This education campaign was driven by the state but the church was responsible for implementing it. The local parishes had to establish and maintain schools. There was thus a close relation between state and church in Sweden for the implementation of universal education.

Graff (1987, 30) argues that the Reformation

... constituted the first great literacy campaign in the history of the West, with its social legacies of individual literacy as a powerful social and moral force and its pedagogical traditions of compulsory instruction in public institutions specially created for the purposes of the indoctrination of the young for explicitly social ends.

Near-universal levels of literacy – making skills in reading compulsory for all citizens – were achieved rapidly in Sweden through a joint effort by the state and the Lutheran Church.

Urbanization, commercialization, and industrialization had nothing to do with the process of making the Swedish people perhaps the most literate in the West before the eighteenth century. (Graff, 1987, 34)

The state church sponsored the literacy campaign in Sweden. Supervision was done regularly and so was personal examination by parish clergy. Hence, the church stood above a system rooted in home education. Not following this law could restrict the possibility of marriage. This state church model of education also achieved something different from other places, a special priority on the literacy of women and mothers. This led to the Swedish mass literacy in form of very high female literacy rates (Graff, 1987).

As in the United States (see Chapter 5), education was seen as a prerequisite for the development of a citizenry capable of governing themselves. Graff also stresses literacy's role for the participatory democracy. Graff (1987, 70) argues that " . . . free, self-governing people must be educated; one must be able to read and write and be trained in critical skills in order to perform the duties of responsible citizenship." Boli (1989, 232) adds that one of "the most striking aspect of the universalism" of the law that established free mass education in Sweden in 1842 was that boys and girls would be treated equally in the new system and that classes would include both boys and girls.

Denmark's long tradition of universal education stemmed from two beliefs. First, the economic well-being of Denmark rested on education (OECD, 1999, 5):

Talk to any Dane, from the taxi driver to the cabinet minister and you will hear the same story: "We have nothing – no ore to mine, no forests to fell, only enough oil to meet our own domestic needs, no waterfalls to send through generators. There is little on the ground or underneath its surface that will sustain us. We have only our people – their skills, their knowledge, their creativity. That is our national asset and we have no choice but to invest in it.

Second, "every child, however destitute, has an inherent and indisputable right to be educated" (Hald, 1857, 45). Denmark enacted a

law in 1814 requiring that every 14-year-old had to pass an examination to prove that (s)he has "received at least the minimum of education demanded by law; so that all children are obliged regularly to
attend the public school" (Hald, 1857, 46). Schools had been run by the
Catholic Church until the Reformation in the early sixteenth century,
when they were taken over by the state. The Lutheran Church worked
with the state to promote universal education (StateUniversity.com).

Most students attended state-run schools, but a set of private
schools. The "*Folkeskol,*" or "folk school," which was run indepen-
dently by parents, sometimes at the level of elementary school but
more often for high school and adult education (A Brief History of
Folk Schools, n.d.):

Nikolai Frederik Severin (NFS) Grundtvig... was a philosopher, poet, theologian, educator, historian, composer of hymns, translator, and social critic.
Education... was one of his primary concerns. Grundtvig believed that the
classical education of the time with an emphasis on Greek and Latin studies,
created a rift between life and learning... schools should bring dignity to
rural people and to the life of the farmer, the majority of Denmark's population at the time. He wanted education to instill a pride in national culture and a love of learning that would be lifelong. In the 1830s, he believed
that... only through the establishment of the folk school would the Danish people be able to build the foundation of skills and the enlightenment
necessary for creating a peaceable and just society.

Christen Kold took up Grundtvig's ideas and founded the "folk school"
movement in the 1830s. These schools were based upon "a deep faith
in the intrinsic abilities of all individuals and a belief that education
should be available to everyone. 'Schools for Life' as Grundtvig called
them were to assist people in understanding their own identity and
to strengthen and empower communities. The folk schools were part
of a decentralized grassroots movement that gave farmers a means for
personal and social transformation ("A Brief History of Folk Schools,"
n.d.). Folk schools served different functions for groups in Danish society: For peasants who were dispersed in small communities distant
from each other, the folk schools were boarding schools for children.
For the "urban merchant class," as well as for the peasants, the schools
"would provide the lower classes of society with the educational level
required for them to be active participants in a modern and less eli-
tist society" (StateUniversity.com; Denmark, n.d.), and for adults, the

folk schools offered practical "learning for life." These schools – which were supported by state grants but were not under state control – as well as state run schools infused people with a sense of national identity. As elsewhere, the push for universal education arose after military defeat. Folk schools spread throughout the country after "1864 when Denmark was forced to surrender a large part of Jutland to Prussia (Germany) after the second war of Schleswig. The loss of territory was another blow to the Danish identity and it spurred a strong nationalism" (Denmark, n.d.).

Denmark has been consistently one of the leaders in mass education in the twentieth century. From its fifth-place ranking in 1870, its mean score has consistently increased over the 140 years to 2010 ($R^2 = .953$ with time). It has also had one of the most equitable distributions of education, as measured by the education Gini, from 1910 – the first year of data for Denmark (ranking second of 27 countries) to 2010 (ranking third of 47 nations). And the Danes' strong commitment to education and equality has paid off in governance. It was tied with New Zealand in 2010 as the least corrupt country in the world (CPI = 9.3). The mean V-DEM corruption score over time is .436. Denmark's score varies from a "high" of .035 in 1901 to a low of .01 from 1969 to 2010. For Denmark, education is clearly associated with less corruption.

The outlier in the Nordic countries was Finland, with just 1.45 mean school years. Most Finns could not write and reading levels were modest. Less than half of children began primary education by 1870 and only 15 percent were able to read and write (Bandle, Elmevik, and Widmark, 2002, 1528). Education was highly unequal with negative educational inequality scores from V-DEM from 1900 (when the time series begins) to 1918. It wasn't until 1945, after World War II, that education in Finland was widely available to all children and educational inequality became very low. In the nineteenth century few young people went to school.

West (1996) writes: " . . . the supply of schooling in Britain between 1800 and 1840 was relatively substantial prior to any government intervention, although it depended almost completely on private funds. At this time, moreover, the largest contributors to education revenues were working parents and the second largest was the Church. Of course, there was less education per child than today, just as there was less of everything else, because the national income was so much smaller . . . [Yet by] 1920, when schooling had become 'free' and compulsory . . . the proportion had fallen to 0.7 percent."

The government enacted a law requiring six years of compulsory education in 1921. The second spurt came in 1945 and beginning in the 1990s, with the fall of the Soviet Union (Finland's nemesis), there was a major spurt to make Finnish education the best in the world (see Chapter 6; Gasrrouste, 2010, 20).

The other major Protestant country is England. England was the leader in the industrial revolution (Gillard, 2011) and it reputedly bequeathed good institutions to its colonies (Acemoglu and Robinson, 2012, 18–19, 27). Yet it lagged behind other European Protestant countries (except Finland) in mean school years. The average education level for England in 1870 was 3.59. And it also lagged behind its colonies in North America and Australia and New Zealand (see Chapter 5).

England was a laggard in the provision of public education. While the United States allocated 90 percent of public education expenditures to primary schooling and Japan spent 69 percent, England allocated only 59 percent to early schooling (Chaudhary, 2007, l8).

England had been at the forefront of education between 1540 and 1700, but in the late eighteenth and early nineteenth centuries fell behind its own colonies and other European countries, including several in Catholic Southern Europe (Lindert, 2004, 113).

There is an alternative account of England's weak performance on early education.

Gillard (2011) called the education system a "haphazard system of parish and private adventure schools." The upper classes "objected to all forms of education for the poor." Many of the schools were run by the Church of England, which refused to allow the children of non-believers to enroll. Even in the first half of the nineteenth century, "the school life of most children was short."

In 1816 3,500 of 12,000 parishes had no school and 5,500 had "unendowed schools of even more variable quality." As late as 1864 two-thirds of English towns did not have a secondary school.

Gillard wrote: " . . . by the start of the 19th century, education was organised, like English society as a whole, on a more rigid class basis." In 1911 only 8 percent of children aged 14–15 were being educated at state schools. By 1938 more than twice as many students went on to higher education in Germany, France, and Switzerland and over 10 times as many in the United States.

England (later Britain) continued to lag behind the United States until 1990. And its rate of increase over time was slower. In a regression of mean school years with year, the t ratio of the slope for the increase for the UK is 20 compared to 34 to the United States, indicating far slower growth.

Why was there so little public education in England in the nineteenth century? Lindert (2004, 114–115, 123) attributed England's relatively poor performance to the centralization of funding of education mandated by Parliament, leaving little room for local communities to invest in educating their children:

Parliament had quietly erected barriers to local government initiative that effectively blocked the creation of local tax-based schools . . . Britain's dependence on central government and wholly private sources for school funding departed from the typical practice of the nations that led in primary schooling . . .

Yet (Lindert, 2004, 113):

England was . . . one of the leaders in basic education *before* the era of her economic world leadership, but not *during* it. England had been one of the leaders in literacy, along with the Netherlands, between 1540 and 1700, when schooling was still mainly private – and meager – all over the world. But across the eighteenth century, English literacy diffused less rapidly than literacy in the North American colonies, Scotland, the Netherlands, northern France, Switzerland, and Italy's Piedmont . . . among the masses, literacy actually retreated from mid-century to the 1785–1814 period.

The greater success of Britain's former colony was attributable to more local control, he concluded.

There is a more straightforward explanation, which is more consistent with the argument I have made in Chapter 2 (and will make throughout the book): England was a highly unequal society in the nineteenth century. Only 5 percent of its farms were family owned. The relationship between land inequality and mean school years is clear in Figures 3.1 and 3.2. Education in England (the UK) is more extensive than we might expect from the share of farms family owned (Figure 3.1). It had by far the greatest education Gini in Europe in 1870 and stands out in Figure 3.2 on the upper left of the graph of educational inequality and percent family farms. More critical than institutional design was economic inequality. Even Lindert and Williamson

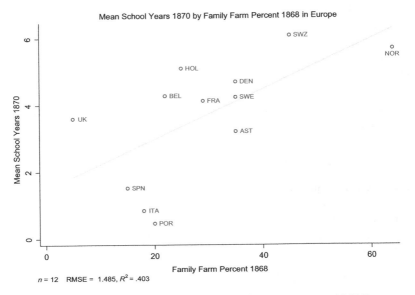

Figure 3.1 Mean School Years 1870 and Family Farm Percent 1868 Europe

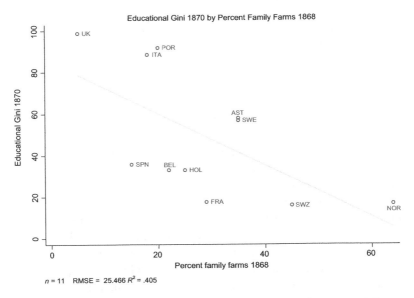

Figure 3.2 Educational Inequality 1870 and Percent Family Farms 1868

(2011, 4) argue that American inequality was lower in the late eighteenth century than the income gap in England (or Wales). And economic equality was the major factor leading to high levels of education in England's former colonies – the United States, Canada, Australia, and New Zealand (see Chapter 5).

Ultimately England (the United Kingdom) "caught up" in education levels – and even surpassed the United States (barely) on the Transparency International CPI – 7.6 compared to 7.1, although Canada, Australia, and New Zealand still ranked higher. The story of education in England is one of how inequality matters, even more than institutional design. England's former colonies topped the mother country in both education and equality.

Mixed Protestant-Catholic Countries

Switzerland, divided by religion and language, nevertheless was the world leader in mean school years in 1870. It also ranked seventh in corruption in 2010 from Transparency International and in 1868 was behind only Norway, Canada, and the United States in land equality. Switzerland was one of the first countries to establish elementary schools that were free and had mandatory enrollments (van de Walle, 1980, 465). Hoffman and Schwartz (2015, 13) attribute Switzerland's "gold standard" of education to its low level of inequality.

Switzerland had been embroiled in a series of civil wars. The conflicts were based upon religious and linguistic differences – with almost equal shares of the population adhering to Catholicism and Protestantism. The two dominant languages are French and German with smaller shares of the population speaking Italian and Romansch (only spoken in Switzerland).

The linguistic and religious divisions were cross-cutting rather than overlapping so that compromise was possible over many issues, including education. Each canton (province) was given control of education, with little power reserved for the central government (Hega, 2011).

The 1874 Federal Constitution established mandatory free education to be run by the cantons (Switzerland in the 19th Century, n.d.) – and the cantons were required to provide schooling to all students without regard to religious background (Hega, 2011).

Switzerland adapted to religious diversity by removing religion from the public schools – thus reserving control over education to the cantons rather than to religious authorities. There were private religious schools but they had difficulty in raising sufficient funding and many were closed (Pahud de Motranges, n.d., 692). Switzerland "solved" the problem of religious education by ensuring schools did not promote any religion.

The Netherlands was also a country divided between Protestants and Catholics. Rather than establishing a secular school system, the Dutch divided their schools between the faiths with each church responsible for educating its own young people. The Netherlands had the fourth-highest level of education (5.09 mean school years) in 1870. Education took root early in the Netherlands. A religious order, the Brethren of the Common Life, was founded by Gert Groote in 1374 as a protest against what he saw as the corruption of the Catholic Church. The Brethren fostered education so that ordinary Dutch people could read the Bible (as did Luther in Prussia).

By the seventeenth century the literacy rate in the Netherlands was substantially greater than in neighboring areas. The Brethren published books and, more critically, set up boarding schools for poor children (Akcomak, Webbink, and tger Weel, 2015). Education was not made compulsory until 1900, with a series of incremental. changes throughout the twentieth century (Garrouste, 2010, 29). From 1870 until the mid-20th century there was a consistent increase in the share of young people attending school. Changes in education policy in 1949 and 1968 were associated with large jumps in levels of schooling. The rate of growth in mean school years was rather modest under pillarization. It began to pick up after depillarization. By 2010 it ranked 17th of the 78 countries in the education database, a decline from eighth place in 1870, before pillarization replaced the secular schools. In 2010, Belgium ranked 22nd in corruption of 178 nations rated by Transparency International, below most of Northern Europe but tied with the United States.

The Dutch system is distinctive because the country has relatively equal shares of Protestants and Catholics. Switzerland, also with an equal share of Catholics and Protestants (but with a Catholic majority), developed a system of secular education that favored neither Catholics nor Protestants. In the Netherlands, three quarters of students attended secular state schools in the late nineteenth century. The Netherlands adopted a system of "pillarization" with separate schools for Protestants and Catholics that lasted until 1968 – and the great majority of students attended private Catholic or Protestant schools. Initially, these religious schools were private, but in 1916 all schools, religious and secular, received full funding from the state (Lijphart, 1968, 52, 110). Pillarization led to social segregation, but led to universal early education (Bundeszentrale fur Politische Bildung, n.d.).

Catholic Europe

The Protestant churches in Northern Europe supported public education more than the Catholic churches. Before the twentieth century, regions with more Protestants had higher literacy rates (Woodberry, 2011). Scandinavia, lowland Scotland, and Iceland were all very poor and yet had broad-based literacy already in the early nineteenth century. The Protestant churches funded religiously financed literacy campaigns and supported public education.

The Catholic Church, which was dominant in Southern Europe, invested in education only where it faced competition (such as in Ireland, North America and in the British colonies) or in a secularizing state such as France. Where competition was lacking in Southern Italy, Spain, and Portugal – education was not a priority. The Catholic Church also feared literacy as this was seen as a means to a Protestant reformation (Gill, 1998).

Italy introduced a law about universal education in 1859. Italy was not a unified nation state and had strong regional differences. The implementation of the school reform was much more efficient in the northern regions whereas little was done in the southern regions before 1900.

Smith adds (1997, 51):

Virtually, the whole southern agricultural population was illiterate. Yet it was impossible to apply the (. . .) law of 1859 which had specified two years' compulsory education, because parents would not have co-operated even if the teachers and schools could have been found. great regional differences in institutional effectiveness between northern and southern Italy.

These regional differences in corruption and the quality of government institutions persist (Charron, Lapuente and Rothstein, 2013). As late as 1911, half of the Italian population was illiterate (Smith, 1997).

There was a lasting impact of what took place in national systems of education during the late nineteenth century and contemporary levels of "good governance" not only between states but also between regions within states. Italy did not rank highly on either mean school years (.84, ranking 31st, below Chile, China, and Russia) or land inequality (18 percent of its farms were family owned). Its Corruption Perceptions Index was 3.9, ranking 67th of 187 countries, between Rwanda and Georgia.

Italy adopted universal education reform early (1859) but it was only implemented in the Northern regions while the Southern parts lagged behind. Few people in the newly united country spoke the Italian language that was thought in the schools. According to one estimation, outside Tuscany and Rome less than 1 percent of the population could understand or speak Italian.

As Clark (1984, 35) writes:

Many aspects of late nineteenth century Italian history – the slowness to eradicate illiteracy, the low circulation of newspapers and journals, the amazing willingness of Italians to emigrate to foreign countries with strange tongues and stranger manner – become more comprehensible if one remembers that Italians did not normally speak the same language, and could not communicate with each other.

The levels of illiteracy remained very high, especially in the southern parts of the country and on its big islands. As late as 1911, the average rate of illiteracy was 38 percent and in places like Calabria and Sicily it was over 65 percent (Clark, 1984, 36; di Scala, 2004, 161).

One factor that made Italy a laggard was that the local municipalities, especially in the southern parts of the country, had very little enthusiasm for the school reforms and that the laws that obliged parents to send their children to school was often not implemented.

According to Clark (1984, 37), "the legal compulsion was a fiction" and in the South, truancy was about 80 percent. "Local councils were indifferent, the teachers were demoralized, the parents were uncooperative, and the local clergy were actively hostile." In Italy before World War II, the Catholic Church was an importance hindrance for the establishment of broad-based universal education. Funding from the central government for education was disproportionally sent to the northern regions and when major new funding was decided in 1912, the outbreak of the war hindered much of the implementation.

The long period of fascism 1927–1944 was not favorable for modernizing or broadening the school system. Large parts of the teaching was political indoctrination of how the fascist movement "managed to rescue Italy from Bolshevism" (Clark, 1984, 246). After World War II, the educational system was in disarray and very traditional.

Clark (1984, 364) gives a very harsh description of the situation.

Fact-laden syllabuses, drawn up by the ministry in Rome, were set to be memorized, pupils were constantly tested, in front of the whole class, on what they could repeat from the textbooks. Those who failed the annual examination were held back to repeat the year, even in primary school, so only about half the children 'graduated' from primary school at the right age. There was no attempt to link the separate subjects, let alone to link schools to the outside world. Teachers in Rome who taught ancient history were not allowed to take their pupils to see Colosseum. This frightful, rigid, unreal, enclosed, boring and profoundly stupid system did its best to anaesthetize successive generation of pupils. One wonder who suffered most from it: the 'failures' who left school as early as possible, stigmatized and barely literate, or the 'successes' arrogantly convinced that what they had learned at school was worthwhile knowledge.

As late as 1951, 13 percent of the Italian population was officially classified as illiterate and in 1971, more than a quarter of the adult population had not gotten the elementary school certificate (Clark, 1984, 364).

Italy and especially its southern and rural regions were plagued by the triple problem of lack of a unified language, dysfunctional institutions for implementing the reforms and the long period of fascist rule which seem to have hindered any modernization of teaching methods.

Unlike Finland, there was not a major spurt in education levels after World War II (see Chapter 6), accounting for the persistence of corruption.

There is a similar pattern in both Spain and Portugal, each with Catholic populations well over 90 percent. The levels of education in 1870 were 1.51 and .46, respectively. Spain's education level ranked 19th of the 78 countries, below its former colony Uruguay. Portugal was tied with its former colony Brazil for 42nd place, well below several of Spain's former possessions in South America (Argentina, Venezuela, Chile, Costa Rica, Cuba, Panama, Honduras, Paraguay, El Salvador, Mexico, Guatemala, and the Dominican Republic). In 2010, Spain and Portugal had CPI scores of 6.1 and 6, respectively, ranking

30th and 32nd. Unlike Italy, Spain and Portugal did increase levels of education and decrease corruption.

Yet each had histories of inequality and low levels of education to overcome. In 1868, 15 percent of farms in Spain and 20 percent in Portugal were owned by families. And education was controlled by the Catholic Church.

Illiteracy in Spain in the late nineteenth century was estimated to be up to 75 percent. Education was "in a dismal state" (State University, n.d., 3). Catholicism was the official religion, as established in 1851 (and lasting until 1931). The Church "had the right to inspect Education, at all teaching centres, in order to ensure the purity of the faith, proper behaviour, and religious education. Moreover, it had the power to prohibit texts were considered detrimental to Catholic doctrine, and to determine what was anti-religious, anti-Catholic or immoral" Griera (2007, 8).

In 1901, all 6–12-year-old children were required to attend school. However, funding was unequal and poor areas were unable to comply with this requirements. In 1940 a quarter of the population was illiterate. There were educational reforms under left-wing governments in 1931–1933 (Garrouste, 2010, 32), but they were largely reversed when the right took power in 1933. The Fascist regime of Generalissimo Francisco Franco, in power from 1939 to 1975, made marginal improvements in education. However, it gave the Catholic Church a dominant role in schooling, even in secular schools (Domke, 2011, 32, 45). With Franco's death in 1975 came a new regime with educational reforms (see Chapter 6).

Despite Spain's relatively low level of education and high inequality, it managed to provide education to its colonial subjects to a much greater degree than did Great Britain – except for the former British colonies of the United States, Canada, Australia, and New Zealand.

Excluding these countries, British colonies averaged .167 years of education in 1870 compared to .753 for Spanish present and former colonies. Apart from the four more developed former British colonies, there is little support for the claim of Acemoglu and Robinson (2012, 18–19, 27) about the superiority of British colonial rule. This advantage to present and former Spanish colonies is even more impressive since Spain restricted the immigration of Europeans to its colonies (Engerman and Sokoloff, 2002).

Portugal had a similar history. It was ruled by António de Oliveira Salazar, a right-wing authoritarian who became prime minister in 1932 and quickly moved to consolidate his power much as Franco did in Spain. Both before and during the Salazar regime, education was controlled by the Catholic Church. An 1844 law establishing mandatory education was never enforced and a 1911 law mandated only three years of schooling. Two other reforms raised the levels to four and five years, but in 1936 mandatory schooling was reset to three years. The literacy rate was just 60 percent, which did represent an improvement of the pre-1910 rate of 20 percent (Garrouste, 2010, 31; Portugal-Education, n.d.). Under Salazar, "educational innovation lagged, illiteracy remained high, vocational training was almost nonexistent, and Portugal reverted to a situation of quasi-feudalism with the most backward economy and education in Western Europe. Only in the mid-1960s did the country make public education available for all children between the ages of six and twelve. The government enacted laws to equalize educational opportunities, but implementation lagged behind." Not until the 1990s did primary school enrollments approach 100 percent (Portugal-Education, n.d.).

Political instability due to wars with Spain and France and a civil war inhibited reform in schooling (Nunes, n.d.). The content of education was, as in Spain, "... authoritarian and anti-liberal, nationalist and Catholic, and embarked on a thorough re-organization of both the economy and the society of Portugal into a so-called corporatist state" (Palma and Reis, 2012, 4).

As with Spain, when the dictator died, political and social reforms rose to the top of the nation's agenda. By the 1990s, Portugal's education levels were beginning to catch up with the rest of Europe (see Chapter 6).

The Great Exceptions: France and Belgium

Two Catholic countries stand out as exceptions to the argument that the Church stood in the way of widespread education: France and Belgium. Mean school years in the two countries were 4.12 and 4.27, respectively. The two states were among the most equal countries in Catholic Europe with 29 and 22 percent of farms owned by families, respectively (ranking tenth and 13th). Northern European Protestant countries were more equal – only England was much less equal and the Netherlands was about as equal. France and Belgium stood out in two other ways: Even though their populations were overwhelmingly Catholic, the state took responsibility for educating children – and the Church had no say in the curriculum. And in both countries, there was a steady growth in mean school years, especially in the last half century. In 2010, France ranked 10th in mean school years and Belgium was 17th. Italy ranked 20th, Spain 25th, and Portugal 41st. France and Belgium were also relatively free of corruption: Belgium's CPI score was 7.1 (ranking 22nd) and France's was 6.8 (ranking 25th). By 2010, the education reforms in Spain and Portugal placed them right below France on corruption, while Italy was ranked lower.

France was an early exception to education levels in Catholic Europe. The French system of mass education was established not only to make "peasants into Frenchmen" but more important to teach them "national and patriotic sentiments" (Weber, 1976, 332).

Green (1990, 79) argued that the new systems for mass education . . .

signaled a decisive break with the voluntary and particularistic mode of medieval and early modern education, where learning was narrowly associated with specialized forms of clerical, craft and legal training, and existed merely as an extension of the corporate interests of the church, the town, the guild and the family. Public education embodied a new universalism which acknowledged that education was applicable to all groups in society and should serve a variety of social needs. The national systems were designed specifically to transcend the narrow particularism of earlier forms of learning.

France succeeded with the same institutions that failed in England: a strong centralized state with "institutions able not only to provide everyone with reading and writing skills, but also with the moral and civic values deemed necessary for the Nation" (Schwartzman, 2003, 9). The French education system in the late nineteenth century (Aghion, Perrson, and Rouzet, 2012, 8):

. . . was mainly private, largely revolving around churches. Teaching was done by priests or more casually by anyone around (be it the baker, the butcher, . . .), who knew how to read. Classrooms were often improvised in the backyard of a farm, with poor equipment and amenities. And a large fraction of registered children never attended school. The result was that a large fraction of the population was either illiterate or unable to understand the content of a text. In 1863, 7.5 million citizens (about a fifth of the French population) could not even speak French properly but only local dialects.

Even prior to the war with Prussia in 1870, French elites were aware of the fact that the French education system had failed to promote national unity.

Ironically, as the impetus for Prussian education was the military defeat in 1806 by Napoleon, the French system reform was spurred by the defeat of Napoleon II by Prussia in 1870, which "prompted the fall of the Second Empire and helped trigger the subsequent educational reforms by the leaders of the Third Republic (Aghion, Persson, and Rouzet, 2012, 9).

Belgium is (and was) an overwhelmingly Catholic country, but it is divided between Flemish and French speakers. Its nineteenth-century equality was about the same as the Netherlands (22 percent of farms were family owned), although it lagged behind the Dutch in mean school years in 1870: 4.27 compared to 5.09. Yet Belgium's level of education ranked eighth of the 78 countries, behind Denmark and just above Sweden (and also France).

What accounts for the relatively high level of education in an overwhelmingly Catholic country? In 1831, following its independence from the Netherlands, Belgium established the "freedom of education," so that anyone – the Church, parents, or other private bodies – could establish a school that would be funded by the state. In 1842 Belgium required every municipality to establish at least one primary school, but attendance was irregular at best. Not until 1890 were children aged 6–14 required to attend school – which was extended to 12–14-year-olds in 1914 (Garroutse, 2010, 16). The Church dominated education policy-making, but the state had established religiously neutral schools that were open to everyone and thus competed with Catholic schools (Witte, Craeybeckx, and Meynen, 2009, 250). The guarantee of education to every child and the competition between the linguistic communities promoted widespread education in Belgium. So did the country's history. Belgium had been ruled by the Netherlands prior to 1831, so the newly independent country "inherited" the colonial power's commitment to education.

Reprise

Developed Europe had higher levels of education than the rest of the world. Its mean level of education was 3.55 compared to .73 for other countries (.47 excluding the United States, Canada, Australia, and New Zealand). Catholic countries did have lower levels of education on average (2.13 compared to 4.5 for Protestant nations). Yet all but one European country was in the top 30 percent of all 78 countries in the data set.

The Protestant–Catholic divide does not explain the differences in education levels in Europe. Protestant countries in Europe do have higher levels of education in 1870 ($r = .437$) than do Catholics ($r = -437$), using 1980 estimates of religious denominations. But land inequality is more important ($r = .635$) – and Protestantism may matter because it is correlated with greater equality ($r = .712$).

Catholic countries are more likely to have higher levels of education if: (1) their economies were more equal; and (2) if their states restricted the role of the Church in educating young people. And there is, unsurprisingly, a connection between the state taking the lead on early education – from the Church – and its level of equality. More equal distributions of wealth empowered secular forces.

The story of developed Europe is thus: (1) its overall level of education was higher in 1870 because it was more equal; and (2) within Europe the most equal countries were the leaders in providing education. This should not be surprising since the countries that made the greatest strides in education also were the most likely to provide other benefits, largely on the basis of universalism, to their publics. Meyer, Ramirez, and Soysal (1992, 131) explain this dynamic:

... mass education became a core component of the nation-state model. Its collective standardization celebrates the unified sovereignty and purposiveness of the collectivity (the state), its individual focus and universality enact the integrated and universal character of society (the nation of citizens), and its secularized culture defines the character of the nation-state as an enterprise that is designed to attain progress.

Education was part of a program of social insurance including worker compensation for injuries, old age pensions, sickness leave, unemployment insurance, and public health for the poor) that were designed to make society more equal. But in turn it was the more egalitarian countries that adopted these programs in the first place (Espuelas, 2014).

Dittmar and Seabold (2015, 7) elaborate on the idea of the Reformation as a fight against corruption:

Luther's theses notably criticized the Catholic church's practice of selling indulgences which were believed to secure the release of dead relatives from purgatory in the afterlife. The proceeds from the sale of indulgences were used to finance church investments (e.g. the basilica of St. Peter in Rome) and consumption. Cash flows on future indulgences were also used to secure loans used by elites to purchase high church offices.

The Reformation – especially the Lutheran Church in Northern Europe – "promoted economic inclusion and directly targeted welfare: they supported the provision of education and social services and set up **anti-corruption safeguards**" (Dittmar and Meisenzahl, 2016, 2, bold in original).

The European countries, and especially the Protestant countries of Northern Europe, started off at the top and continued to grow at a faster rate than other nations in the world. Most of the laggards – England, Spain, Portugal, and especially Finland (see Chapter 6 on the latter three countries) – had consistent growth in education and their rate of increase exceeded most other nations. The socially rich became richer even as much of the world lagged behind.

4 | *Education Beyond Developed Europe*

The keys to educational development in Europe (and other Anglo-American countries, see Chapter 5) are economic equality, Protestantism, and state capacity. Economic equality leads people to demand public services, including education, from the state. Protestantism provides a favorable climate for literacy, and the state was the vehicle that promotes secular education and schooling for both the rich and the poor – and for both boys and girls (see also the discussion of education in the United States in Chapter 5).

These same factors are the foundation for the control of corruption. Where incomes are more equal, political leaders will have fewer opportunities to be the patrons in a system of clientelistic politics. State capacity leads to less corruption in at least two ways. First, in a weak state, local leaders, what Olson (1993) called "roving bandits," can extort the population without being checked. A central state authority is hardly a guarantee of honest government. Yet it is likely to be a necessary, if not sufficient, condition for controlling the bad guys. Second, colonies – or recent former colonies – will not have an independent capacity to control corrupt "bandits," and colonial powers will have few reasons to intervene to ensure honest government. The local "roving bandits" are not a threat to the colonial powers, who may care little about the welfare of the indigenous population. A weak (or nonexistent) central authority controlled by the local population is an invitation to theft.

Outside the developed countries are a mixture of some countries that were always (or mostly) independent but less well-off as well as many "countries" that were colonies in 1870 or had been ruled earlier in the nineteenth century by European powers – in Asia, Africa, and Latin America. For almost all of these countries, colonies or independent, the story of their nineteenth-century education levels is similar: Relatively small shares of the population were educated and the schools were more likely to be run by religious authorities than by the state. Education by religious authorities was aimed more at indoctrination than at original thinking – or teaching the skills needed for gainful employment. Religious education was usually aimed at establishing the church as an alternative source of power to the secular state – and as an institution that reinforced existing inequalities.

I present discussions of several independent countries – Japan, Turkey, Russia, Bulgaria, and Hungary – and move to discussions of India, Africa, and Latin America. I chose these countries based upon their importance to my overall argument – and for the availability of historical information. They largely support my thesis – and I will extend my argument with details about other countries that have become less corrupt–and more highly educated – in Chapter 6: Finland, Japan (again), South Korea, Botswana, Georgia, Hong Kong, Singapore, Taiwan, Estonia, Mauritius, and Slovenia. This is a diverse set of countries and together they tell the story of how education is a force against corruption.

Japan

While Japan had a central authority (the *shogun*), his authority was limited. From 1603 to 1868, a feudal system run by local lords ran schools that were primarily aimed at the children of the *samurai*, members of high military castes. Other schools aimed at commoners required parents to pay fees to have their children educated. The local feudal governments did little to promote public education until 1870 (Dore, 1964).

A national primary school system was only established in 1872, with only six years of education required by 1907 – and just nine years as late as 1947. Even as government policy mandated educational opportunities for all boys, many peasant families in rural areas could not afford the mandatory fees (Anderson, 1975, 40). Education for girls was adopted only by 1941 (Adams, 1970, 36, 44). Education in Japan was largely restricted to boys from wealthy families until the end of World War II, when the entire system was redesigned under pressure from and management by the United States. The reform of the education system went hand-in-hand with broader land reform in Japan, as with South Korea and Taiwan. And these reforms were a key factor in the reduction of corruption in Japan (see Chapter 6).

Turkey

Under the Ottoman Empire, which lasted from 1299 to 1922, Turkish society was a highly inegalitarian society, divided between a "ruling elite" and the peasantry. Most schools were religious, run by the Muslim authority, the *waqf*, and the curriculum was largely religious. The smaller number of secular schools were run by the military. These schools also served a small number of students. These parallel school systems competed with each other for the few boys (and only boys) who received an education. In both systems, only the children of the wealthy were educated (Frey, 1964; Kilicap, 2009). The religious and military establishments "crowded out" the state, which played little role in education. As late as 1928, only 3.7 percent of the population was in school, with a literacy rate of less than 11 percent (Frey, 1964, 218). The quality of education was low: The Islamic schools were unregulated with no established standards (Kuran, 2014, 12). The military schools had difficulties finding qualified teachers (Szyliowicz, 1969, 152).

The *waqfs* were the agencies of religious charity in Islamic societies. The *waqf* was "an unincorporated trust established under Islamic law by a living man or woman for the provision of a designated social service in perpetuity. Its activities are financed by revenue-bearing assets that have been rendered forever inalienable" (Kuran, 2001, 842). The *waqf* and related Islamic institutions were essentially private funds, run by wealthy landowners, which provided public services that ordinarily might be run by state institutions (Kuran, 2014, 18). At the founding of the Republic of Turkey in 1923, three-quarters of the arable land belonged to *waqfs* (Kuran, 2001, 842). In the Ottoman Empire (Turkey), only 7 percent of their contributions were devoted to education, with the bulk of the money going to food support for the poor – which kept them dependent upon religious leaders (Cizakca, n.d., 34).

The *waqfs* were rife with corruption. They were unregulated and accountable to no one, run entirely by the founders. Assets were extensive – up to half of all real estate in some regions in the Middle East – and sheltered from public authorities, who turned a blind eye in return for bribes. Embezzlement of *waqf* funds was "common and acceptable" (Kuran, 2013, 400, 402). State authorities had little control over these religious authorities. Since the *waqfs* controlled substantial amounts of public land and provided many essential services, they were beyond the reach of secular authorities. Even in contemporary Turkey, the educational system is marked by corruption: In 2010/2011 people saw education as the most corrupt government institution. Over a quarter of Turks said that they paid bribes to educational institutions in 2013, compared to 17 percent across all countries and 4 percent in the European Union (Hyll-Larsen, 2013, 55).

The corruption of the *waqf* led to a more widespread disrespect for the law: "Traffic regulations, rules against littering and tax laws are openly flaunted in the Middle East even today. This is partly because in a huge set of contexts circumventing the law has been tolerated, even accepted" (Kuran, 2013, 402). The interconnection of inequality, a weak state, and an education system that was left to religious and military authorities led to high levels of corruption in Turkey that persist.

Russia, Bulgaria, Hungary

These three countries were Communist regimes that made great strides in education following the take-over by the collectivist governments. Prior to the Communist revolution in Russia in 1917 and the take-over of the Bulgarian and Hungarian regimes by the Soviet Union after World War II, all three countries were largely rural and had low levels of education. There was little mobility and few opportunities for education in pre-revolution Russia: " . . . imperial Russia developed the political strength to fix serfs more tightly to their lords on the . . . lands" (Lindert, 2008, 367). Russia was primarily an agricultural economy and most peasants were uneducated. Barely more than 20 percent of the population could write and count in the late nineteenth century (Cherkasov, 2011, 139). Mean school years remained low in comparison to European countries until well after the 1917 revolution. Russia did not catch up with the rest of Europe until 1950. As recently as 1930, mean school years in Russia were 2.51, a figure closer to Paraguay (2.44) than to the European laggard, Finland, of 3.6 – or to either Bulgaria (4.2) or Hungary (5.1).

Bulgaria and Hungary were also agricultural societies, although Hungary had a somewhat higher level of education in 1870 than did Bulgaria. Bulgaria was under Ottoman rule from 1396 to 1878, culminating in a rebellion in the latter year and the establishment of an independent state. Before the reforms, education revolved around rote memorization of religious texts.

One of the first goals of the new government was to establish a widespread education system. However, only a third of villages had established primary schools by the turn of the twentieth century (Bulgarian Properties, 2008; Education: Bulgaria, n.d.). The pace picked up in the early twentieth century: the 1870 education level doubled by 1920 and had tripled by 1930.

Hungary was more urbanized than Bulgaria. There was continuous conflict with Austria, leading to an unsuccessful war of independence in 1848 and the establishment of Austria-Hungary. In 1850 compulsory education of just three years was established, but spending on schools increased by only 30 percent and less than 2 percent of the state budget was devoted to education (Ministry of Education and Culture [Hungary], 2008). Education was controlled by the churches until the middle of the nineteenth century – and there were no coeducational schools until 1916. Before World War I, only a quarter of Hungarian children completed fourth grade and they were mostly from wealthy families (Braham, 1970).

What distinguished education in Russia, Bulgaria, and Hungary under Communist rule was the emphasis on ideology and rote learning. Education was not designed to give students opportunities to make their own way in the world, nor did the curriculum promote independent thinking or the moral values that underlay honesty in government. The Ministry of Education and Culture of Hungary (2008, 10) described the Communist education system as "an obedient tool of communistic indoctrination" marked by "brutal totalitarian methods." Education in an authoritarian regime is not a route to lower corruption. To the extent that the education system is itself corrupt, the opposite may be true. Even as mean levels of education were relatively high compared to many other countries, schooling did not serve as a route to greater honesty in government.

There is no evidence that corruption has fallen significantly in either Russia or Bulgaria since the fall of Communism, but there is evidence from Transparency International scores that Hungary had already become relatively less corrupt by 1996 (with a TI score of 4.9, better than Italy or Spain) and in 2010 was 4.7. Hungary's mean level of education in 1990 was 9.9, comparable to other European countries such as Belgium and Ireland. Since the level of education in

Hungary was already high, I cannot establish a relationship between mean school years and corruption for Hungary. However, higher education has increased dramatically and the central control of curriculum was abolished. So there is likely at least an indirect connection between educational reform and lower levels of corruption.

India

India is renowned for its intellectual contributions in literature, science, economics, and many other fields. Yet, it is also a laggard in how widespread educational opportunities are. In 1870 the mean school years for India was .08, lower than Madagascar, Malaysia, or Sierra Leone. By 2010, average education had risen to 4.8, but this was still equal to Malawi and Nigeria and below Ghana and Myanmar.

The historically low levels of education in India reflect the legacy of colonial rule by Great Britain. The colonial power invested very little in educating Indians. Even at Indian independence in 1947, 88 percent of the population was illiterate. Maddison (1971, 6) wrote: "The [British] elite with its classical education and contempt for business were quite happy establishing law and order, and keeping 'barbarians' at bay on the frontier of the raj."

Britain abolished traditional Indian schools (*madrasahs* or *pathashalas*) in the nineteenth century and replaced them with curricula imported from England and taught in English and targeted toward the upper castes (Altbach and Umakoshi, 2004, 15; Chaudhary, 2007, 2), Education funding was geared to secondary schools, attended by a small elite. Primary schools received 34 percent of education funds, compared to 90 percent in the United States, 59 percent in England, and 69 percent in Japan (Chaudhary, 2007, 8). Only one in ten children were enrolled in primary schools in the late nineteenth century, but even by 1941 only a third of eligible children were in school. Male literacy was less than 20 percent by 1931 and female literacy was below 5 percent (Chaudhary, 2012, 6; 8).

The colonial power Great Britain governed India with little respect for local culture.

Governor General Mayo wrote in 1892 (quoted in Acharya, 1995, 671):

In Bengal we are educating in English a few hundred Babus at great expense to the state. Many of them are well able to pay for themselves, and have no other object in learning than to qualify for government employ. In the meanwhile, we have done nothing towards extending knowledge to the million. The Babus will never do it. The more education you give them, the more they will keep to themselves, and make their increased knowledge a means of tyranny.

Young girls were not educated. An English observer, John Murdoch (1891), wrote at the turn of the twentieth century that women did not need education. They were not equal to men, they held superstitious beliefs, and their role was to attend to household duties.

The major factor underlying the low levels of education in India was neglect by the colonial power. Britain simply didn't invest much in public services such as education when colonials didn't look like them (see Chapter 2 for this relationship more generally). When Indians had control over their own services, they were more attentive to people's needs. Iyer (2010, 697) argues that "colonial rulers ... set up poor institutions in places where they do not intend to settle over the long term." Britain did not impose direct rule over all parts of its colony, so some areas controlled their own budgets. Iyer (2010, 703) shows that "districts that were part of the British Empire have 37% fewer villages with middle schools, 70% fewer villages equipped with primary health subcenters, and 46% fewer villages with access to good roads ... ". Local elites may have been more generous than the colonial powers, but they were reluctant to spend much. Landed elites, Chaudhary (2012, 15), "were reluctant to support public education because they had to bear a disproportionate cost in terms of land taxes, the main source of local revenues for public primary schools. Educated elites belonging to the new urban intelligentsia were unlikely to promote mass education because it would increase competition for the much sought after [government] jobs." The bulk of the population was not well served either by the colonial or local officials – who sought to protect government positions for themselves.

Colonial government in India, as elsewhere, was more designed to exploit resources for the colonial power than to provide public services or good government for the local population. The legacies of low levels of education were poverty, inequality, and corruption.

Africa

Colonial exploitation was most dramatic in Africa, where poverty, inequality, and corruption are pervasive. Africans had an average of

.16 years of schooling in 1870 compared to 1.68 for all other countries and 2.88 for non-colonies. The mean corruption score in 2010 is 2.82 compared to 43.91. The 2004 Solt net Gini index is 43.4 compared to 37.3 for all other countries.

The major colonial powers were the British and the French, although there were also Portuguese, Belgian, German, and Italian colonies. I shall examine early and contemporary education across African countries – and then will show that how early levels of inequality – as measured by the share of a country's population sold as slaves – led to lower levels of education over time – and also to more corruption.

Indigenous governments had few resources to spend on public goods – and colonial powers had little interest in providing services such as education. The only source of schooling for most Africans was the support of missionaries. Malinowski (1943, 649) argues that "education was started in Africa by the Christian missionaries and that even up to the present it still remains almost exclusives ly in missionary hands." Ferguson (2011, 263) and Woodberry (2012) argue that Protestant missionaries were the dominant providers of education in Africa – and elsewhere. "Non-missionaries invested little in education regardless of the colonizer," Woodberry (2012, 251) argues. "Most whites wanted a small indigenous elite they could control and thus wanted most education to be limited to manual training."

Woodberry argues that most education was provided by missionaries – conversionary Protestant missionaries, in particular. Yet French Catholic missionaries were also active in Africa; and both British (Protestant) and French (Catholic) missionaries faced resistance by indigenous populations. While missionaries were the dominant providers of education, their limited resources and resistance by the local populations meant that only a small share of Africans benefited from their largesse.

While the British welcomed and facilitated Protestant missionaries, the French were hostile to Catholic missionaries in their colonies and tried to restrict their activities. The French believed in the separation of church and state and thus opposed missionary education – so much so that the French Law on the Separation of State and Church in 1905 withdrew all subsidies to missionaries (Wietzke, 2015). The French provided few resources for African schools because they wanted to train a small elite to serve as administrators (Frankema, 2012, 337).

France contributed just 2 percent of annual revenue for the colonies in French West Africa and just .29 percent was devoted to education

(Huillery, 2014, 32). The share of government expenditures devoted to education was the same in British Africa (Frankema, 2011, 142).

The French and the British had different attitudes toward Africans – and their education. France did build schools in Africa, but they mostly served expatriots and Africans who already spoke French and who identified with the French language and culture (Balch, 1909; Mumford with Orde-Brown, 1970, 28–29, 63, 68). They had "little patience with the completely uneducated African. Hence they often seem harsh and cruel." Africans "who are little educated have a marked confidence in the British official, feeling that their point of view and freedom to live in their own way are sympathetically studied even if equality is not given" (Mumford with Orde-Brown, 1970, 68).

The French saw black Africans as having only "an elementary civilisation," in the words of an inspector-general in French West Africa (Charton, 1970, 97). While British officials may have been less openly biased, they were not much more tolerant in their racial views. The mission schools were to be boarding schools: "Physically removing children and placing them in boarding schools on mission grounds became a key strategy for missionaries trying to solve not only the problem of geographical access to schools but also that of contaminating influences from elders" (Bledsoe, 1992, 188).

British missionaries sometimes worked with government officials but most of the time there was no coordination between secular and religious organizations (Mpka, n.d.). If there was more education provided in British Africa compared to the French colonies, it was only because the British worked with, rather than against, the missionaries.

Muslim Africans often resisted the missionaries' efforts to convert them – and to focus education on religious instruction (Asagba, 2005, 151; Mpka, n.d.). In Algeria, the French government avoided conflict with the local Muslim population by turning educational responsibility over to European settlers, who had little interest in providing schooling to the African population (Heggoy, 1973, 183).

Heggoy (1973, 196) summed up the dilemma of education in French Africa: The French wanted to develop their Algerian subjects, to assimilate them; the Algerians generally wanted to remain what they were, Algerian Muslims – they did not want to become Frenchmen. The French wanted tranquility in Algeria; the Algerians were not opposed to peace, but preferred resistance to French initiatives – peaceful or not – to the alternatives they subconsciously perceived. As a result,

French efforts made little difference. Then, when Algerian attitudes towards modern education changed, probably after World War I, it was already too late; nationalism, which was anti-colonial and anti-French, grew simultaneously with the demand for a French-type of education . . . progress for Algerian education usually only occurred as a result of Arab and Berber pressures on the French government. Until the 1880s, little progress was made because the Algerians themselves refused to send their children to French schools. Then, France gave control over local affairs in Algeria to the European settlers. These colonials were generally antagonistic to any reform in favor of the natives. When Algerians changed their minds and began wishing for access to modern education, they found change difficult to achieve. Colons resisted their demands and the government in Paris was generally weary of challenges to the dominant Europeans. As a result, demands made in the 1930s had little effect until 1944, when France announced plans to build enough schools to enroll about half of the Algerians of school age by 1964. Not until 1958 were plans devised to approach schooling for all Arab and Berber children. The language issue, which was also clearly expressed in the 1930s, finally led to the 1947 law which made Arabic an official language in Algeria and provided the framework, but not the personnel, to teach that language at every level of Algerian education.

In much of Africa, traditional education was oral, not written, designed to teach young people the skills needed to survive in an agrarian society, but the colonists did little to respect this heritage (Mpka, n.d.). The few students who did receive public education were almost all boys (Robertson, 1977, 213).

Education in the British colonies was less conflictual than in the French areas. Yet the issues of religion and language also led to resistance by many indigenous people. Mean education levels were marginally higher in British Africa (.20 years) than in French Africa (.11 years), but both were very low. Education by British missionaries was also aimed at creating British subjects: "beside Jesus life and the religious notion, the African children were taught the British Constitution, the Geography of Britain, and English literature. For instance literary works were presented by the teachers as the greatest literary achievements in the world, and were taught in such a way that they caused the Africans. admiration for English values and their alienation from their own oral tradition" (Aissa and Djfari, 2011, 8).

Malinowski (1943, 651) wrote that the African was "made aware that . . . he was not the brother of his white fellow-Christian – not even the younger brother, but rather someone to be shoved aside at the white Christian's fraternal pleasure and convenience . . . ". Germany also had missionaries in Africa. But it withdrew them during World War I. Baldwin (2015) finds that areas where there were more Protestant missionaries prior to their departure did promote greater political activity but "did not result in . . . higher levels of education or greater wealth in the twentieth century."

The minuscule support for education by all colonial powers was part of a broader pattern of exploitation. Colonialism led to a "severe deterioration in living standards," a reduction of up to 50 percent, and a sharp increase in inequality as the colonial powers extracted mineral and agricultural resources and a "mass expropriation of land" (Helding and Robinson, 2012, 3, 19, 21).

The greatest exploitation of Africa was not the taking of land or resources, but of people – sent to the "New World" as slaves. Nunn and Wantchekon (2011) have developed estimates of the share of a country's population captured and sent to the West as slaves. They show that slave exports in a country lead to lower levels of generalized trust today. Slave exports are a proxy for the level of inequality in a country and I posit that countries that have sent more slaves to the New World will have lower levels of change in mean school years from 1870 to 2010. I do not argue that such exports will affect the level of education in 1870 – since each of these countries did not make their own education policy in the late nineteenth century. A more appropriate question is whether slave exports affected longer-term education outcomes, so I focus on the change in mean school years – and there is support for this linkage: Greater shares of a country's population exported as slaves lead to smaller changes in education levels from 1870 to 2010 ($r^2 = .33$, N = 22, see Figure 4.1). And the change in school years leads to less contemporaneous corruption ($r^2 = .21$, N = 21), although this relationship is weaker (see Figure 4.2).

Is there a stronger, perhaps causal, link? I estimate a regression system for contemporary corruption, with mean school year change instrumented by slave exports, the European population share, press freedom, and status as a former British colony (see Table 4.1). I have just shown that education levels were higher under British rule. In Chapter 2 I showed that the European share of a country's

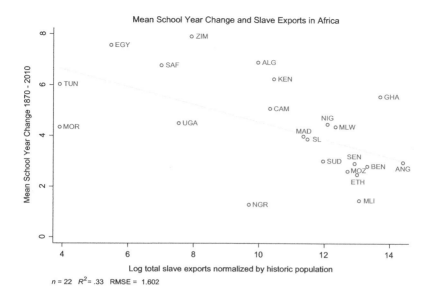

Figure 4.1 Mean School Year Change 1870–2010 and Slave Exports in Africa

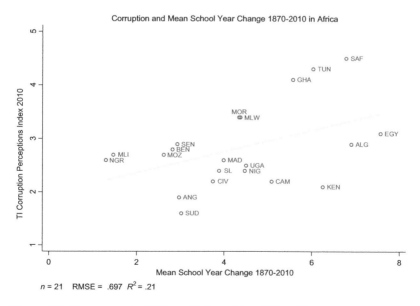

Figure 4.2 Corruption in 2010 and Mean School Year Change 1870–2010 in Africa

Table 4.1 *Instrumental Variable Estimation of Corruption Perceptions in 2010 in Africa*

Variable	Coefficient	Standard error	t ratio
First stage: Estimation of mean school year change, 1870–2010			
European population share	.118**	.053	2.22
Press freedom	.019	.016	1.18
Slave exports by historical population	− .237***	.098	− 2.42
Former British colony	1.451***	.561	2.59
Constant	4.874**	1.616	3.02
Second stage: Estimation of corruption			
Mean school year change, 1870–2010	.413****	.122	3.39
Former British colony	− .541+	.329	− 1.65
Press freedom	− .026****	.008	− 3.46
Constant	2.714****	.474	5.72

Notes: $R^2 = .320$; R.M.S.E. $= .594$; N $= 22$; **** $p < .0001$; *** $p < .05$; + in wrong direction.

population was the strongest predictor of education levels. For the second stage, the equation for corruption, I employ the instrument for change in mean school years. Following the main model in Chapter 2, I include press freedom – under the argument that a free press will uncover misdeeds by a government. And I include British rule again – expecting that the same factor that will lead to greater education will also predict lower corruption.

In the first stage, slave exports are a strong predictor of change in education levels: The greater the share of slaves exported, the smaller the change in mean school years over time.

Former British colonies are more likely to have a greater change in education levels as does the European share of the population. The press freedom measure, which enters the model, is *not* significant. For the second stage, the instrument for mean school year change is a strong predictor of contemporaneous corruption. So is the measure of press freedom. However, the British colony dummy *has the wrong sign*. Former British colonies may have provided more education, but they do *not* have less corruption in this model. We thus should not make too much of the "better" result for British rule in the first stage either.

The African countries offer strong support for the long-term effects of inequality. The story here is straightforward: Colonial rule was built on expropriation and inequality, often brutal. Inequality led in the long term (as well as the short term) to lower levels of education – and in turn to greater corruption.

Even as some African countries increased their mean levels of education from 1870 to 2010, they did not "catch up" to the more well-off nations (see Figures 5.12 in Chapter 5 and 6.4 in Chapter 6). And the country with the second-greatest gain, South Africa (see Figure 4.2), is plagued by the poor quality of its schools. Education spending has increased sharply but an increasing share of students are repeating grades. The mean school year share for South Africa had risen to 7.88, in between Thailand and Portugal. Yet half of first grade students reach their senior year in high school and South Africa's schools were ranked next to last of 140 countries by the World Economic Forum – even as. Teachers are regularly absent. An adviser to former President Thabo Mbeki said: "One of the ironies of South Africa is that if education is the great liberator, it is precisely in those poor areas where you need education that teaching and learning are at their weakest" (McGroarty and Parkinsobm 2016). Russia, Bulgaria, and Hungary under Communism, and South Africa all show that simply sitting young people in schools is not sufficient for education to serve as a tool for economic advancement and for fighting corruption.

Latin America

Latin America poses a challenge to my overall argument for several reasons. Mean levels of education are higher than in other colonies. The colonial history in Latin America was different: Independence came earlier and the major colonial power promoted rather than restricted education. And the two countries with the highest levels of European population, Argentina and Uruguay, have relatively high levels of education that track each other closely over time. However, Uruguay has a much lower level of corruption than does Argentina – contrary to the argument I have made.

Inequality in Latin America was historically *lower* than in many other parts of the world. Inequality was lower in Mexico, Bolivia, and Columbia than in most European countries – or the United States – in the early nineteenth century (Williamson, 2015, 11–12).

Inequality fell after independence for most Latin American countries (Williamson, 2010). Independence, mostly from Spain (but also Portugal for Brazil), came earlier than for colonies in Africa or Asia. By the early nineteenth century (1810–1821), most Latin American countries had become independent. Latin American countries were wealthier than other present and former colonies – with GDP per capita in 1820 (Maddison, 2003) at $651 compared to other colonies at $511 and non-colonies at $931.

Education levels in Latin America were considerably greater than in other present and former colonies: .79 compared to .27. Latin American countries spent less on primary education than did other countries at similar levels of income (Lindert, 2008) – but the overall wealth and lower inequality led to greater overall levels of education than in other colonies.

Latin American countries had substantial European populations. Across the 15 countries for which there are data, the average share of Europeans in the population in 1900 was 30 percent, compared to 13 percent for other colonies. Argentina and Uruguay had 60 percent of their population of European background and Chile had 50 percent. The lowest share of European population was 15 percent in Mexico. The correlation between mean school years in 1870 and the European population share in Latin America is .684 (N = 15), .785 without Brazil (a Portugese colony, see below).

Education and literacy rates varied among Latin American countries: In Argentina, Chile, Costa Rica, Cuba, and Uruguay, literacy rates ranged from 30 to more than 40 percent compared to Mexico and Brazil (22 and 26 percent) and Bolivia, Guatemala, and Honduras (at 11 to 17 percent). The share of students of the total population ranged from 1 to 9 percent (Engerman and Sokoloff, 2012, 133–134). Engerman and Sokoloff (2012, 34–35) explain patterns of inequality and education levels by factor endowments – the distribution of sugar, coffee, rice, tobacco, and cotton plantations across Latin America. Nugent and Robinson (2010, 50, 70) dismiss this argument and attribute differences to variations in laws protecting small landholders, while Williamson (2010) argues that inequalities in Latin America varied over time and are not attributable to climate, but rather to political decisions following independence.

While the English, and especially the French, invested little in education for their colonists in Asia and Africa, Spain was proactive in promoting education in its colonies. The Spanish Cortes enacted legislation decreeing free public education in its colonies (Fitchen, 1974, 105). Spain promoted education in Cuba Premo (2005, 81) wrote about Peru: "Institutions such as . . . schools were as important to Spanish colonial rule as were tribunals and palaces, and they were as central to the lives of Lima's ordinary inhabitants as they the private residences in the city."

By the middle to the late nineteenth century, almost all Latin American countries established systems of universal education (Frankema, 2009, 361) – even if they funding and attendance lagged behind this goal. Almost all Costa Ricans were illiterate as late as 1864, but there was a gradual decline when the state made primary education free and compulsory for both boys and girls in 1885. By 1927 two-thirds were able to read (Evans, 1999; Rankin, 2012, 70–71).

Fewer Brazilians were educated (.46) than were residents of any other Latin American country except Peru (.28). Brazil is the largest country in Latin America and was a Portugese rather than a Spanish colony. Portugal was not as active in promoting education as was Spain – its own level of schooling was the same as Brazil's. Even as Brazil became independent in 1822, it did not develop a system of elementary education for the rest of the century – even by 1900, only a third of the children were enrolled in school – and most of them were born outside the country and attended private schools (Schwartzman, 2003. 11–12). The low level of education in Brazil was "inherited" from the former colonial power. When Brazil was enmeshed in a web of corruption scandals, local people attributed the problems to their former colonial power: "[Corruption] was inherited by us from the Portuguese people who first came to Brazil and developed throughout the years, surpassing the corruption levels of our colonizers" (Novais, 2012). A Portugese navigator, Pedro Álvares Cabral, brought gifts to claim indigenous lands (Romero, 2016, A6). The same dynamic over time seems to apply to education – although by 2010 Brazil had surpassed Portugal in levels of education.

The mean levels of schooling in Argentina and Uruguay in 1870, at 1.51 and 1.61, were almost identical to that of the former colonial power, Spain (1.5). Argentina and Uruguay each had 60 percent Europeans in their populations. Chile followed at 50 percent – and a mean level of education of .94 years, about the same as Bulgaria, South Korea, and Japan. Costa Rica was not far behind with an average

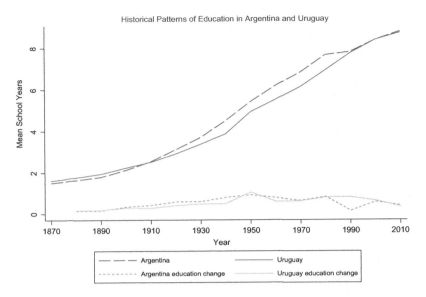

Figure 4.3 Historical Patterns of Education in Argentina and Uruguay

education level of .9, despite having only 20 percent of its population of European origin. While Costa Rica was not wealthier than other Latin American countries, it was by far the most equal: A quarter of all farms were owned by individual families compared to 15 percent in El Salvador, the second most equal.

The Great Anomaly

Argentina and Uruguay are the countries in Latin America with the greatest levels of education – and the largest share of the population of European background. In 1870 they stood out among Latin American nations – and among former colonies (outside of the Anglo-American nations) more generally.

The patterns of education levels and change in levels in Argentina and Uruguay track each other very closely. Argentina had small advantages over Uruguay until 1990 when the two countries "tied" once again. In both Argentina and Uruguay, universal education was established to integrate immigrants from Europe and to instill a sense of identification with the nation and to create a sense of social solidarity (Ignacio and Hamilton, 2005; Arocena and Sutz, 2008, 13).

Yet there is a great anomaly. Uruguay's 2010 TI score was 6.9, in between Belgium and France. Argentina's TI corruption score is 2.9, which makes it tied with Algeria and Senegal and was barely above the median for former colonies, but below the median for Latin American nations.

Why is Uruguay less corrupt? Neither factor endowments nor Institutional design is not the answer. Argentina and Uruguay were similar in terms of climate and resources. Throughout the twentieth century, both Argentina and Uruguay had periods of military rule and democracy, although the dictatorships in Argentina were more ruthless.

Buquet and Piñeiro (2014) argue that low levels of corruption in Uruguay reflect the transition from clientelistic to programmatic parties in the 1960s. This argument seems reasonable, but tests of the linkage between programmatic parties and corruption (see Chapter 2) failed to provide support for this argument (see, however, the models for the American states in Chapter 5). The more fundamental problem with the Buquet-Piñeiro thesis is that Uruguay was less corrupt than Argentina well before the changes in the party systems in the 1960s. The V-DEM corruption score for Argentina in 1900 was .224, compared to .112 for Uruguay. Argentina's score was equal to many African countries, while Uruguay tracked Canada, the United States, and Finland.

An alternative account focuses on inequality. While the differences are not large, inequality has been consistently higher in Argentina than in Uruguay. In 1870 the Gini index was 52.2 in Argentina and 48.1 in Uruguay. A "pseudo-Gini" index, reflecting income from diverse sources including investments and property, showed greater disparities: 39.1 for Argentina and 29.6 for Uruguay (Williamson, 2010, 236, 247). Even as the mean school years for the two countries track each other closely, the share of the population in school was higher in Uruguay (8.48 percent) than in Argentina (6.57) in 1895 (Engerman and Sokoloff, 2012, 134).

Public policy in Uruguay has been more focused on inequality. Abad and Lindert (2015, 25) argue: "What shows up even more clearly in the history of social spending is a consistent Uruguayan tendency toward equalizing incomes ... Uruguay's social spending has been highly progressive throughout the last hundred years." While social spending has been relatively high compared to other Latin American countries for both Argentina and Uruguay, it has been greater in Uruguay and more specifically focused on education (Abad and Lindert, 2015, 41, 44). Land ownership was more concentrated in Argentina than in Uruguay and economic power was more dispersed among a "divided elite" (Chavez, 2003, 421). Uruguay had Latin America's first welfare state, with government control of the railroads, gas stations, water and mail services, and even the production of rum (Krauss, 1998). Argentina had greater inequality: Rural areas such as Cordoba and Entre Rios had more equitable distributions of wealth than did Buenos Aires in the nineteenth century (Gelman, 2013). The regional concentration of inequality in urban areas in Argentina was fertile ground for corruption.

More recently, in 1991–2001, the poverty rate in Uruguay was 5.6 percent, compared to 18.7 percent in Argentina. Uruguay spent 18 percent of its GDP in the 1990s on social security and welfare compared to 7.6 percent for Argentina (Huber and Stevens, 2005, 4, 5).

The differences between Uruguay and Argentina are thus consistent with my argument, even if they are not as clear from comparisons of aggregate data. The message from this comparison is that the factor underlying education, economic equality, matters for corruption.

Reprise

In independent countries, in former colonies – in India, Africa, and Latin America, the roots of education over time stem from historical levels of inequality. Colonialism exacted a particularly strong price. The colonial powers had little interest in providing education or any other social service to the colonists – unless the colonists looked like them (were of European background). The weak education systems in these countries made ordinary people dependent upon the patrons in a clientelistic system – and thus perpetuated corruption.

Colonialism, as the statistical model and the qualitative narratives show, has long-lasting effects. Historical inequality and the failure of the colonial powers to deliver basic services (such as education) to the local population have long-lasting effects. Inattention to the needs of the population – through poor governance – sustains itself.

5 | The United States and Other "New" Anglo-American Countries

The United States and other English-speaking former British colonies – Canada, Australia, and New Zealand – offer a key test of the argument that good institutions lead to strong economic growth and to better governance. These four countries – and notably the United States and Canada – had among the highest levels of education by the measure of mean school years I have been employing. In 1870 Canada ranked second, behind only Switzerland, and the United States ranked fourth. New Zealand was 11th and Australia 14th. By the early twentieth century, Canada and the United States moved into the top two places and by mid-century, the American advantage had become substantial. Other data (see below) indicate an earlier American advantage. In the early twenty-first century, these four countries were also among the least corrupt according to the TI Corruption Perceptions Index for 2010: New Zealand ranked 2nd (behind Denmark), Canada 5th, Australia 7th, and the United States 17th among the 78 nations in the sample. They were also among the most prosperous, as measured by gross domestic product per capita adjusted for purchasing power parity in 2000: The United States was 2nd, Canada 9th, Australia 16th, and New Zealand 19th.

I focus primarily on the United States in this chapter, though I also will consider Canada, Australia, and New Zealand. There are two reasons for examining the United States in greater detail. First there is more historical information – both qualitative and quantitative – on the development of universal education in the United States. Data on school attendance both nationally and across the states will allow me to test the arguments linking inequality and education to better governance. Time series evidence on education, inequality, and corruption is available *only* for the United States – and there is a clear linkage among these three key elements in my argument.

While the United States was an early leader in universal education, many children were (in the current popular language there) "left behind." School attendance rates were 150 percent higher where public education was the most widespread in 1870 (New Jersey) compared to the state with the fewest (Mississippi) across the 35 states for which there are data in 1870.

Adjusting for population density – since transportation to schools was difficult in rural areas – there was a difference of 244 percent between Nebraska and Rhode Island. Land inequality in 1860 was 150 percent higher in Florida than in Maine and Nebraska. The diversity of the American states makes them, in the words of the late Supreme Court Justice Louis D. Brandeis, "laboratories of democracy." The availability of data for most of the American states allows me to estimate a model explaining contemporary corruption from these historical levels of education and inequality. As in Chapter 2, I find strong support for the cross-sectional relationship between contemporary corruption perceptions and historical levels of education and inequality.

Second, in the United States, more so than almost anywhere else, there were explicit connections among education, equality, and good governance. Education was perceived as a means for young people to advance into professional jobs that required literacy and rewarded them with middle-class incomes. Schooling also developed the skills people needed to govern themselves. Beyond enabling people to govern themselves, education was seen as the path to *good governance*. In at least one town – and especially in one state – universal education was seen as the "cure" for the "disease" of corruption. According to the "Wisconsin Idea," scientific learning can teach doctors how to cure tuberculosis and scientific learning can teach public officials and citizens how to eradicate corruption.

I turn to a discussion of education, equality, and corruption in the United States and then to comparisons with Canada, Australia, and New Zealand. Benavot and Riddle (1988, 200) argue that the United States, Australia, Canada, and New Zealand had the most extensive public schooling in the world. But first, a slight digression on why institutional accounts of early education tell at most a share of the explanation of the story.

The Foundations of Education in the Anglo-American Former Colonies

Why did these former British colonies fare so well? Acemoglu, Johnson, and Robinson (2001, 1266, 1395) point to democracy and property

rights in the United States, Australia, and New Zealand as the keys
to success for these countries. These institutional factors are far more
important than economic ones, they argue (Acemoglu and Robinson,
2012, 43).

We should not be so quick to accept the argument that institutions
inherited from Britain were the key to understanding the performance
of these countries. First, the institutions of these nations were not uniform. The United States declared independence in 1776. Canada did
not become independent until 1865. Australia separated from Britain
in 1901. New Zealand statehood emerged in a sequence of events, from
a Maori (native) declaration of independence in 1835, the establishment of the country as a British Crown Colony five years later. From
1852\to 1860 there was a white–Maori war from 1852 to 1860 with
troops for the white population provided by a "New Zealand government." After the war there was a decision not to become part of the
new nation of Australia. New Zealand ultimately became an independent country, climaxing in New Zealand citizenship in 1948 and full
separation from Britain in 1986.[1] The four former British colonies did
not have a common institutional structure.

Inheriting the benefits of British rule isn't a good explanation either.
For most of the indicators Britain was more of a laggard than a leader.
For mean school years in 1870, the United Kingdom was well behind
Canada and the United States, ranking 12th. Even when Great Britain
finally crashed the top 10 (in 1920), it still lagged behind its former
colonies, which ranked first (Canada), second (the United States), third
(Australia), and sixth (New Zealand).

There is an irony in the story of institutions and education for Britain
and its former colonies. Strong national state institutions have been
important elements in the development of universal public education
(see Chapter 3). However, England's strongly centralized government
led to lower levels of mass education (see Chapter 3). In the former
colonies, education was the province of local (or state or provincial)
governments. In each of the countries, there was a conflict between
religious and secular authorities. And in each, the secular forces pre-
vailed, so that schooling was available to most young people – and the
curriculum helped young people get jobs requiring more than simple
literacy. Education thus promoted greater equality as well as laying on
a foundation of a more equitable distribution of wealth.

An alternative account is that public education was built upon egalitarian social structures – notably in the United States – without a

history of feudalism (Sombart, 1976). In 1868, Canada and the United States ranked second and third in the percent of farms owned by families, behind only Norway. (There are no data for Australia or New Zealand.) The skills learned in public schools furthered economic equality. And they also fostered good governance. The curriculum was designed to foster good governance.

I first turn to estimates of corruption over time from content analyses of newspaper front page stories on fraud. There are also census data on school enrollment and economic inequality (the share of income for the top 1 percent of the country). I first show bivariate plots and then estimate an instrumental variable model for the three measures for 1913–1974, the years for which there are data on all three measures. There is strong support for an argument that economic equality leads to greater school enrollment, which in turn leads to lower levels of reported corruption. More education in turn leads to greater equality – but without at least relative economic equality, countries – or states – won't adopt universal education.

I also present data on the American states and estimate a model of contemporary corruption perceptions across the states by public school enrollment rates and land inequality in the late nineteenth century. This is a replication of the cross-national model of Chapter 2. There is also strong support for the claim that widespread education not only pro- motes education, but also is most likely to be found in states with the greatest level of equality. While the United States was one of the most equal countries in 1868, there was substantial variation in inequality across the states. The Northeast and Midwest were the most equal and the South the least equal. This is not surprising since slaves in the South- ern states were excluded from public education. States with the highest ratio of slaves to total population also had lower levels of public educa- tion. Even in a nation with uniform rules for elections and democratic decision-making, variations in inequality and racial politics played a major role in accounting for variations in education levels.

I turn next to the "Wisconsin Idea." I outline how political lead- ers and academics drew a linkage between education and less corrup- tion. Once state leaders were committed to this idea, Wisconsin educa- tion levels increased dramatically and outpaced those of neighboring states. I cannot establish causality, but the corrupt political machine in Milwaukee fell to a series of "good government" Socialist party may- ors as the state expanded public education. And then I turn to a brief account of education and corruption in Canada, Australia, and New Zealand.

Universal Education in the United States

The United States was an early leader in educating young people. By the mid-nineteenth century more children were in school in America than almost anywhere else (Go and Lindert, 2010, 3). One estimate put the United States in undisputed first place (Goldin and Katz, 2008, 130), an advantage heralded by a leading social scientist and an eminent historian before comparative data were available. Seymour Martin Lipset (1966, 21) proclaimed: "This country has led the world by far in the proportion of people completing different levels of mass education from early in the 19th century..." Henry Steele Commager wrote (1950, 37): "What was unique – or shared only by the Scotts – was [the American's] passion for education...his school system was the oldest in the world and the most successful." Even as the American edge narrowed later in the century, it expanded again as more teenagers attended high school there than anywhere else (Goldin and Katz, 2008, 130).

The American public, especially in the Northern states, was willing to tax itself to provide for schools. Unlike most of Europe (notably Britain) and the American South, local governments could respond to demands for public education by taxing their citizens to provide universal education (Go and Lindert, 2010, 1, 12). Institutions did matter: Ordinary Americans had more political voice in choosing to tax themselves than did Europeans or Latin Americans (Engerman and Soloff, n.d., 10; Go and Lindert, 2010, 13).

American education was distinguished by (Goldin and Katz, 2008, 133, 166):

- Widespread availability regardless of income.
- Greater gender equality: An almost equal share of girls and boys attended public schools.
- The separation of church and state, so that the curriculum was secular rather than religious.

In the middle of the nineteenth century, states enacted legislation requiring that local districts provide funding for public schools (Goldin and Katz, 2008, 161). By 1850, almost every Northern state had passed legislation making it possible or mandatory for localities to provide free education for all children (Engerman and Sokoloff, n.d., 13). Between 1830 and 1870, school enrollment rates for 5–19-year-old whites rose from 35 to 61 percent (Cremin, 1980, 178).

Goldin and Katz (2008, 133) argue: "U.S. schooling was not an elite system in which only a small number of bright young boys could attain an upper secondary school education." In part, this was attributable to the political institutions that empowered the middle class.

Yet even more critical was the distribution of income. Lindert and Williamson (2011, 4, 23, emphasis added) argued:

American inequality was much lower in 1774 and 1800 than in England or Wales, especially among free whites. Among all American households, slaves included ... the richest 1 percent had only 7.1 percent of total income, and the Gini coefficient was 0.437. Without the slaves, the top 1 percent of free households had only 6.1 percent of total incomes, and the Gini was 0.400. Compare colonial American inequality with that of the United States today, where almost 20 percent of total income accrues to the top 1 percent, and where the Gini coefficient is about 0.5 ... That colonial America was a more egalitarian place is even more apparent when we compare modern America with colonial New England (Gini 0.35), the Middle Atlantic (Gini 0.38), and, surprisingly, the free South (Gini 0.33). Within any American colonial region, free citizens clearly had much more equal incomes than do today's Americans ... Free American colonists also had much more equal incomes than did West Europeans at that time. The average Gini for the four northwest European observations ... is 0.57, or 0.14 higher than the American colonies. Indeed, there was no documented place on the planet that had a more egalitarian distribution in the late 18th century was also lower in the Northern colonies than in the United States today ...

The educational system was also open to both boys and girls. By the turn of the twentieth century, even high schools had a 50–50 gender balance (Goldin and Katz, 2008. 133). The literacy rate of young women in the Northern states exceeded that of any European country (Go and Lindert, 2010, 11).

Education was seen as a vehicle for both economic advancement and for citizenship. The United States had neither a feudal past (Sombart, 1976) nor a system of apprenticeship, whereby young men would learn a trade under the tutelage – and obligation – to craftsmen and craftswomen. Apprentices would be bound to their communities for the rest of their lives. However, young Americans were far more mobile and they could make their own way in the world in positions that paid more and gave them more freedom. By the early twentieth century, a quarter of young men and women held jobs that required a high school education or more. Each additional year of secondary school led to gains of 10 percent or more in salaries. The school system was open to all – even those who had fared poorly early on were given second chances to gain the skills necessary to gain diplomas (Goldin and Katz, 2008, 29, 133, 167, 177, 183).

The public school system in the United States rested more upon the equitable distribution of wealth than just upon the access to political influence. The American public saw schooling as the foundation of economic equality. Horace Mann, the nineteenth-century politician and educational reformer, in his Fifth Report as Secretary of the Massachusetts Board of Education [in 1842] wrote: "Education, then, beyond all other devices of human origin, is the great equalizer of the conditions of men ... It does better than to disarm the poor of their hostility toward the rich; it prevents being poor" (quoted in Bowles and Gintis, 1976, 28). Cremin (1976, 86) made a similar argument almost a century and a half later: "[the American educational system ... afforded more varied and extensive opportunities to many who had previously enjoyed rather limited opportunities." The public school system was the pathway to widespread literacy. Where schools were mostly private, only the wealthy could afford them and this exacerbated economic inequality (Engerman and Sokoloff, n.d., 14).

Beyond promoting economic advancement and equality, education in America promoted the teaching of moral values and citizenship and participation. Where churches ran schools, moral education was a natural part of the curriculum. Yet American schools were distinctive by the separation of church and state. Even as members of New England Protestant churches or synagogues in Iowa were substantially more likely to have their children attend high school (Goldin and Katz, 1999, 711), the curriculum was secular. Public schools taught values such as "punctuality, achievement, competitiveness, fair play, merit, respect for adult authority" (Cremin, 1976, 51). They also groomed boys and girls with the "education needed to allow Americans to perform civic duties such as voting and to prepare them to run for office and to lead the nation" (Goldin and Katz, 2008, 135–136).

Kaestle and Vinovskis (1980, 183), in a study of the public schools in Lynn, Massachusetts in the mid-nineteenth century, write:

Moral education was one of the chief aims of education in Lynn throughout the nineteenth century. The ideology that supported this goal had as one of its central tenets that social morality depended upon individual morality, and therein lay the main contribution of the school system in legitimizing the social and economic system. This belief was apparently widely accepted.

A local newspaper for manual laborers, the Lynn *Awl*, argued in an editorial on March 1, 1845, in favor of a library for shoemakers: "It is this that will empty our poor houses of their inmates, and free our jails and prisons of the corrupt and vicious; for there is a close connection between ignorance and vice" (quoted in Kaestle and Vinovskis, 1980, 173). Kaestle and Vinovskis (1980, 173) commented: "The workers expected the public school system to . . . provide the opportunity for their children to rise a bit in the world, while inculcating values that would lead to respectability and morality."

What was distinctive about working-class towns, they argue (175), was the lack of class conflict and the belief that schools were central to the development of the moral character of each person. Education prepared ordinary people not just to govern themselves, but also to govern themselves well. Thomas Jefferson, one of the founders of the American Republic, the third president of the United States (1801–1809), and the founder of the University of Virginia, wrote in a letter to Pierre Samuel Dupont de Nemours in 1816: "I believe [the human condition] susceptible of much improvement, and most of all in matters of government and religion; and that the diffusion of knowledge among the people is to be the instrument by which it is to be effected."[2] I shall argue below that leaders in at least one state (Wisconsin) explicitly linked education and the fight against corruption.

Education, Inequality, and Corruption

Widespread public education in the United States rested on a foundation of relative equality. Educational inequality fell rapidly so that by early in the twentieth century the education Gini had fallen to about .15, where it remained throughout the next 100 years. I calculated a measure of "educational Gini advantage" for the United States, which is the difference between the worldwide average education Gini and the American inequality index (Figure 5.1). Early in the twentieth

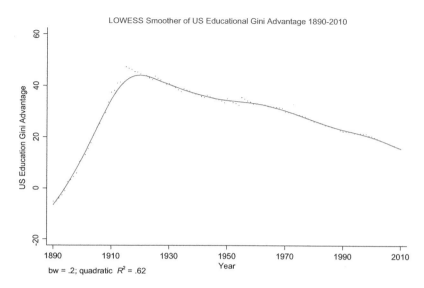

Figure 5.1 United States Educational Inequality Advantage

century the United States established a strong lead over the rest of the world, with a Gini index of .4, lower than the rest of the world. The United States maintained an advantage of .3 until the 1970s, when it fell slightly. It remained around .2 until 2005, when it fell to approximately .15. The United States still has less educational inequality than most other countries, even as it is no longer the most equal. Over time the American "lead" declined not because educational inequality rose in the United States but because it fell throughout the world.

Equality was relative compared to most other countries. There was considerable inequality in education across the American states in the nineteenth century (see Figure 5.2, from data developed by Thomas, Wang, and Fan, 2001). Southern states were less equal than the North because of the legacy of slavery and an economy based upon large plantations dominated by a small number of property owners (Lindert and Williamson, 2011, 17, 23). The schools funded by, attended by, and teaching virtue to ordinary citizens were absent in the South. Attendance rates were three times as high in the North, even after slavery was abolished (Goldin and Katz, 2008, 133).

The plantation economy of the South and the Industrial Revolution in the North led to the development of corrupt political regimes in

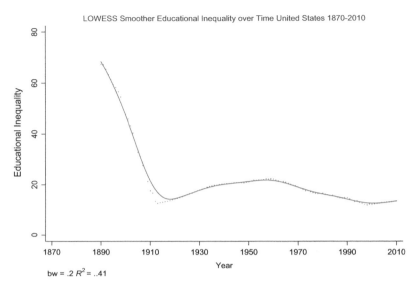

Figure 5.2 Educational Inequality across Time in the United States

both places. The immigrants who came to the United States fell prey to political machines. Journalists and historians wrote extensively about corruption in both politics and business (Josephson, 1938; Steffens, 1931). The Industrial Revolution led to a demand for workers that could not be filled by native workers. The burgeoning economy led to large-scale immigration. The immigrants often needed help getting adjusted to their new country. Many became dependent upon corrupt machine leaders for jobs and for social services and legal assistance. In return, the immigrants were expected to be loyal to their benefactors (Merton, 1968, 131), in big cities and especially in the South, where African-Americans had few rights and many needs, political bosses enriched themselves while exploiting poor people.

Corruption thrived on both inequality and a less educated public. Key (1936, 407) argued many years ago: "Much of what we consider as corruption is simply the 'uninstitutionalized' influence of wealth in a political system" (quoted in Scott, 1972, 33). The share of the foreign-born population was one of the strangest determinants of school enrollment: Foreign-born parents were less likely to have children attending school (Kaestle and Vinovskis, 1980, 131).

Over time, the corrupt political machines of the big cities lost power. Political power in the South shifted away from the rich landholders as the plantation economy gave way to a more diverse economy of agribusiness and services. The descendants of slaves either moved to the North or to the Democratic Party in the South after the Voting Rights Act of 1965 removed legal barriers to African-American electoral participation. By the mid-to-late twentieth century, the corrupt machines had fallen from power – and education was close to universal. In Uslaner (2008, 236–241), I linked the decline of the urban machine to the increase in education for the children of immigrants.

The political machines provided basic services for the Irish, Italian, and Jewish immigrants in large American cities such as New York and African-Americans in the South (Cornwell, 1964). The decline of the machines (notably the Tammany Hall organization in Manhattan) took place at the same time as enrollment in colleges spiked upward. There is no statistical causal connection since it has been difficult to measure corruption and data on college education at the City University of New York (CUNY) colleges are not available. But my argument about New York was based upon one critical fact: Education at the colleges of the CUNY system was free. Young people were not dependent upon political leaders to defray tuition – and after attending college, they could find their own jobs and not be dependent upon political leaders as their parents were. As Wolfinger (1972, 395) argued: " ... growing prosperity and education are diminishing the constituency for machine politics."

Can I provide stronger evidence for this argument? Since my earlier work, I have uncovered data sets on corruption and inequality over time – in addition to the historical measures of education that I have employed throughout this book. The data on corruption over time come from Glaeser and Goldin (2006). Their measure is an annual index of mentions of "fraud" and "corruption" in large newspapers across the country from 1816 to 1974, divided by mentions of "politics" (to provide a common base).[3]

The income inequality data are the shares of income of the top 1 percent of the American population from 1913 to 2012 (Saez and Zucman, 2014) I estimate annual school attendance data from 1870 to 2010 using data on school attendance over time from Goldin (2006, 2–431–2–432). Since this data set only has estimates by decade until 1950 (with annual data thereafter until 1994), I interpolate figures by year

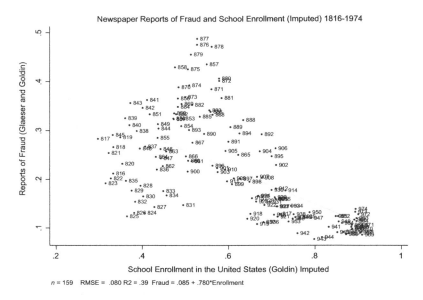

Figure 5.3 Newspaper Reports of Corruption and School Enrollment (Imputed and Adjusted for Population Density), 1816–1974

through imputation using year as the predictor variable. This interpolation guarantees a strong positive trend over time, but mean school years by decade are almost perfectly correlated with time ($r^2 = .98$). The Goldin measures, derived from US Census data, are almost perfectly correlated with the Morrison-Murtin estimates by decade ($r^2 = .92$). I use the Goldin estimates because they are the most commonly employed by students of American education.

I first show bivariate relationships. Since each data set has different numbers of observations, these plots will show more complete information than the resulting multivariate models. The Glaeser-Goldin measure of corruption has a moderately strong relationship with mean school years for 1816–1974 ($r^2 = .39$, see Figure 5.3). The outliers are in the early years of the time series. The r^2 between corruption and school attendance increases to .54 for the time series after 1830 and to .64 after 1840. The relationship between corruption and inequality from 1916 to 1974 is stronger ($r^2 = .45$, Figure 5.4). And there is a very strong relationship between school enrollment and the income share of the top 1 percent from 1913 to 1974 ($r^2 = .81$, Figure 5.5).

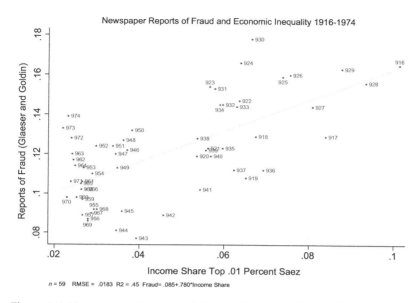

Figure 5.4 Newspaper Reports of Corruption and Economic Inequality, 1916–1974

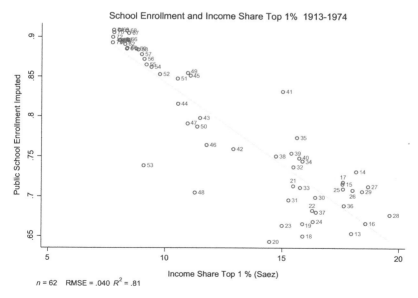

Figure 5.5 School Enrollment and Economic Inequality, 1913–1974

Table 5.1 *IV Regression of School Enrollment and Inequality on Newspaper Reports on Fraud, 1913–1974*

Variable	Coefficient	S.E.	t ratio
First stage: Estimation of School Enrollment			
Top 1 percent income (Saez)	−.017****	.002	−8.59
Educational inequality	.005+	.002	1.90
Constant	.911****	.069	13.19

Notes: R^2 = .792; R.M.S.E. = .04; N = 53; *** p < .0001; + Not in predicted direction.

Variable	Coefficient	S.E.	t ratio
Second Stage: Estimation of Newspaper Reports on Fraud			
School enrollment	−.135***	.054	−2.52
Educational inequality	−.002**	.001	−2.17
Constant	.286****	.026	10.90

Notes: R^2 = .460; R.M.S.E. = .04; N = 53; *** p < .0001; *** p < .01; ** p < .05.

I estimate an instrumental variable regression for corruption (newspaper reports of fraud) for the years 1913–1974 – the years in which there are data for all measures – in Table 5.1. For the first stage, the dependent variable is school enrollment by year. The predictors are the income share of the top 1 percent and a measure of educational inequality from Foldvari and van Leeuwen (2011).[4] Both are significantly related to school enrollment, although the income inequality measure has a much greater effect. For the second stage, both school enrollment and educational inequality are negatively related to corruption (R^2 = .46 for the second stage). There is strong support for a linkage from economic inequality to school enrollment to corruption.

While I cannot demonstrate causality, there is some evidence for the primacy of equality on education. I lagged both inequality and school attendance by 10 years. The correlation between lagged inequality and current education is −.631, considerably greater than the correlation between current inequality and lagged education (−.375). Education *does* lead to less inequality, but the level of inequality comes first.

I find even stronger support for linkages among contemporary corruption and historical levels of inequality and education by using a cross-sectional instrumental variable model for the American states. My goal is to estimate a model that replicates the cross-national analysis of Chapter 2 but also includes some measures that reflect the American context. The first-stage estimation is for school enrollment in 1870, as in the cross-national model of Chapter 2. The key predictors are land inequality in 1860 (also as in the cross-sectional model of Chapter 2) and the ratio of slaves to population. Slaves were not eligible for education. Even as slavery was abolished in the Thirteenth Amendment in 1865, the negative effects of slavery persisted long after slavery was abolished (Nunn, 2007). Both measures were developed by Nunn (2007).

The second-stage estimation is for a measure of contemporary corruption (see below), so that the model reflects the same dynamic as those in Chapter 2. In both the first and second stages, I include two additional variables. First is the adoption of the merit system for appointing state bureaucrats. Even though the Pendleton Act established a civil service system patterned after Great Britain's at the federal level in 1883, states were much slower in enacting these reforms. Merit systems were expected to replace patronage appointments to bureaucratic offices – and thus to reduce the power of machine politicians. Only a quarter of the states had adopted the merit system by 1933, according to the measure developed by Ruhil and Camoes (2003), which I employ.

The second is a measure of the state party system that is similar to those of Cruz and Keefer (2010). This is Mayhew's (1986) widely used measure of "traditional party organization (TPO). Traditional party organizations – and public employees appointed politically rather than by a merit system – are based upon patronage rather than policy (parties) or academic qualifications (state employees). States without merit systems or with high scores on the TPO should have higher levels of corruption. For the corruption equation, I also include a measure of the number of newspapers covering politics in 1880 per capita. A diligent press might, as I argued in Chapter 2, lead to lower levels of corruption. This was the hope of "muckrakers" such as Lincoln Steffens (1931). This measure comes from Glaeser and Ward (2006).[5]

The first question is how to measure each of these variables across the American states. Estimating corruption is especially problematic. There are two major measures of government corruption: the indictment and conviction rates of political leaders and newspaper reporters' subjective estimates of corruption (Boylan and Long, 2003), which is closest to international estimates of corruption by Transparency International. The Boylan-Long measures for 47 states in 1999 have Rhode Island and Louisiana as the most corrupt. Rhode Island has a traditional patronage-oriented Democratic machine that is dominant in state politics. Charges of corruption are common. The Dakotas and Colorado rank as the most honest, with Minnesota 7th, and Wisconsin 12th.

An alternative measure of corruption is the share of public officials indicted or convicted (Meier and Holbrook, 1992). The most corrupt states in 1995 were Florida and Virginia and the least corrupt were New Hampshire and Vermont. This measure has little face validity – and the rankings of the states vary dramatically over time (Dincer and Johnston, 2015, 8). The two measures are *not* identical: Florida and Virginia rank 14th and 26th respectively on the Boylan-Long measure and the overall correlation between the two measures is just .259. The reporters' measure seems to be the better one, since it has greater face validity. Prosecution indicators may reflect the personal priorities of prosecutors (Boylan and Long, 2001, 3–4; Dincer and Johnston, 2015) or political leaders (Bologna, 2015) – and it may simply be more difficult to gain an indictment and conviction in a heavily corrupt state. Thus, I rely upon the reporters' perception measure, which seems less troubled by endogeneity issues (such as whom to prosecute and whom to convict) and has greater face validity.

For school enrollment in 1870, I rely upon census data. I adjust enrollment figures by population density – first because the available data are not adjusted for state population size, but also because school attendance in rural areas would be underestimated if I did not take distances into account.[6] I present a plot of perceived corruption in 1999 and 1870 school attendance adjusted for population density in Figure 5.6. The relationship seems modest ($r^2 = .24$) but without two outliers on the bottom left of the graph, the r^2 increases to .40. There are also moderate relationships ($r^2 = .32$ and .39) between corruption perceptions in 1999 and land inequality in 1860 (Figure 5.7) and between land inequality and school attendance (Figure 5.8).

In the instrumental variable model, inequality and the ratio of slaves to the total population are strong predictors of 1870 school enrollment by population density across the 34 states for which there are data (Table 5.2). The first-stage regression has an $R^2 = .565$. The

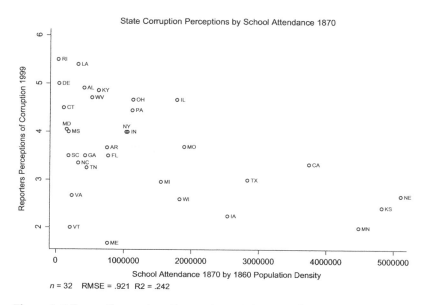

Figure 5.6 State Corruption Perceptions (1999) and School Attendance (Adjusted for Population Density), 1870

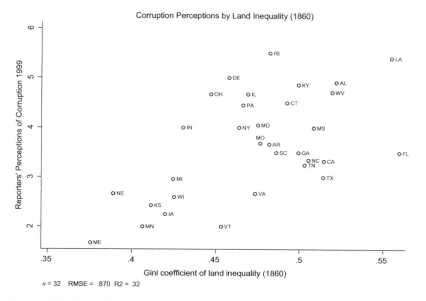

Figure 5.7 State Corruption Perceptions (1999) and School Attendance (Adjusted for Population Density), 1870

Table 5.2 *IV Regression of School Enrollment and Inequality on Reporter Perceptions of Corruption, 1999*

Variable	Coefficient	S.E.	t ratio
First stage: Estimation of school enrollment by population density			
Land inequality 1860	− .359**	.164	− 2.19
Ratio slaves to population 1860	− .120**	.059	− 2.03
Merit system adoption year	− .0001	.0004	− .38
Traditional party organization	− .004	.005	− .76
Constant	.719	.843	.85

Notes: $R^2 = .565$; R.M.S.E. $= .03$; N $= 34$; ** $p < .05$.

Variable	Coefficient	S.E.	t ratio
Second stage: Estimation of reporters' corruption perceptions			
School enrollment per capita	− 15.492****	4.304	− 3.60
Traditional party organization	.460****	.079	5.81
Merit system adoption year	− .001	.009	− .12
Newspapers covering politics 1880 per capita	420.782	1337.624	.31
Constant	7.540	18.627	.40

Notes: $R^2 = .571$; R.M.S.E. $= .68$; N $= 34$; **** $p < .0001$.

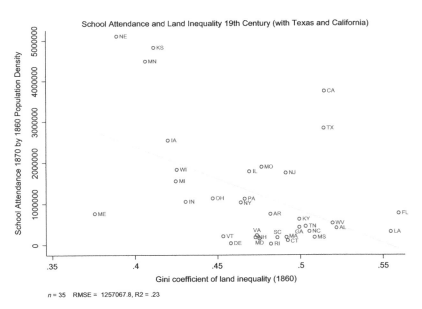

Figure 5.8 School Attendance (Adjusted for Population Density) by State 1870 and Land Inequality, 1860

instrument for 1870 school enrollment is also a strong predictor of reporter perceptions of corruption at the end of the twentieth century. States with traditional party organizations are also much more likely to be perceived as corrupt. Neither newspaper coverage nor the early adoption of a merit system for state employees is a significant predictor of contemporary corruption (see also Uslaner, 2008, 228–229). An alternative measure of the adoption of state merit systems from Ting *et al.* (2012) yields almost identical (non-significant) results.

Across countries and across the American states, there are strong links from inequality to lower enrollment in public schools to higher levels of corruption. This dynamic also holds over time in the United States. Do political leaders see this linkage as clearly as I do? In at least one case in the United States (and elsewhere, see Chapter 6), they do.

The Wisconsin Idea: Education and Better Governance

Corruption was widespread in the nineteenth and early twentieth century in the United States. The state of Wisconsin was (Howe, 1912, xii):

...not unlike other states. Its legislature was discredited and corrupt. The biennial bartering of legislation, of place and privilege, the boss and machine control were not dissimilar from conditions disclosed in other states.

Its largest city, Milwaukee, was not the most corrupt city in the country, but it ranked above average in Menes's (2006, 67) ratings of the corruption of big cities in America. Buenker (1998, 146) wrote that private businessmen provided most city services in contracts that were "long on insider benefits and short on public responsibility."

Then something happened. Howe (1912, xii) wrote:

In a few years' time Wisconsin has become the most efficient commonwealth in the Union. Of the honesty of the legislative and administrative departments there is no question. Executive offices are filled with trained men who are animated by enthusiasm for the public service.

By 1900 Milwaukee "was a non-machine city" (Menes, 2006, 85, n. 17).

What changed politics and administration in Wisconsin?

The "big picture" answer is what became known as the "Wisconsin Idea." Loving (n.d., 2) writes: " ... the Wisconsin Idea offers a set of values – self-governance, integrity, egalitarianism, truth and inter-personal trust . . . " More specifically, it highlights the role of expertise from the public university, but also education more generally, that public policy should be based upon expert judgment rather than partisan disposition.

A legislative committee on industrial and agricultural training reported in 1911 (quoted in McCarthy, 1912, 148, emphasis in original):

We may pass all the resolutions we want to, but the only way to cure political corruption in our cities is to cure it in the way we are stamping out tuberculosis – *by education.*

Dr. George Kerschensteiner of Munich wrote (quoted in McCarthy, 1912, 148):

Reformers in America are striving to get some knowledge of why corruption is rampant here. We are fighting political corruption and physical disease at the same time. We may have reform periods or spasms; we may create temporary organizations for the purpose of reforming government; we may deliver lectures, or our magazines may lead in pointing out the defects in government, but we will never get a true sense of obligation to the state until we teach that obligation. If we teach this in college or the high school we will not hit the mark. How can we, when four-fifths of the boys and girls do not go to high school or college? We never can completely fight disease, political or physical, unless we teach these four-fifths, in some way, how to fight.

Much of the discussion of the Wisconsin Idea focused on what contributions the University of Wisconsin could make toward improving public policy (McCarthy, 1912, 132, 138). The linkage of education with good governance extended to education more generally. High school enrollment doubled from 1890 to 1906, the number of high schools also doubled, while the number of graduates increased four-fold. From 1885 to 1922 the number of public libraries increased ten-fold. Public schools became public resources – serving as community centers in the evening (Buenker, 1998, 371–372, 393–394).

The growth of public education and clean government was spurred by ideas from Germany and Scandinavia, as well as by political move-ments that reshaped politics in Milwaukee and the state. The writings of George Kerschensteiner of Munich were just one instance of North-ern European influence. McCarthy (1912, 12, 22) wrote:

Germans have shown us the way; we need not adopt all their methods, but we will do well to accept their philosophy, for there is no patent on it... Every Norwegian, Swede or Dane who pays a visit to-day to the Scandinavian countries returns an easy convert to the ideals which seem to have dominated Wisconsin during the last decade or more...

Germany (then Prussia) was the first country to adopt universal education, while the Scandinavians were also among the earliest adopters of mass schooling (see Chapter 3). The adoption of policies from these countries was not surprising in Wisconsin: 14 percent of state residents in 1880 had parents born in Germany, followed not so closely by Minnesota (7 percent). Eight percent of Wisconsinites had fathers born in Scandinavia, second only to Minnesota (22 percent).[7]

The political movements that led to increased education and the linkage with clean government were the Socialist party in Milwaukee and Progressivism in the state. The Socialists won power in Milwaukee in 1910 – and maintained the mayoralty until 1940. Unlike their more ideological counterparts in Europe, Milwaukee's Socialists focused on education, libraries, parks, the minimum wage, and eight-hour days for city workers. The city regularly won awards for good governance – and the "leftists" worked with business, even as they canceled sweetheart contracts (Dreier, 2012).

The Progressive movement in the state – and ultimately in other Midwestern states with large Scandinavian and German populations (Minnesota, North Dakota, and South Dakota) – started as a more liberal branch of the Republican Party. It too focused on good government but also policies to benefit the child, who was "the carrier of tomorrow's hope whose innocence and freedom made him singularly receptive to education in rational, humane behavior" (Wiebe, 1967, 169). The first governor from the Progressive movement was Robert LaFollette, who served from 1901 until he was elected to the Senate in 1906. LaFollette was the central sponsor of the Wisconsin Idea and he took the idea to the nation in 1924 when he ran as a third-party candidate for the presidency. The Progressives split with the Republican Party in the early 1930s and its leaders, the sons of LaFollette, ultimately switched to the Democratic Party.

Did the Wisconsin Idea really matter for universal education? I present data on public education in Wisconsin and several similar

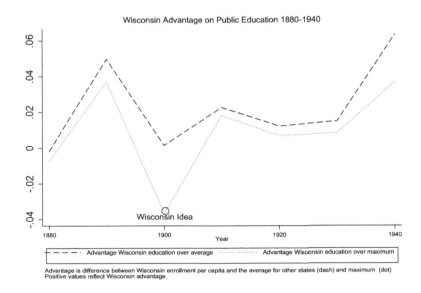

Figure 5.9 The Wisconsin Advantage on Public Education, 1880–1940

states with reputations for corrupt government – Ohio, Illinois, and Pennsylvania. In Figure 5.9, I present a measure of the "Wisconsin advantage" over the other three states from 1880 to 1940. Early on Wisconsin had a lead in public education that rapidly eroded. By 1910 Wisconsin's "advantage" – the difference between Wisconsin and the other states – was negative. Wisconsin had fallen behind the comparison state with the most education and it was effectively tied with the other three states. After 1910, when the Wisconsin Idea was formulated, the state took the lead over the other three states, with advantages becoming increasingly positive. The Wisconsin Idea was not just a theory. It meant much more spending on education and it made Wisconsin a leader in public education.

Since the Progressive Party focused primarily on clean government and structural reform, support for it is a reasonable proxy for public support in a state for anti-corruption initiatives. Of course, public preferences are hardly the same thing as actual performance and vote choice clearly reflects other factors (including evaluations of LaFollette himself, attachment to the traditional parties, and the Progressives' strong commitment to an activist role for government in the economy).

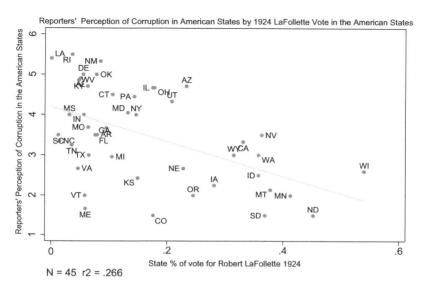

Figure 5.10 Reporters' Corruption Perceptions in the American States (1999) and 1924 LaFollette Vote

The LaFollette vote nevertheless is the best available proxy for (lack of) corruption seventy years earlier.

While the fit with reporters' corruption perceptions is not overwhelming ($r^2 = .266$, see Figure 5.10), the LaFollette vote is part of a more general syndrome of honest government, trust, and equality – even though it is measured almost three-quarters of a century ago. The Progressive vote in 1924 is strongly related to state-level estimates of trust in the 1980s and 1990s ($r = .696$ and $.564$ – and cross-nationally trust is the strongest predictor of honesty in government [Uslaner, 2008]). Goldin and Katz (1999, 718) find that education across the American states in 1928 is strongly correlated with Putnam's aggregate measure of social capital. Progressivism was part of a more general syndrome of factors associated with support for education and for good governance.

I have demonstrated support for linkages between historical levels of education and contemporary corruption – statistical and in the way policy-makers see the fight against dishonesty in government. The story here is not one of how institutions shape corruption. For both the longitudinal and cross-sectional analyses, there was little to no variation in

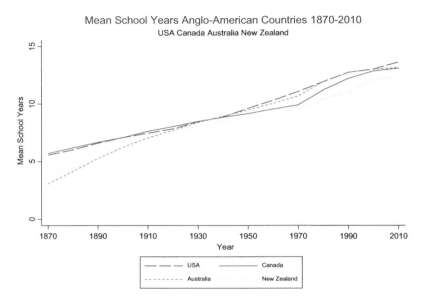

Figure 5.11 Trends in Mean School Years: United States, Canada, Australia, New Zealand

the institutional context. The major institutional variable – the adoption of the merit system across the states – was an insignificant predictor of corruption. I turn now to some cases where there is institutional variation – Canada, Australia, and New Zealand – but still high levels of universal education even before their formal independence and low levels of contemporary corruption.

Canada, Australia, and New Zealand

All four Anglo-American democracies display similar patterns of education trends over time (Figure 5.11). The correlations among the time trends for the four countries range from a "low" of .979 (Australia–Canada) to a high of .994 (Australia–New Zealand). All of the correlations are .99 or higher after 1900. Is this simply a reflection of the common heritage of British rule?

No. In Figure 5.12 I show the trends of education for the United States and three other former British colonies: India, Jamaica, and South Africa. These time trends are also highly correlated: The lowest correlation is between India and the United States (r = .949). But

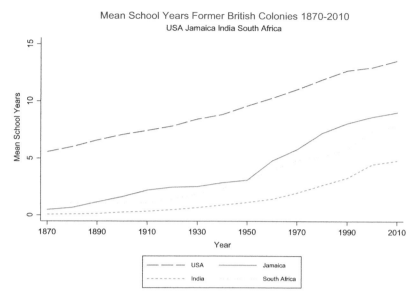

Figure 5.12 Trends in Mean School Years: United States, Jamaica, India, South Africa

the levels of education are very different for these four former British colonies. Over time, each has "caught up" with the United States but still all lag considerably behind the leader. India is a particularly notable laggard – each percentage gain in American education levels is associated with only a .57 increase in Indian education. The average gain for the other Western countries ranges around 1.00, indicating parity in growth rates.

Compared to the United States, there is far less documentation on education for Canada, Australia, or New Zealand. There are commonalities in the development of education with the United States despite the differences in institutional structures. The United States became independent almost a century before Canada did and more than a century for Australia and New Zealand.

The most important similarities between Canada and the United States were the movements to shift schooling from the church to the state, to ensure public funding of education, to require all children to attend school, and to establish uniform standards throughout the country. Schools were seen as the source of moral education as well as developing more mundane skills that would help young people find employment (Mathien, 2001, 2, 3, 13, 29, 31). In "New France" (Quebec), the immigrants in the early eighteenth century were mostly illiterate – and there were sharper conflicts between the Catholic Church and the state than in English Protestant Canada. At independence, Quebec was the only province without a Minister of Education (Canadian Encyclopedia, n.d. a). There were also conflicts between missionaries and the First Nation (indigenous) populations (Anuik, 2006).

In Australia, education was under the jurisdiction of each state. As in Canada, the government did battle with church authorities for control over education. From 1851 to 1895, the Australian states withdrew public funding for church-run schools and established a predominantly secular curriculum. The central government, even before independence, enacted the Education Act of 1851. Under this legislation, local governments were required to establish publicly funded schools. The local boards were responsible for running the schools but there was a common curriculum and the central government retained the right to inspect schools, but not to dictate teaching standards. Education was not universally free even into the twentieth century, but most fees were eliminated and each colony established requirements for compulsory education.

Australians, like Americans and Canadians (and likely New Zealanders), saw education as a force for making young people good citizens capable of governing themselves. Unlike the United States and Canada, there was less consensus on whether the children of working-class parents needed to be given such moral education (McCreadie, 2006). Many well-off parents sent their children to private schools and there were substantial differences between the quality of public and private schools (Vick, 1992, 69).

The development of education in New Zealand was similar, though more delayed. While most immigrants from Scotland and Ireland were literate, few Maori (indigenous) New Zealanders were – and only a small number were educated at missionary schools. War between the Maoris and the white government in the 1850s disrupted policy-making generally, including on education (Cumming and Cumming, 1977, 306). As in Canada and Australia, there were conflicts between church and state authorities. Catholic and Protestant clergy blocked attempts to enact legislation to establish universal state-run education. In both Australia and New Zealand, many communities were remote and had few schools – often with few teachers: Half of New Zealand students in 1877 attended primary schools with one or two teachers (National Commission, 1972; "Story", n.d.).

The central government – still under British rule – enacted the Education Act of 1877, which took the responsibility away from the provinces and the churches. Education was to be free, secular, and compulsory This act led to a strong spurt in enrollment but students still had to pass entrance examinations (Look4, n.d.). While enrollment increased dramatically, attendance was generally sporadic. Regional disparities continued into the early twentieth century, when attendance levels finally approached 90 percent. The major factor leading to more uniform educational standards was the economic prosperity that made education funding both desirable and possible (National Commission, 1972, 25–26, 29).

Canada, Australia, and New Zealand all developed extensive education systems. The evidence is not strong, but it seems to indicate that the public education system was most fully developed in the United States. Education was widespread in Canada as well. Yet it was less extensive in "New France" (Quebec) because of the dominant role of the Catholic Church. In Australia and New Zealand, there was more prolonged conflict between religious and secular forces as well as between classes, even though there is little evidence that Australia and New Zealand were less equal than Canada or the United States. But the key result is that the three other countries "caught up" with the United States – and rather rapidly. In 1870, the United States had a substantial lead in the average years of secondary education in the Morrison-Murtin data. Australia was a laggard, with an average of .66 years of secondary education compared to 1.39 for the United States. Thirty years later, these four countries were largely at parity (with Canada slightly behind and Australia in the lead).

A likely explanation for the initial weaker performance by Australia and New Zealand is institutional. Neither country was independent by 1870, so one might argue that both lacked the institutional means to require that local jurisdictions enforce equitable education. Nor could they order religious authorities to cede control to the secular state. However, this account is flawed in at least three respects. First, Canada had achieved independence only in 1865, and it already had education levels at or greater than the United States by 1870. Second, much of the policy-making on education in Australia and New Zealand (as well as in Canada) preceded formal independence. Third, the trajectories of Australia and New Zealand toward parity with the United States and Canada were set long before the independence of the former countries.

Reprise

There is strong evidence for the link between historical levels of inequality and education and contemporary corruption in the United States. The longitudinal data support the claim that inequality, education, and corruption follow similar time trends. With few variables measured over time, it is more difficult to establish a causal order. But the data I present indicate that these three measures are part of the same syndrome.

The comparisons of the United States with Canada, Australia, and New Zealand provide some support for this argument, although the linkages are more difficult to establish since information on early education and education for these latter countries is more sparse. The patterns for the United States and Canada seem most similar (see Figure 2.4 in Chapter 2, the graph of 1870 mean school years against corruption perceptions in 2010). New Zealand and Australia are outliers on this graph. Yet it was not long before these countries "caught up" with the United States and Canada on education. There are no data for Australia and New Zealand for the share of farms owned and run by families in the nineteenth century. However, in another data set on economic inequality (van Zandem *et al.*, 2011), Australia and New Zealand had in 1910 Gini indices of inequality of approximately .4, about the same as Canada (and Norway and Denmark).[8] By 2010, all four of these nations had low levels of corruption. They ranked 1st (United States), 4th (Australia), 5th (Canada), and 11th (New Zealand) in 2010 mean school years.

What distinguished these countries, Acemoglu and Robinson argue, was the protection of property and the rule of law. Yet there was substantial variation in when each adopted property rights and it is not clear that the development of such institutions preceded the provision of universal education.

The United States was first, with property rights guaranteed in the Fifth Amendment to the US Constitution (ratified in 1791). In Canada, Nova Scotia and New Brunswick protected property by law in 1758. New Brunswick did not do so until 1858; Alberta, Manitoba, and

Saskatchewan followed in 1870 (Canadian Encyclopedia, n.d. b). By then Canada already had widespread education. Even before independence, Australia accepted the Berne Convention, an international agreement on property rights that was negotiated in 1886. These rights were officially protected in 1928, although the various states adopted such rights at different times, often late into the twentieth century (Sainsbury, 2003, ch. 2). New Zealand enacted a Land Transfer Act in 1870 and a more detailed Town and Country Planning Act in 1953 (Boast, 2013, 167, 173). Even then, more formal protections of property rights were offered in Parliament in 1988 in the proposed Protection of Personal and Property Rights Act 1988 and again in 2005 in the New Zealand Bill of Rights (Private Property Rights) Amendment Bill (New Zealand Legislation, 1988; New Zealand Parliament Hansard, 2005).

What distinguishes these countries – and some others in Northern Europe – was less a common institutional structure than a commitment to equality through the early development of social transfers (Espuelas, 2014, 3). Despite different histories and varying institutional contexts, these countries seem to have wound up at similar places in both education and corruption.

Finally, a note of caution. Despite the spread of education, in each of these countries persistent inequalities remain. In all four countries, indigenous populations remain isolated with far less access to education and employment. The native population is smaller in the United States, but African-Americans remain segregated from the white majority with lower graduation rates and worse outcomes on a wide range of socioeconomic outcomes (Massey, 2007). These four countries may be among the leaders in universal education, but inequalities persist. There is still a legacy of slavery in the United States.

I turn now to what may be the most pressing questions: Can countries that start out far behind on mass education catch up? If so, how and why? And does "catching up" lead to less corruption?

Notes

1 See http://www.teara.govt.nz/en/self-government-and-independence.
2 From "Thomas Jefferson on Educating the People," at http://tcfir.org/opinion/Thomas%20Jefferson%20on%20Educating%20the%20People.pdf.

3 I am grateful to Claudia Goldin for sharing these data.

4 I am grateful to Bas van Leeuwen for sharing these data.

5 I am grateful to Edward L. Glaeser and especially Bryce A. Ward for providing this and other measures.

6 The school enrollment data for 1870 come from https://usa.ipums.org/usa/resources/voliii/pubdoc. The adjustment for population density is based upon data from www.demographia.com/db-state1900.htms/1870/1870a-11.pdf.

7 See n. 5 for the source of these data.

8 The United States, which ranked third on land inequality, had a Gini of .51 in the van Zanden *et al.* data.

6 | *Is Path Dependence Forever?*

Not necessarily. The past is not set in stone. The legacy of the past exerts a strong pull (for the countries that provided education a century and a half ago) or a strong drag (for those countries that lagged behind). The good news is that cross-national educational inequality fell sharply from 1890 to 2010. But the bad news is that:

- countries with high levels of corruption at the turn of the twentieth century largely remained corrupt in the early twenty-first century.
- there remain substantial gaps in mean education levels for most countries.
- most of the countries with low levels of education in 1870 did *not* catch up to the leaders.
- initially, there is at best a modest relationship between the rate of change in education levels and the 1870 mean school years, but:
- the relationship is much stronger if one excludes countries with the highest levels of education a century and a half ago. Outside the countries with the highest levels of education, the countries that caught up the most were the ones that had relatively more education a century and a half ago.
- overall, there are upward trends in mean school years for every group of countries, but the initial "leaders" – the Anglo-American countries excluding Britain and Northern Europe – showed the greatest increases in education, while African nations lagged behind every other group.

The overall story is that levels of education have become more equal since 1870 but the rates of improvement – for both terms of honesty in government and education levels – are substantially greater for the countries that were initially the best off. Very few countries that lagged behind "caught up."

Some countries *do* catch up. Their education levels increase much more than the average – and they become less corrupt. There are three such countries in the data set: Finland, Japan, and South Korea. And there are also several countries "outside the box" (for which there are no data) that also seem to have "conquered" corruption: Botswana, Georgia, Hong Kong, Singapore, and Taiwan.

What distinguishes these countries? First, in each country, the fight against dishonesty in government was linked, sometimes very explicitly, with programs to increase the social welfare of their citizens – mostly through programs that promoted widespread education. The link between social welfare reform and corruption rested upon one of two foundations. Almost always anti-corruption drives were linked to broader social movements to challenge leaders who had enriched themselves at the expense of ordinary citizens. Dishonesty in government was part of a broader syndrome of battles between a wealthy elite and a mass public lacking in both economic and political power.

Why did some countries with low levels of education and high corruption "beat the system" while most others did not? The common denominator of most of the success stories is external threat. The first country to adopt widespread education was Prussia. King Frederick II established an expensive school system to promote loyalty to and identification with the Prussian state following a humiliating military defeat by Napoleon. When faced with threats from outside, regimes have sought to win the loyalty of their citizens by both domestic reforms and more honest government (Aghion *et al.*, 2012; Uslaner, 2008, 206). External conflict may (as many of the cases show) destroy the political institutions of countries. So new structures will be established. The redesigned institutions may be better able to provide public services – since the leaders want to establish greater loyalty among the citizenry. In some cases, the institutions may be rebuilt by external forces (such as the American role in restructuring Japanese education after World War II). External threats, especially if they have led to war, destroy institutions and test public loyalty, as in France and Denmark (see Chapter 3).

In some cases (Botswana, Hong Kong, Singapore, Taiwan), governments respond to external threats by winning the loyalty of their publics through more extensive welfare regimes and more honesty in government. Sometimes countries can overcome the inequality/corruption trap without external threats (see the discussion of Spain and Portugal especially), but these cases seem to be the exception.

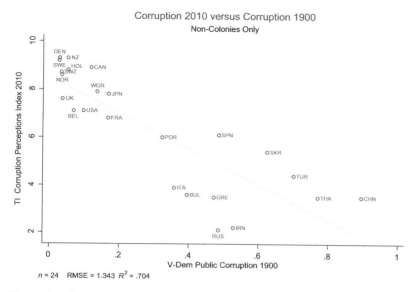

Figure 6.1 Corruption Levels Over Time (1900–2010) V-DEM and Transparency International Estimates: Non-Colonies

Trends in Governance and Education

Corruption persists over long periods of time because of what Uslaner (2008, ch. 2) calls the "inequality trap": High inequality leads to low trust and then to high levels of corruption – which in turn leads to more inequality. It becomes difficult to break this cycle and corruption persists over long periods of time. Until now it has been difficult to trace corruption levels prior to 1980. There is a new data set, V-DEM (Coppedge, 2015), that has historical estimates of a variety of measures, including corruption, from 1900 to the present. While the V-DEM estimates are expert judgments, so are contemporary measures such as the Transparency International indices.

Corruption persists over long periods of time. The 2010 Transparency International and the 1900 V-DEM estimates (using the v2x_corr measure) are strongly related (see Figure 6.1): $r^2 = .70$. I exclude countries that were colonies at the turn of the century since they were not self-governing. The major outlier is Russia; excluding it increases the r^2 to .76.

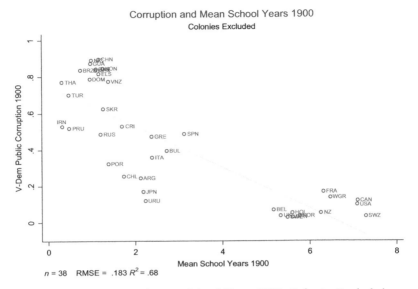

Figure 6.2 Corruption and Mean School Years 1900: Colonies Excluded

The V-DEM data let us examine the historical roots of corruption. Excluding colonies, there is a strong relationship between levels of education and corruption in 1910 (see Figure 6.2): $r^2 = .68$. **The level of education in a country shaped corruption in 1900 and this effect persists over time.** The European share of a country's population and the percent family farms both lead to less corruption, but these measures are so highly correlated ($r = .72$) that neither is estimated precisely in a regression.

The connection between education and corruption endures over time because both corruption and education levels persist. There is good news. Educational inequality has declined sharply from 1890 to the present. The mean education Gini (from Van Zanden *et al.*, 2011) has fallen from over 60 to less than 30. And this reflects both within- and between-country inequality (Figure 6.3).

While the overall level of education has dropped substantially, the pattern has been uneven. I plot the mean school years from 1870 to 2010 by region in Figure 6.4. The Anglo- American countries (excluding the United Kingdom) started tied with Protestant Europe but quickly rose to have the highest level of education in the world. The

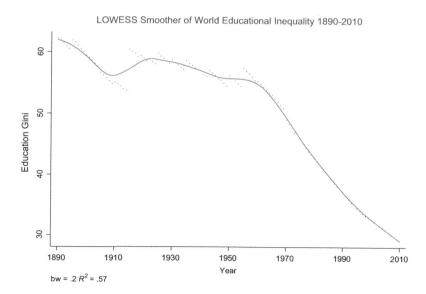

Figure 6.3 Educational Inequality Over Time (1890–2010)

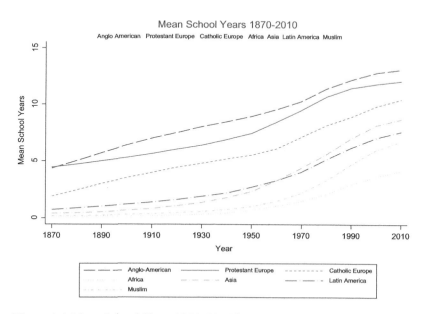

Figure 6.4 Mean School Years 1870–2010 by Region

gap with Protestant Europe grew smaller in the second half of the twentieth century, but it still persists. These two regions started out ahead and remained there – with the highest levels of growth in education. Catholic European countries lagged behind and they still do. Their mean levels of education have risen, at approximately the same rate as European Protestant countries, but not enough to catch up.

Asian nations grew at almost the same rate as the Anglo-American nations. In the second half of the twentieth century, their rate of growth was substantially greater than any other region (5.9 compared to 4.5 for other regions). The rise of education levels in Asia is part of the larger story of economic growth in Asia – and of policies that put schooling and greater equality at the center of political reform (You, 2015). Latin American education levels also grew substantially in the mid-twentieth century, though not as strongly as Asian countries. Lagging behind are Muslim countries in Asia and Africa and especially black African nations. The legacy of colonialism was particularly strong in these two regions. Black African colonies did not gain their independence until the second half of the twentieth century – Ghana was first in 1957 – and the colonial powers did little to provide an economic, educational, or institutional infrastructure.

A more precise measure of a country's "progress" in attaining universal education comes from regressing its mean school years for each decade from 1870 to 2010 on a marker variable for each decade. The higher the regression coefficient, the steeper a country's gain in education levels. I present the coefficients for each country in Figure 6.5. Here there is evidence of the lasting effects of colonialism. Colonies – as of the turn of the twentieth century – had a mean regression coefficient of .038 compared to .057 for other countries (Australia and New Zealand were coded as non-colonies). The 15 countries with the smallest coefficients were all in Africa (including Morocco). The mean coefficient for African countries is .027, compared to .06 for Northern Europe. Only one of the ten largest coefficients came from a developing country (Malaysia in 10th place). Japan, South Korea, Finland, Russia, Bulgaria, Chile, and the United Kingdom had the greatest coefficients, ranging from .098 to .072. These were the countries that had the greatest advances in education over time (see Figure 6.4).

The larger story is that educational inequality – both across and within nations – has declined significantly since the late nineteenth century. However, the countries that had the highest mean levels of

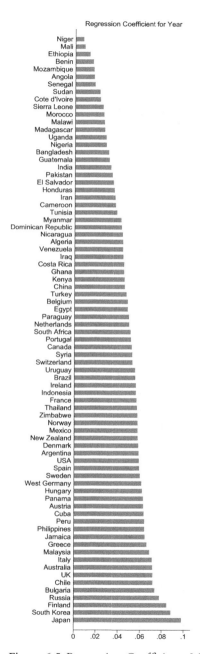

Figure 6.5 Regression Coefficients Mean School Years by Year

education in 1870 still are have the most educated children today. And the countries with the least corruption in 1900 still have the most honest governments today. There was a linkage between education and corruption over a century ago and it persists to this day.

The countries that had the greatest increases in the mean level of education from 1870 to 2010 were mostly the countries that had the most widespread schooling in 1870. The countries that had the smallest gains were former colonies in Latin America and especially Africa. The biggest gains came in Western nations (Anglo-American and both Protestant and Catholic European countries) and countries that had *not been colonies*. Asian countries, especially countries that had not been colonies, had the greatest increases in mean levels of education: Japan (12.2) and South Korea (11.9) had the largest increases, followed by Malaysia (9.5), Indonesia (7.9), and Thailand (7.7). Malaysia was a British colony and Indonesia had been ruled by the Dutch. However, each had a long history of independence before being colonized in the early nineteenth century.

The smallest gains came in former colonies: Latin America (average of 4.9 years) and Africa (3.5). Latin America had greater increases than African countries because they had gained independence more than a century earlier. They had greater state capacity to provide public services such as education. This is not simply a case of a more benevolent state providing social welfare programs (including education) to its citizens. As long as colonialism persisted, the ruling powers had little incentive to provide benefits to the people in these states. Where there were substantial European populations – as in South Africa and to a lesser extent Zimbabwe – the gains were greater.

Three nations with middle-to-low levels of education in 1870 showed the largest increases over time: Finland (10.6 year increase), South Korea (11.8), and Japan (12.2). Contemporary Finland ranks among the four very least corrupt countries at 9.2. Japan is tied for 17th and South Korea is tied for 39th place. These are all much higher transparency scores than expected based upon their 1870 levels of education. I present graphs of education levels and rates of change in mean school years for Korea and Japan (Figure 6.6) and Finland (Figure 6.7).

These three "deviant" cases increased mass education in a way that fits the story of state capacity and equality. The movement for universal education in Korea first came as a reaction against the Japanese occupation that ended in 1945. The Japanese rule limited access to

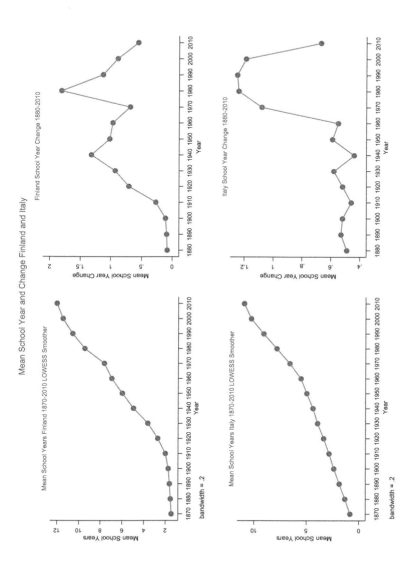

Figure 6.6 Mean School Year and Change: South Korea and Japan

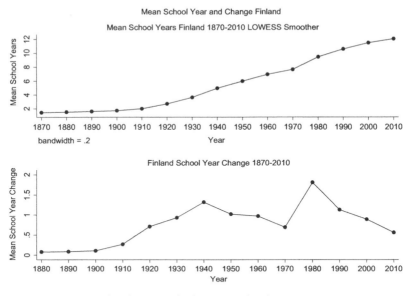

Figure 6.7 Mean School Year and Change: Finland

education in Korea, but reform attempts were put aside when China intervened on behalf of North Korea and started the Korean War in 1949. When the war ended in 1954, education spending soared as the political elite saw education as the key to economic development. Free compulsory primary education was adopted in 1954 and was achieved by 1959.

An expanded public education system including free textbooks was implemented by 1971. In 1968, the state replaced the comprehensive examination system for middle school admission with a more egalitarian lottery. By 1980, 96 percent of students in primary schools went on to middle schools and 85 percent of middle-school graduates went to high school. The trigger events for mass educational policies were the need for state-building coming from the threats from the conflict with North Korea.

Japan's rise in education levels was more directly a response to external events. After Japan lost World War II, the United States Occupation Government drew a new constitution to create a liberal democracy. The United States Education Mission to Japan, 27 prominent scholars, had the task of "develop[ing] a new education appropriate to a liberal democratic state." The Occupation Government dictated that Japanese schools eliminate militarist and nationalist materials. Schools emphasized equal opportunity for all students and adopted a learning style in which children of different abilities and personalities worked together in small groups to promote equality (Okano and Tsuchiya, 1999, 59).

Japanese reform was not entirely determined from without. Japan's education system had been highly structured by class, with limited opportunities for commoners (Anderson, 1975; see Chapter 3). The American intervention started the reform movement. By the 1960s teachers, parents, and civic groups organized to demand "high school education for all" (Okano and Tsuchiya, 1999, 40). The big spurt in mean school years in Japan (Figure 6.5) came after this movement was organized, not simply after the American-imposed reforms. The push for more equal education was made easier by the egalitarian distribution of income – if not social status – in Japan. The Gini index (Solt) after benefits are taken into account was .25 or lower for most of this period.

The Finnish history is a combination of external threat, internal strife, and an ambition, after independence from Russia in 1917, to orient the country toward Western Europe and especially toward the other Nordic countries. Finland had been an integrated part of Sweden for 600 years until 1809 when Sweden's defeat against Russia meant that Finland came under Russian rule. However, Finland never became an integrated part of the Russian Empire but managed to keep some autonomy and the right to follow its own (that is, the Swedish) laws as a Grand Duchy. Swedish was then the "official" language, mostly spoken by the ruling elite. From the 1860s onward, a strong Finnish nationalist movement appeared very much centered on the language issue. In 1892, the Finnish language, spoken by peasants and workers, achieved equal legal status with Swedish. Since Swedish and Finnish are completely different languages, the language issue delayed the introduction of broad based schooling.

After declaring independence from Russia in 1917, class-based political conflicts escalated into a gruesome civil war in 1918. The lack of full nationhood until 1917, the difficult language question, and the civil war all served to delay the introduction of mass education in Finland compared to the other Western European and especially Nordic countries. The rapid increase of education during the 1920s and 1930s can be explained by a combination of the threat felt from the Soviet Union and a strong willingness to orient the country to Western Europe and the Scandinavian countries.

The major educational reforms in Finland were adopted in the 1980s, in the waning years of the Soviet Union. To a considerable extent, these reforms were aimed at integrating immigrants and providing them with the skills needed to be successful in a country that was already one of the most equal in the world – it ranked second on Solt's 1980 net Gini index (Sahlberg, 2007). Even as the society has become less homogenous – with the share of foreign-born Finns doubling between 1991 and 2003 and the number of people whose first language is not Finnish tripled – the country developed an education system where high standards are set for all students. The standards are high for teachers as well: They must have a Master's degree – and all teachers are treated as equals (Sahlberg, 2007, 153; Sahlberg, 2011, 37). Sahlberg (2007, 148–151) links the development of the education system to Finland's place as the least corrupt country in the Transparency International rankings.

Each of these countries have relatively low levels of corruption in the 2010 Transparency International index: Finland ranked 4th, Japan 18th, and South Korea 40th among the 178 countries in the full TI data set. And all three became markedly less corrupt in the V-DEM data from 1900 to 2010: Finland's score on the 0–1 measure fell from .106 to .033. South Korea's score declined from .625 to .209, while Japan fell to .111 from .169. As education levels rose, corruption declined for all three of these countries. The zero-order correlation between mean school years and the V-DEM corruption index from 1900 to 2010 were −.61 for Finland, −.89 for South Korea, and −.94 for Japan.

The three cases follow the pattern of stressing mass education as a result of increased ambitions for state-building following a perceived threat to the nation. There were other countries with somewhat smaller increases in mean school years: Australia, Bulgaria, Chile, Cuba, Greece, Italy, Malaysia, and the United Kingdom all had increases of nine or more years.[1] Yet only Chile had more than a minimal decrease in corruption. Malfeasance in government *increased* from 1900 to 2010 in Bulgaria and Malaysia. Why was there no connection between education and corruption in these countries? Why did higher levels of education in these countries *not* lead to less corruption?

One plausible argument is that there is a threshold effect – Finland, South Korea, and Japan all had greater gains in the mean level of education than the other countries. But this would then lead to why there is such an effect. A better explanation would be the following:

- Australia and the United Kingdom were already among the least corrupt countries in the 1900 (1910) V-DEM data: Australia ranked 10th of the 65 countries in the data base in 1910 and the UK ranked 6th in both 1900 and 1910. There was little room for major improvement.

- Bulgaria and Cuba were Communist countries – Cuba still is – and Communist countries had higher levels of corruption that persisted after the authoritarian regimes fell (in Bulgaria, not Cuba; cf. Uslaner, 2008, ch. 4).

- In neither Greece nor Malaysia were gains in education tied to any broader reforms in social welfare programs. Education in Greece increased from an average of 1.41 years of schooling in 1870 to 10.7 in 2010, about the same level as Italy. But it still ranked as relatively corrupt: Its V-DEM score was .47 in 1900 and .42 in 2010 and its Transparency International score was 3.5 in 2010. Fragoudaki (2015, 2) argues: "...during the 1950s and 1960s, the educational system reproduces social inequality." Greece was "a widely uneducated society" and "the content of education...in Greek schools in the 1950s could be described as transmitting grammatical knowledge on dead languages, and blunt political propaganda" (Fragoudaki [2015, 3]. Even as the mean level of education increased dramatically (the average school year measure increased from 7.45 in 1980 to 10.7 in 2010), education was highly unequal in Greece, with small numbers of working-class students completing secondary school even in the 1980s (Fragoudaki (2015, 3). In Greece, the mean school year measure hid inequalities in the society – and thus there was not a direct relationship between mean school years and corruption.

- Malaysia stands in contrast to Singapore (see below), which separated from it in 1965 – and pursued a widespread system of social reforms, including more extensive education.

- Of these countries, only Italy had faced external threats. As with Japan, it was on the losing side of World War II. Yet its change in corruption from 1900 to 2010 was a meager-.053 and its corruption index in 2010 was 3.9, ranking 67th, behind Rwanda. After World War II, the educational system was in disarray and very traditional.

Clark (1964, 364) described the Italian education system:

Fact-laded syllabuses, drawn up by the ministry in Rome, were set to be memorized, pupils were constantly tested, in front of the whole class, on what they could repeat from the textbooks. Those who failed the annual examination were held back to repeat the year, even in primary school, so only about half the children 'graduated' from primary school at the right age. There was no attempt to link the separate subjects, let alone to link schools to the outside world. Teachers in Rome who taught ancient history were not allowed to take their pupils to see Colosseum. This frightful, rigid, unreal, enclosed, boring and profoundly stupid system did its best to anaesthetize successive generation of pupils. One wonders who suffered most from it: the 'failures' who left school as early as possible, stigmatized and barely literate, or the 'successes' arrogantly convinced that what they had learned at school was worthwhile knowledge.

As late as 1951, 13 percent of the Italian population was officially classified as illiterate and in 1971, more than a quarter of the adult population had not obtained an elementary school certificate (Clark, 1964, 364). The long period of fascist rule seems to have hindered any modernization of teaching methods.

World War II led to major changes in domestic politics and policy in Japan – with a corresponding decrease in corruption. There was not a similar transformation in Italy. Post-World War II Italy was marked by social and political tensions. Davis (2015, 6) wrote:

The collapse of Mussolini's regime had reignited pre-fascist rural conflicts which were now exacerbated by population increases and mass rural unemployment. These discontents focused above all on the need for land to work or farm, resulting in collective occupations of uncultivated estates and repeated violent clashes between the laborers and the police and security forces. In Sicily the landowners recruited mafia and other criminal groups to combat the rural laborers and peasants and the rising tensions and death tolls caused many to fear that the south was on the brink of civil war.

Secessionist movements arose in both the North and the South – and the economic disparities between the "two Italys" became greater after the war and especially from 1992 to 2013.

Italy's average level of education lagged behind the rest of Catholic Europe until the twenty-first century and its corruption (from V-DEM) scores were more than twice as high as other Southern European countries (.30 compared to .12) and ten times higher than Northern Europe

(.03). Italy had substantially higher levels of inequality than other countries in Catholic Europe after World War II and slightly higher in 2010. The net Gini (Solt) for Italy remained above average compared to other countries in Catholic Europe – and the great variations across regions (North versus South) exacerbated political tensions and led to instability in politics: Since 1945, the average government in Italy has lasted just 18 months (Browne, 2014). The country was politically split between the dominant Christian Democrats and the Communists – and reforms were made difficult because of continuing strikes and violence (Salvatore, 2011). While domestic political movements led to social programs, especially on education, that reduced inequality, Italy was wracked by ideological and regional conflicts and political instability. Corruption remained unchecked: The 2010 V-DEM estimate was not much different from the 1900 score (.30 versus .36).

There is additional support for this argument in examining two countries that faced domestic turmoil but not external threats: Spain and Portugal. Both were led by Fascist dictators from the 1930s to the mid-1970s. When Francisco Franco died in 1975, Spain began a transition to democratic rule. When António de Oliveira Salazar was incapacitated in 1968, Portugal's path to democracy was more indirect – and marked by a military coup (as in Greece) – and a government that veered sharply to the left.

Corruption in Spain, as measured by V-DEM, fell sharply. In 1900, 1950, and 1970, its score ranged from .49 to .52. After the death of Franco, the score fell to .09 in 1980 and .07 thereafter – the lowest in Catholic Europe and not far from the scores in Northern Europe. The mean school year score for Spain increased from 6.4 in 1970 to 10.3 in 2010. Portugal also had a decline in corruption – from .32 in 1900 to .15 in 1980 – where it stayed with minor variations to the present. Its education level increased from 4.19 before the end of Salazar's reign (1970) to 7.3 in 2000 and 2010. Portugal remained more corrupt than Spain with lower levels of education.

Spain and Portugal both developed democratic government. In 1978, three years after the death of Franco, the Spanish Constitution made education a fundamental right of all citizens. In 1985 Spain enacted the Organic Law on the Right to Education, which established a right to free education and made schooling compulsory (Rolwing, 1997, 22). By 1990, further reforms led to 16 years of compulsory education and by 1991 there was almost universal literacy (Flecha, 2011,

33–35). The education reforms were part of a broader program of decentralizing power from the center and away from both the military and the Catholic Church (Hanson, n.d., 19) – as well as a broader set of reforms in social welfare policy. Arriba and Moreno (2002, 9) argued: "Universal access and equal treatment were, thus, the two ideological foundations of the regional legislation on welfare provision. Traditional public beneficence was to be 'updated' so that stigmatisation of beneficiaries could be avoided."

Portugal also had lower corruption and greater levels of education when the dictatorship ended. Portugal's path to democracy was much different from Spain's. In Spain, King Juan Carlos, the designated successor to Franco, led the country to democratic governance without conflict. Portugal faced a civil war and the military, backed by the Communist Party, ruled the country from March 1975 until the parliamentary elections of 1976. Civilian rule – and democracy – put Portugal on what seemed to be a path similar to Spain.

Yet the transition to democracy did not have effects in Portugal as great as in Spain.

Corruption fell from .32 in 1900 to .15 in 1980, and the mean level of schooling rose from 4.19 before Salazar was incapacitated to 5.67 in 1980 and to 7.36 in 2010. The decline in corruption and the rise in education levels were both significantly lower than in Spain – and Portugal still had a high dropout rate in the early twenty-first century (OECD, 2014). The new Portugese constitution guaranteed "compulsory, free, and universally accessible" education and tuition-free universities (Brauges, 2012, 331). Illiteracy remains high and the overall social welfare system is weak (Pereirinha, 1995, 174–175). "Government social policies seeking to limit socioeconomic disparities do exist, but they are poorly funded and are not very effective in preventing poverty" (Sustainable Governance Indicators, 2014).

In neither Spain nor Portugal was there an external threat. The Communist revolution in Portugal was a domestic battle, not run by a foreign power. The comparison of the two Iberian countries must take this into account. The more general argument is that two seeming similar cases – dictatorships with relatively low levels of education and high corruption – had different paths toward better outcomes. Spain had a stronger transition to less corruption with higher levels of education and a more comprehensive welfare state than Portugal. Democracy *per se* was not the key to these results.

Education matters most when it is tied to a broader set of social reforms – and these reforms are more likely to matter when they are enacted in the face of external threats. Such threats lead to "rally effects" and a greater sense of identification with the nation – which in turn leads to better governance (Darden, 2013). As I argue below, external threats matter, but they are not always present.

Thinking Outside the Box (or the Data)

Botswana, Georgia, Hong Kong, Singapore, and Taiwan are not in the data set. But they each have reduced corruption substantially, and these efforts can be tied to both increased social welfare, notably education, and to external threats. I consider each of these cases and then also briefly discuss some other countries that have reduced corruption – but where the literature (scholarly or popular) on how they did it – or how they increased education – is sparse. These countries are Barbados, Bhutan, Brunei, Estonia, Israel, Mauritius, Qatar, Slovenia, and the United Arab Emirates. Each of these countries rank in the top 22 percent (almost the top fifth) of all nations in the 2010 TI Corruption Perceptions Index. And most also had advanced in providing education.

The two most well-known cases of the reduction in corruption are Hong Kong and Singapore. Notably, neither is a democracy. Singapore ranked 3rd among 178 nations in the 2010 Transparency International index and Hong Kong was 13th, above most Western European countries. Both countries had relatively high levels of inequality and high levels of corruption.

And both instituted widespread anti-corruption campaigns, with strong anti-corruption agencies with strict enforcement, heavy penalties for violating the law, and generous salaries for public servants to make sure that they did not fall prey to the lure of payoffs. Yet these factors are not sufficient to explain *why* Hong Kong and Singapore could conduct strong anti-corruption campaigns when other states could not.

Corruption had long been common in both Hong Kong (Lo, 2001, 21) and Singapore, where "[e]xtortion, blackmail, kidnappings, murders, rapes, you name it, they did it in Singapore . . . Murders took place with alarming regularity – in the streets, coffee shops, and in housing estates . . . we have changed dramatically, almost metamorphosed from a society caught in the grip of criminals . . . to the orderly and secure haven we have today" (Lee, 2003). In both places, corruption was seen as part of Chinese culture (Lee, 1981, 358–359).

What led to the anti-corruption campaigns in Hong Kong and Singapore? Both faced an external threat – from China – although some new research challenges this claim for Singapore.[2]

The high levels of inequality led to radicalized labor movements and leaders in both places saw China as the source of the challenges to their authority. In both Singapore and Hong Kong, the leaders sought to gain the support of the people against the unions by adopting a mix of free market and state-centered economic policies designed to increase wealth and reduce inequality. They also focused on efforts to build separate, more inclusive, Singapore and Hong Kong identities. If people were wealthy, they would have little interest in Communism. A stronger welfare state would reduce the allure of the radical unions and their followers.

Singapore and Hong Kong both still have relatively high levels of inequality, but the rates have been cut by almost 20 percent from 1965 to 1990 (though they increased by 40 percent in Hong Kong – from 37.3 to 52, by 1996 according to the WIDER estimates).[3] Other high performing Asian economies only reduced their (lower levels of) inequality by 12 percent.

Unemployment by 1990 was almost non-existent. Singapore has increased education spending by a factor of 90 in the effort to produce a social safety net (and to defuse political tensions) amidst a high level of inequality (Quah, 2001, 291). While Hong Kong has favored a less active welfare state than Singapore, it has succeeded in sharply increasing the share of its income that goes to the middle class (Lo, 2001, 22; Campos and Root, 1996, 46). In both Hong Kong and Singapore, according to the leading student of corruption in Asia (Quah, 2013, emphasis added), "The first reason for the high level of government effectiveness in Singapore and Hong Kong is their favorable policy contexts . . . both countries are city-states with small populations, high GDP per capita, no housing shortage, **high government expenditure on education**, low level of corruption, and high degree of political stability."

Following World War II and the ending of the Japanese occupation, South Korea began a program of land reform. In both South Korea and Taiwan (see below), the "prime motivation . . . for launching land reform was to cope with communist threats from North Korea and the

Chinese mainland." The United States also pressed both countries to enact land reform (You, 2015, 86). The land Gini fell by half in Korea (You, 2015, 89).

Land reform, You (2015, 90) argues, "facilitated the expansion of education, which in turn contributed to the development of professional bureaucracy, active civil society, industrialization and economic growth" in Korea and Taiwan. Primary school enrollment increased by more than 100 percent from 1945–1955 even though the Korean War "led to the destruction throughout the country" (90). These reforms made the entreaties of North Korea and China less attractive to the peasants who now owned their own land. They also allowed the government to develop autonomous – and honest – government institutions since the reforms reduced the role of clientelistic leaders (91).

There is a similar dynamic in the anti-corruption campaign in Taiwan. Taiwan had high levels of corruption (Göbel, 2015). Galor *et al.* (2009, 162, 164) argue, as does You, that in Taiwan, Korea, and Japan, land reform and "significant education reform" were part of the same movements toward a stronger welfare state and greater equality. The government redistributed land to individual farmers. The number of students increased by 6 percent each year from 1950 to 1970. Funding for schools more than doubled during this period.

Many younger Taiwanese felt that the government – run by ethnic Chinese who had fled the mainland – was too corrupt and had limited their opportunities for advancement. They sought "equal opportunity in the access to education … and … envisioned a political system that was democratic and free of corruption" (Göbel, 2015, 10–11). As in Korea, expansion of education was part of the same reform program as was the campaign against corruption. And both were fueled by the need to assert a Taiwanese identity and a Taiwanese prosperity that could withstand threats from the mainland.

Taiwan is now marked by low inequality – a Gini index accounting for welfare benefits – of 30 in the Solt data set, a figure that has been relatively constant since 1964. As with South Korea, the land Gini in Taiwan also fell from about .60 in 1950 to between .39 and .46 in the 1960s (You, 2015, 89). Its level of corruption is also relatively low – tied for 33rd at 5.8 on the 10-point scale. Mainland China is tied for 78th place with a score of 3.5.

In both Korea and Taiwan, land reform and expansion of public education were part of a broader movement toward greater equality and lower corruption. What distinguished these countries was the clear linkage from equality to education to honesty in government.

Botswana is Africa's greatest success story in combating corruption. It is tied with Taiwan for 33rd place in the 2010 Transparency International rankings. Only one other African country (Mauritius) is in the top 50. Despite high inequality, Botswana experienced a period of sustained economic growth with declining inequality (Riley, 2000, 153). Between 1966 and 1990, income per capita rose at the fastest rate in the world (Guest, 2003, 26). Its per capita income is still low at $3,000, so the fight against corruption and toward greater equality is still a work in progress.

Botswana has tremendous mineral wealth through its diamond mines. But it is landlocked and completely surrounded by Namibia, Zimbabwe, and South Africa – all of which were in the early years of Botswana's independence (1966) run by white racist regimes. So Botswana followed the path of Hong Kong and Singapore in developing an honest government and an open economy that is a welcoming place for foreign investment.

Botswana did not start out with great advantages. The British colonial administration "provided more or less nothing in terms of education" and other public goods (Heldring and Robinson, 2012, 19). An independent Botswana made major investments in education and other public goods (Acemoglu, Johnson, and Robinson, 2003, 84). Acemoglu *et al.* (2003, 85–86) argue that such investments can be traced to institutional design – democracy and property rights.

However, there is no straightforward link from good institutions to the policies that benefit a large share of the population. Other countries, including some in Africa, have strong institutions but do not invest in education or have low levels of corruption (Uslaner, 2008, 195). Botswana's investment in education and other public goods may have not reduced inequality – at least in the short run – but it led to the creation of an indigenous elite to serve in both government and business. And this, together with a business climate of honesty, provided a bulwark against possible threats from its neighbors who would envy its mineral resources.

The final case is the former Soviet Republic of Georgia. Widespread protests erupted against a corrupt and oppressive regime "left over" from the Soviet era. The new president, Mikheil Saakashvili, set out to reduce corruption, especially petty corruption. In 2003, the time of the Rose Revolution, Georgia ranked 124th of 133 nations by Transparency International. "[T]he level of corruption built into the infrastructure of the bureaucracy disrupted daily life and hampered access to public services." (Ferris, 2014).

The campaign against corruption led to a ranking of 55th of 177 countries in 2014, above Italy and the Czech Republic. The reforms put limits on party spending for elections and making party funding available on the Internet as well as a crackdown on corruption by bureaucrats.

Former officials accused of bribery were put on trial, as were about 1,000 public employees, including members of parliament and some deputy ministers. By 2008, there were signs of a return to close ties between business and government and a return to some "elite corruption." And Saakashvili was accused of centralizing power in the executive and running an authoritarian government (Mungiu-Pippidi, 2015, 155). However, the drive against corruption had already led to a longer-term decline in corruption, even as Georgia remains a "borderline case" of combating corruption. Among the cases I consider, Georgia was the only one with a score of less than 4 (3.8) on the TI scale – ranking 68th out of 178 countries, ranking between Italy and the four-way tie of Brazil, Cuba, Montenegro, and Romania.

Beyond reducing corruption, the new regime focused on improving public services (Kupatadze, 2015, 2–10, 17).

Education funding became a top priority. A World Bank (2012, 75–76) report stated:

Education funding in Georgia dried up following the collapse of the Soviet Union. By the time of the Rose Revolution, all educational institutions suffered from a lack of books, barely qualified teachers, and crumbling infrastructures. Salaries were so low – a university professor earned about GEL 60 a month in 2002, less than half the minimum subsistence level – that bribe taking was considered an acceptable way to get by. Students paid bribes to get into universities, to pass exams, and to get their diplomas. Although the quality of education was usually poor, having a university degree conferred a certain social status and granted access to jobs . . . Bribes were so common that people negotiated them right on campus.

The new government focused on expanding higher education as part of its anti-corruption program.

A centralized examination system made it more difficult to bribe officials to get higher grades. The number of universities increased by tenfold. Since higher education was considered the most corrupt institution, reforming it played a central role in the reforms of the Rose Revolution. The central government also took over the funding of primary education, which had previously been left to local governments (World Bank, 2012, 76–77, 81, 85). As in Hong Kong and Singapore, the schools were seen as important elements in the struggle against corruption.

Young people would be required to take civic education courses emphasizing honesty in government (Slade, 2012, 47–48).

The Rose Revolution was a rebellion against a corrupt regime.

Georgia was also in the grip of Russia. Its president, Eduard Shevardnadze, had agreed to a secret agreement with the Russian state gas company Gazprom, giving it control of Georgia's gas distribution system for 25 years (Management Systems International, 2005, 9). Russia was supporting separatists in South Ossetia and Abhkazia and effectively controlled the border with Georgia – from which it flooded the Georgian economy with Russian currency (Papava, 2006, 659). The Rose Revolution, a popular movement based upon Georgian identity and independence, was a rebellion against a corrupt government that people believed was too close to Russia, on the one hand, and too weak to defend Georgia, on the other hand.

Other Countries

The other countries that have reduced corruption include (with their TI scores in 2010 in parentheses): Barbados (7.8), Estonia, (6.5), Israel (6.1), Mauritius (5.4), Qatar (7.7), Slovenia (6.4), and the United Arab Emirates (6.3). All are in the top 15 percent of the TI scale. They are not included in the Morrison-Murtin education data base. However, the V-DEM data base does include most of these countries. It does not have a measure of mean years of education, but does have an indicator of educational inequality at both 1900 and 2010. For the 61 countries with data on both mean school years and education inequality in 1900, the correlation between these two measures is .754. For 2000, the correlation across 77 countries is .741. Educational inequality is thus a reasonable proxy for mean school years.

Barbados is one of the great success stories on corruption, with a score in 2010 between Austria and Germany (tied for 15th) and Japan (18th). There are many citations to the low levels of corruption but few discussions about what has produced such honesty. One compelling account is a public philosophy in Barbados emphasizing social cohesion and a shared vision for the country's population – what I would see as generalized trust in people who are different from yourself (Uslaner, 2002, ch. 2). This idea of a social contract gave the government more leeway in enacting pro-growth economic policies – and that also led to greater honesty in government (Clair *et al.*, 2013).[4]

Barbados was also an early leader in providing education to its children. Early in the twentieth century – and well before independence – Barbados was responsible for educating its children (Sokoloff and Engerman, 2000, 228). A reform commission in 1932 established a system that soon became the foundation for universal access to public education (UNESCO, 2006). The gains in educational equality were very strong over the course of the twentieth century. Barbados's score in 1900 on the V-DEM educational inequality index was −.938. The index is a standardized score and negative values were below average. By 2010, it had risen to 2.20, greater than Germany's score and equal to the United Kingdom's. There is no direct evidence linking increases in educational equality and honesty in government, but the "social contract" thesis suggests that there likely is a connection. Barbados also shows the limitations of the factor endowment explanations. Its economy, like many others in the Caribbean, was based upon large slave plantations producing sugar (Engerman and Sokoloff, n.d., 6).

Estonia and Slovenia have the best CPI scores of any former Communist country – at 6.5 and 6.4, ranking 26th and 27th of the 178 countries. Estonia stood out among former Soviet countries. It has strong anti-corruption provisions with criminal penalties for public officials who engage in corruption and strong requirements for disclosure of assets and conflicts of interest as well as public disclosure of campaign financing. All government procurement is done online with publicly available information about contracts (European Commission, 2014). These legal restrictions cannot explain the low level of corruption, since many, if not most, are consequences rather than causes of government honesty.

What makes Estonia so honest is the ethnic heritage of its population. Unlike other citizens of the former Soviet Union, Estonians are ethnically Nordic – Swedish and Finnish – and Estonians see themselves as espousing Nordic values and attitudes toward government (Bennich-Björkman, n.d., 4, 29). Sweden and Finland are tied for third place on the TI Index (at 9.2). Kalniņš (2015, 5) argues that "[the] Estonian people had less of a tolerance for corruption than in many other parts of the former Soviet Union, especially for corruption in the form of bribery, in particular bribery in a monetary form. An anecdotal story tells of Georgian students who had come to study at the Tallinn Polytechnic Institute during the Soviet era. They came to Estonia because there they could get their diplomas by actually studying, while at home they would have had to buy their diplomas and they were too poor to do so... The social pressure to hide engagement in corruption and proceeds from corruption allegedly acted as a constraint and has been in place supposedly well before the collapse of Soviet rule in Estonia." An Estonian added: "a bribe, in whatever form, especially in a monetary form, always, including the Soviet time, was considered an ugly thing. [...] To boast with one's corrupt relations was never considered a good tone with us."

This social pressure against corruption is similar to Jante Law (see the discussion of Denmark in Chapter 3), a set of rules for a fictional Danish community that laid out the moral guidelines for Nordic society. Jante Law is a set of rules for a fictional Danish community that lay out the moral guidelines for Nordic society. Two of the ten key social norms are: You shall never indulge in the conceit of imagining that you are better than we are; and You shall not believe that you are more important than we are (Booth, 2014, 83), The anti-corruption morality of the Estonian people was the same as for other Nordics. And most Estonians had access to Western interpretations of the world since Finnish television was widely available and Estonian and Finnish languages were very similar (Kalniņš, 2015, 6).

Estonia was incorporated into the Soviet Union later than most other states in the area. It had longer periods of independence, "during which time national identity was intensely nurtured through **mass schooling and education**" (Bennich-Björkman and Likiæ-Brboriæ, 2012, 65, emphasis added).

Education is very important to Estonians. In the late nineteenth century, education was widespread in Estonia, with 94 percent literacy.

The Western culture of Estonia led people to resist the doctrinaire education imposed by the Soviet Union in favor of a Western model (Estonia.org). Estonians rank 13th in world rankings on science on one index, 11th in math and reading and tied for fourth and seventh places on another ranking. Eighty-nine percent of 25–64-year-olds have completed at least secondary school, compared to an average for the Organization of Economic Cooperation and Development (34 Western and Asian countries) of 75 (Shepherd, 2010; Estonia Public Broadcasting, 2015; OECD, 2013). There is no V-DEM educational inequality score for Estonia in 1900. In 2010, the score was 2.54, equal to the values for Ireland, the Netherlands, and Sweden.

Slovenia is the other former Communist state with a high score on the CPI. Slovenia was formerly part of Yugoslavia. Following the death of Yugoslav leader Tito, Slovenia moved away from the other states. It developed strong economic ties with the West – notably Austria and Italy (its neighbors). Economic integration with Western Europe required honesty in business relations – and this quickly spread to the public sector. Slovenia declared independence from Yugoslavia in 1991.

Slovenia had long been wealthier than the other Yugoslavian states. By 1991, it also had higher level of education. Following independence, a major reform initiative centered upon social welfare and especially education (Flere *et al.*, 2004, 47), Education had long distinguished Slovenia from other Yugoslavian states. Even before independence, education reform had led to universal schooling (Gabriè, 12, 21). Slovenia's story was thus similar to that of Estonia. Its CPI score was almost identical and its educational inequality measure for 2010 was 3.32, better than any of the other 167 countries except Japan (3.49).

Slovenia and Estonia had become European countries – highly educated and uncorrupt. And Slovenia had escaped the fate of many former Communist countries. These nations were marked by low inequality under Communism (although the quality of the data are questionable). The rise of market regimes led to sharp increases in inequality for almost all of these nations (Uslaner, 2008, 105). In 2010, according to the Solt net Ginis, Estonia had a middle ranking on inequality (.32), but Slovenia was among the most equal (.25) – ranking seventh of 105 nations.

Mauritius fares well on the TI CPI with a score of 5.4, the second-best in Africa after Botswana. Mauritius is an island nation off the east coast of Africa that had been colonized by the Dutch, the French, and the British before gaining independence in 1968. Perhaps most notable for its high ranking on the CPI are its strong economic growth and its open markets, making it the most competitive economy in sub-Saharan Africa (World Economic Forum, 2014, 42).

Mauritius had long been a leader on education in British Africa. Frankema (2011, 142) wrote:

Although the absolute per capita educational expenses in Mauritius in 1925 (£0,15) were low compared to New Zealand (£2,03), they were a factor of three to ten times higher than in the rest of British Africa. In terms of the relative share of educational spending, which was around 10%, Mauritius even belonged to the select group of industrialized countries that were moving towards the creation of extensive welfare systems.

After independence in 1968, there was a long economic boom in Mauritius. The growth rate of the Mauritian economy was greater than 6 percent in the 1990s. The GDP per capita (in terms of purchasing power parity) was $11,287. Mauritius ranked first in economic competitiveness in Africa, and 23rd worldwide (OECD, 2006).

The economic boom led to a program of social reform emphasizing education. And the main goal of education was, according to the World Bank (n.d., 5, emphasis in original) was the "[**enforcement of the principles of good governance and accountability.**" Further reforms in 1996 guaranteed education for all children. In 2005, the government established free public education for all and mandated at least 11 years of schooling (UNESCO, 2008). Mauritius advanced dramatically in educational equality. In 1900 its score was −.48. By 2010 it had increased to 1.68, almost equal to that of Austria and greater than Botswana. While Mauritius had the second-best CPI score in Africa, it was not "free of corruption." A Transparency International (2014) report still found corruption "pervasive and ingrained" (according to cables leaked from the American Embassy), widespread public disapproval of government efforts to curb dishonesty, weak enforcement of anti-bribery statutes, reported linkages between contributions to political parties and government contracts, and substantial direct payments by private firms to obtain government procurements.

Yet Mauritius seems less corrupt than most other African nations. Reports of petty corruption are rare. Even grand corruption seems less common (and less expensive) than in other developing countries.

Only a tiny number of countries have "beaten" corruption – Finland, Hong Kong, Singapore – and perhaps Barbados. But the other countries discussed here have reduced dishonesty, some substantially. And these small steps are more realistic targets than "curing corruption" (Johnston, 2015, ch. 3).

Beyond the Data in this Study

In addition to these countries, the CPI shows high scores for Qatar, the United Arab Emirates, Israel, Bhutan, and Brunei. But there is little literature on either their corruption patterns or education, so I do not discuss them. This list of countries – in addition to Georgia, Hong Kong, and Singapore – provide some evidence that democracy is not the key to reducing dishonesty in government: Only Israel is a democracy among these nations. But there is greater support for the linkage between education and corruption. For the ten countries that have beaten or reduced corruption (Barbados, Botswana, Estonia, Finland, Georgia, Japan, Mauritius, Slovenia, South Korea, and Taiwan), the average education inequality score in 2010 is 2.56, equal to that for Sweden. The simple correlations for corruption in 2010 and educational inequality in 1900 and 2010 are .686 (N = 61) and .806 (N = 77). In some cases, there is a direct linkage between reforms in corruption and education. Even without a direct linkage, the two sets of reforms largely occur at the same time.

Evidence on education is sparse for these countries. Education inequality in Qatar increased from a very unequal −.488 in 1900 to a highly equal 2.862 in 2010. But data are not available for other countries. Corruption fell from .351 (1900) to .184 (2010) for Bhutan and from .195 (1950) to .149 (2010) for Israel.

These countries do seem to have expanded educational opportunities for its young people. In each of these countries, education has become both free and compulsory for both elementary and secondary schools.

Education in Israel was made compulsory and free from the founding of the state, when the 1949 Compulsory Education Law was enacted. In the late 1960s, compulsory education was extended to age 16 and free education to age 18. However, two sectors of the population receive less education – the *Haredim*, or ultra-Orthodox, who maintain their own schools that emphasize religious education over secular subjects, and Israeli Arabs. In 1935, before the state was founded, only 20 percent of Muslim children were enrolled in schools. By 2006, 83 percent of Israeli Arabs were enrolled in secondary schools, compared to 93 percent of Jews (Volansky, 2007) Nevertheless, Israel has made major gains in education and its level of education is comparable to developed Western countries.

The high level of education in Israel is not surprising, Jews, as "the people of the Book," have been at the forefront of universal education (at least for boys) for centuries. For Jews, as for Protestants, "the main goal [of education] was to make every male child able to read the Torah in the synagogue." Education also gave Jews skills in working with "business letters, sale and purchase contracts, partnership deeds, and loans," among the few professions that were not barred for Jews throughout their history in Europe (Botticini and Eckstein, 2005, 13, 19).

In both Qatar and the United Arab Emirates, education is universal and free. Early education in Qatar was exclusively religious. Upon independence in 1956, the Ministry of Education was created. By the 1980s education had become free and universal (Qatar-Educational System-overview, n.d.). The situation was similar in the United Arab Emirates, with universal education for Qatari citizens established after a major program building public schools in the 1960s and 1970s. The UAE became independent in 1971. Universal secondary education was established in 2000/2001 (Embassy of the United Arab Emirates Cultural Division, ND; UNESCO, 2010/2011). Education in Brunei was also exclusively religious until 1954, when a government five-year plan was established, leading to the National Education Policy of 1962 and the establishment of the National Educational System in 1985 that gave the government control of education. By 2012, secondary school enrollment reached 94 percent (Borgen Project, n.d.).

Education in Bhutan mostly took place through religious authorities, the Buddhist monasteries prior to 1959. Only a small number of students received education. In the 1960s, public education for the larger population was adopted and widespread education was adopted as part of the Dragon King Jigme Singye Wangchuck's program of "Gross National Happiness (GNH)," which was enacted in 1972. The GNH program provided universal and free education for all Bhutanese children (Bhutan Ministry of Education, 2012).

Each of these countries faces external threats, although it is difficult to establish a connection between the threats and the development of early education. Israel has been in a state of war with its Arab neighbors since its independence in 1949. Qatar worries about attacks from the Islamic State (ISIS) and Iran and has entered into a defense pact with Turkey (Cochrane, 2016). The UAE is also concerned about attacks from ISIS and Iran (Al Rashedi, 2004–2005).

Bhutan has not faced any direct confrontation, but it is closely tied to India, which is seen as an ally against possible aggression from Pakistan and China (Globalsecurity.org, n.d.). China has asserted territorial rights over Bhutan and India is the small kingdom's defender (Benedictus, 2014). Brunei is a different story: It faces no threats from other nations or forces. However, there was an internal revolt (supported by China) in 1962 to protest a proposed merger with Malaysia, Singapore, Sarawak, and North Borneo (Sabah). The government put down the rebellion, but has maintained a state of emergency since then (Majid, 2007; Radio Australia, 2012).

It may be difficult to establish a direct causal connection between education and external threat. However, in each case education helps provide a greater sense of identification with the nation, which is a key factor in reducing corruption (see Chapter 1).

Reforms and External Threat

For two of the "new" cases, there is a clear link between reforms and external threat. The secessionist provinces of Abkazia and South Ossetia led to military conflicts with Russia in 2008. But the tensions and military conflicts within Georgia had wracked the country for more than a decade before the Russian invasion to support the secessionist South Ossetians. As Schmidt-Braull and von Kopp (2007, 286–287) wrote: "Schools were either destroyed or occupied by refugees during the civil war. As a consequence, the enrolment of children entering the first grade of primary school decreased." During this period, the Georgian government fell in the Velvet Revolution and the new regime made education reform its top priority.

Estonia also faced a military threat from Russia. Even without military action, Estonians remain on the alert to a possible attack. Estonia, with a population of 1.3 million and only 6,000 soldiers, has a very high rate of gun ownership, so that citizens can be on guard in the event of Russian military action against this former Soviet state that is now a NATO member. The Estonian Defense Force organizes training exercises among its 25,000 members to stand against Russia (Kramer, 2016). Some Western military analysts have warned that it would be easy for Russia to enter some cities with ethnic Russian majorities and thus to threaten the new regime. Russia has threatened to support referenda that would call for separation for the areas with majorities of Russian speakers (GlobalSecurity.org, n.d.). While there is no direct link with either anti-corruption or education policies, having a clean government that delivers on basic social services such as education will reinforce the support of the citizens who disapprove of separatist movements.

These additional cases lead to a more nuanced argument. Most of the countries where we see less corruption – and reforms in education – did face external threats. However, some countries with lower levels of corruption *did not face external threats*. There is no evidence of such threats for Barbados, Mauritius, or Slovenia – or for some other countries I do not include because of lack of information – Bhutan and Brunei. This does not mean that external threat doesn't matter. The overwhelming majority of countries that have reduced corruption substantially *did* face outside threats. But it opens up the possibility that the fight against corruption can be successful even in the absence of external threats. Inequality does not seem to be the key to a successful anti-corruption strategy in these states: While it is low in Slovenia (.25), it is much higher in Bhutan (.39) and especially Barbados (.48). Perhaps it is economic success: Barbados, Brunei, Mauritius, Slovenia, and the two Gulf Arab countries (Qatar and the United Arab Emirates) are all wealthy, either absolutely or relatively to other countries in their areas. Yet Bhutan is relatively poor.

We are thus left with a partial explanation of how countries "beat" corruption. External threat seems the most potent factor. But it is neither necessary nor sufficient – since many countries facing outside enemies have done little to combat corruption. Notable "exceptions" are the former Soviet states of Armenia and Azerbaijan (long at war with each other) and Ukraine (which lost Crimea to a Russian invasion in 2014). While Slovenia escaped external conflict, other former Yugoslavian states – Bosnia, Croatia, Kosovo, and Montenegro – fought each other but did not battle corruption. External threats may provide an opportunity to rebuild a nation's economic, social, and political systems but it is hardly a guaranteed "silver bullet."

Economic success may also provide a rationale – or even a need – for better governance, as well as the means to finance the educational system that usually accompanies reductions in corruption. It too is not a prerequisite. Some countries have great wealth but the money is sometimes squandered if corruption is high. This often occurs if a country's wealth is in natural resources, which may be quickly extracted, sold or stolen, and the wealth transferred out of the country. This is the "resource curse" (Frankel, 2010). Oil is a commodity that is stolen in countries such as Nigeria, Angola, and Venezuela, all of which have high levels of corruption and inequitable distributions of wealth. Some countries that have large oil resources – Norway, Qatar, the United Arab Emirates, and Brunei – are wealthy oil-producing nations with low levels of corruption.

External threats and both wealth and an equitable distribution of income are potential paths to reducing corruption. But others may exist even as these alternative causes are not evident – most likely because there are so few cases of countries that have "conquered" corruption.

Reprise

Both corruption and education are "sticky." Countries that had more widespread education and honest government a century or more ago have higher levels of education and less corruption today.

Path dependence is not forever. I discussed a number of countries that have increased education levels and combated corruption. So reform is possible. Yet it is not easy. Investment in education is expensive. And it takes political will. But the larger lesson is that, however difficult, change is possible. I don't accept the argument that biology is destiny. Some of the most successful fights against corruption as well as increasing education come in states that are not endowed with the climate and resources that the factor endowments account would have us believe. Nor is there a strong linkage between a particular form of institutional design – notably democracy – and levels of education or the quality of government and democratic institutions.

Lipset (1959), Glaeser, Ponzetto, and Shleifer (2007), and Murtin and Wacziarg (2014) – among others – provide support for the argument that universal education leads to democratic government, rather than the other way around.

Corruption is difficult to "cure" for the same reason that *relative* education levels mostly remain the same. While all countries have higher levels of education than 140 years ago, the ordering has not changed much except in a handful of cases. Path dependence reflects the economic resources, rather than the natural resources, of countries. The wealthier and especially the more equal countries could afford to educate their publics 140 years ago – and also today.

They also faced demands from their citizens to provide public services, and political leaders found that they needed to provide goods such as education to keep the favor of their publics. Economic growth and education empowered people to become masters of their own fate – they did not have to rely upon corrupt leaders for their well-being. It was wise for leaders to recognize such demands: Education built identification with the state – and thus potentially greater loyalty to leaders.

As in the United States, education also opened new occupations requiring skills such as reading, writing, and arithmetic – and these positions were more highly paid. This "new" economic system led to greater economic equality – and ultimately to demands for clean government.

Many of the anti-corruption reforms discussed in this chapter were part of more general movements that included demands for more egalitarian land and wealth distribution as well as better service delivery, especially in education. So the linkage between education and clean government may reflect a broad syndrome of "good governance."

On the other hand, today's states that were colonies were often neglected by the colonial powers. There was little investment in public services – notably on education. The colonial powers were more interested in exploiting the resources of the areas they governed – *except where a large number of their own citizens had moved to the colonies.* This lack of investment had long-term consequences. Poor and unequal states, once independent, did not have the resources to invest in education (or other public services). Low education and especially great inequality were fertile grounds for the emergence of corrupt leaders, who could deliver targeted benefits to their own constituents (often members of their own tribes) rather than pursue more expensive policies that would benefit wider constituencies.

Path dependence can be broken, but deviations from the expected course are most likely to occur with a triggering mechanism – notably an external threat. Such threats may lead current leaders to change course and recognize that they must defend their rule by enacting reforms, as happened in Botswana, Hong Kong, and Singapore. Or it may lead to the development of opposition movements that can seize popular discontent to demand reforms in both governance and service delivery, as in South Korea, Taiwan, and Georgia. Or it can stem from reforms that are imposed from outside – as with Japan – but these will not be successful unless there is support from the local population.

Path dependence may not be forever for all countries. Yet, for most, as William Faulkner wrote: "The past is never dead. It is not even past."[5]

Notes

[1] The V-DEM data for Australia and Cuba are for 1910.

[2] See Fernandez and Seng (2008) and Pingtjin (2013) for arguments that the labor unions were allied with radical Chinese students, but not with Communists in China. For a rebuttal, see "Lim Chin Song was never a Communist...?" at http://unravelling1987.blogspot.com/2014/10/lim-chin-siong-was-never-communist.html.

I am grateful to Chong Ia Ian of the National University of Singapore for bringing this dispute to my attention.

[3] See https://www.wider.unu.edu/project/wiid-%E2%80%93-world-income-inequality-database.

[4] See also the story on the social contract in Barbados on the American public radio program *This American Life* at http://www.thisamericanlife.org/radio-archives/episode/410/social-contract.

[5] See http://www.goodreads.com/quotes/12124-the-past-is-never-dead-it-s-not-even-past.

Appendix

Table A.1 *Mean School Years by Country, 1870*

Country	Mean School Years 1870
Algeria	0.4
Angola	0.01
Argentina	1.5
Australia	3.06
Austria	3.2
Bangladesh	0.08
Belgium	4.27
Benin	0.07
Brazil	0.46
Bulgaria	1.65
Cameroon	0.02
Canada	5.71
Chile	0.94
China	1.01
Costa Rica	0.9
Cote d'Ivoire	0.04
Cuba	0.83
Denmark	4.69
Dominican Republic	0.49
Egypt	0.15
El Salvador	0.6
Ethiopia	0.02
Finland	1.45
Germany	5.44
France	4.12
Ghana	0.04
Greece	1.41
Guatemala	0.51
Honduras	0.64

Table A.1 *(cont.)*

Country	Mean School Years 1870
Hungary	2.58
India	0.08
Indonesia	0.05
Iran	0.29
Iraq	0.1
Ireland	2.65
Italy	0.84
Jamaica	0.51
Japan	0.97
Kenya	0.21
Madagascar	0.14
Malawi	0.4
Malaysia	0.11
Mali	0.04
Mexico	0.56
Morocco	0.05
Mozambique	0.06
Myanmar	0.03
Netherlands	5.09
New Zealand	3.91
Nicaragua	0.54
Niger	0.01
Nigeria	0.01
Norway	5.68
Pakistan	0.08
Panama	0.78
Paraguay	0.63
Peru	0.28
Philippines	0.14
Portugal	0.46
Russia	0.9
Senegal	0.06
Sierra Leone	0.11
South Africa	1.1
South Korea	1.11
Spain	1.51
Sudan	0.06

(cont.)

Table A.1 *(cont.)*

Country	Mean School Years 1870
Sweden	4.23
Switzerland	6.07
Syria	0.29
Thailand	0.17
Tunisia	0.3
Turkey	0.26
United Kingdom	3.59
United States	5.57
Uganda	0.04
Uruguay	1.61
Venezuela	1.1

References

Abad, Leticia Arroyo and Peter H. Lindert. 2015. "Fiscal Redistribution in Latin America since the Nineteenth Century." Unpublished paper, University of California, Davis.

Acemoglu, Daron, Simon Johnson, and James A. Robinson. 2001. "The Colonial Origins of Comparative Development: An Empirical Investigation," *American Economic Review*, 91:1369–1401.

2002. "Reversal of Fortune: Geography and Institutions in the Making of the Modern World Income Distribution," *Quarterly Journal of Economics*, 117:1231–1294.

2003. "An African Success Story: Botswana' in Dani Rodrik (ed.), *In Search of Prosperity: Analytical Narratives on Economic Growth*. Princeton, NJ: Princeton University Press.

Acemoglu, Daron and James A. Robinson. 2012. *Why Nations Fail: The Origins of Power, Prosperity and Poverty*. New York: Crown Business.

Acharya, Poromesh. 1995. "Bengali 'Bhadralok' and Educational Development in 19th Century Bengal," Economic and Political Weekly (April 1):670–673, available at www.jstor.org/stable/4402564.

Akcomak, I., Semih, Dinand Webbink and Bas ter Weel. 2015. "Why Did the Netherlands Develop So Early? The Legacy of the Brethren of the Common Life," *Economic Journal*, DOI: 10.1111.

Adams, Don. 1960. "Problems of Reconstruction in Korean Education," *Comparative Education Review*, 3:27–32.

Adserà, Alícia, Carles Boix, and Mark Payne. 2003. "Are You Being Served? Political Accountability and Quality of Government," *The Journal of Law, Economics, & Organization* 19:445–490.

Aghion, Phillipe, Torsten Persson, and Dorothee Rouzet. 2012. "Education and Military Rivalry." Unpublished paper, Harvard University available at http://scholar.harvard.edu/aghion/publications/education-and-military-rivalry.

Aissa, Djamila and Yasmina Djfari. 2011. "The Role of Colonial Education in Retrospect: The Gold Coast Case in the Era of Imperialism," at http://research.uni-leipzig.de/eniugh/congress/fileadmin/eniugh2011/dokumente/Mechanisms-of-British-Imperial-Aissat_and_Djafri-2011–04–15.pdf.

Al Rashedi, Major Musallam M. 2004–2005. *The UAE National Security Strategy in the 21st Century*, Future Warfare Paper. United States Marine Corps School of Advance Warfighting, Marine Corps University, at www.dtic.mil/dtic/tr/fulltext/u2/a508432.pdf.

Altbach, Philip G. and Toru Umakoshi. 2004. *Asian Universities: Historical Perspectives and Contemporary Challenges*. Baltimore: Johns Hopkins University Press.

Anderson, Ronald S. 1975. *Education in Japan: A Century of Modern Development*. Washington: US Department of Health, Education, and Welfare, available at www.eric.ed.gov/ERICWebPortal/recordDetail? accno=ED131057.

Angeles, Luis and Kyriakos C. Neanidis. 2014. "The Persistent Effect of Colonialism on Corruption," *Economica*, doi: 10.1111/ecca.12123.

Ansell, Ben, and Johannes Lindvall. 2013. "The Political Origins of Primary Education Systems," *American Political Science Review*, 107:505–522.

Anuik, Jonathan. n.d. "Forming Civilization at Red River: 19th-Century Missionary Education of Metis and First Nations Children," at http://iportal.usask.ca/docs/Prairie%20Forum/Forming%20Civilization%20at%20Red%20River%20(v31no1_2006_pg1–15).pdf.

Aristotle. 1962. *The Politics of Aristotle*. Edited and translated by Ernest Barker. New York: Oxford University Press.

Arocena. Rodrigo and Judith Sutz. 2008. "Uruguay: Higher Education, National System of Innovation and Economic Development in a Small Peripheral Country." Lund University Research Policy Institute, available at www.fpi.lu.se/_media/en/research/UniDev_DP_Uruguay.pdf.

Arriba, Ana and Luis Moreno. 2002. "Spain: Poverty, Social Exclusion and 'Safety Nets'," European Project FIPOSC ('Fighting Poverty and Social Exclusion in Southern Europe: Dilemmas of Organization and Implementation') Programme 'Improving the Human Research Potential and Socio-economic Knowledge Base', Research Directorate General, European Commission, HPSE-CT-2001–60020, at http://digital.csic.es/bitstream/10261/1508/1/dt-0210.pdf.

Asagba, Joseph O. 2005. *The Untold Story of a Nigerian Royal Family: The Urhorobo Ruling Clan of Okpe Kingdom 1500–2000*. Lincoln, NE: Iuniverse, Inc.

Balch, Thomas Willing. 1909. "French Colonization in North Africa," *American Political Science Review*, 3:539–551.

Baldwin, Kate. 2015. "Missionaries and Democracy: Inferences about Mechanisms from a WWI-Era Shock." Presented at the Annual Meeting of the American Political Science Association, San Francisco, September 3–6.

Bandle, Oskar, Lennart Elmevik, and Gun Widmark. 2002. *The Nordic Languages: An International Handbook of the History of the North Germanic Languages*. Berlin: Walter de Gruyter.

Baten, Joerg and Jan Luiten van Zanden. 2008. "Book Production and the Onset of Modern Economic Growth," *Journal of Economic Growth*, 13:217–235.

Bauer, Michal, Christopher Blattman, Julie Chytilová, Joseph Henrich, Edward Miguel, and Tamar Mitts. 2016. "Can War Foster Cooperation?" National Bureau of Economic Research, NBER Working Paper 22312, at www.nber.org/papers/w22312.

Bechert, Insa, and Markus Quandt. 2009. *ISSP Data Report: Attitudes towards the Role of Government*. Bonn: GESIS. Liebniz-Institute für Sozialwissenschaften. Working Paper 2009:2.

Becker, Sascha O. and Ludger Woessmann. 2009. "Was Weber Wrong? A Human Capital Theory of Protestant Economic History,"*Quarterly Journal of Economics*, 124:531–596.

Benavot, Aaron and Phyllis Riddle. 1988. "The Expansion of Primary Education, 1870–1940: Trends and Issues," *Sociology of Education*, 61: 191–210.

Benedictus, Brian. 2014. "Bhutan and the Great Power Tussle," *The Diplomat*, at http://thediplomat.com/2014/08/bhutan-and-the-great-power-tussle/.

Bennich-Björkman, Li. n.d. *State Formation and Democratic Consolidation in the Baltic States: a Political Perspective on the EU Membership*, at www.snee.org/filer/papers/25.pdf.

Bennich-Björkman. Li and Branka Likiæ-Brboriæ. 2012. "Successful But Different: Deliberative Identity and the Consensus-Driven Transition to Capitalism in Estonia and Slovenia," *Journal of Baltic Studies*, 43:47–73, DOI: 10.1080/01629778.2011.639148.

Bhutan Ministry of Education. 2012. "National Education Policy," at www .gnhc.gov.bt/wp-content/uploads/2011/05/NEP-2012–21st-March .pdf.

Bledsoe, Caroline. 1992. "The Cultural Transformation of Western Education in Sierra Leone," *Africa: Journal of the International African Institute*, 62:182–202.

Boix, Carles. 2008. "Civil Wars and Guerrilla Warfare in the Contemporary World: Toward a Joint Theory of Motivations and Opportunities." In Stathis Kalyvas, Ian Shapiro and Tarek Masoud, eds.., *Order, Conflict and Violence*. New York: Cambridge University Press.

Boast, R.P. 2013. "Property Rights and Public Law Traditions in New Zealand," *New Zealand Journal of International and Public Law*,

11:161–182 at http://poseidon01.ssrn.com/delivery.php?ID=9681200
7001709601606709400807108208112701506601206503809910306
5095067127118101095000019101125033110002058114102112069
0310821200130100540300010090710750830671100870040370031
2600103011608311211211900308011608710208112508909600706
60061260960270310250S4&EXT=pdf.

Boli, John. 1989. *New Citizens for a New Society: The Institutional Origins
of Mass Schooling in Sweden.* Oxford: Pergamon.

Bologna, Jamie. 2015. "Executive Influence over Reported Corruption Con-
victions: Are Conviction Rates a Biased Measure of State Level Corruption?" at http://papers.ssrn.com/sol3/papers.cfm?abstract_id=2662208.

Boppart, Timo, Josef Falkinger and Volker Grossmann. 2014. "Protestantism and Education: Reading (The Bible) and Other Skills," *Economic Inquiry*, 52:874–895.

Booth, Michael. 2014. *The Almost Nearly Perfect People.* New York:
Picador.

Borgen Project, n.d. "Education in Brunei," at http://borgenproject.org/
education-brunei/.

Botero, Juan, Alejandro Ponce, and Andrei Shleifer. 2012. "Education and
the Quality of Government." NBER Working Paper, available at www/
nber.org/papers/w18119.

Botticini, Maristella and Zvi Eckstein. 2005. "Jewish Occupational Selec-
tion: Education, Restrictions, or Minorities?," *Journal of Economic History*, 65:1–27.

Bowles, Samuel and Herbert Gintis. 1976. *Schooling in Capitalist America.*
New York: Basic Books.

Boylan, Richard T. and Cheryl X. Long. 2003. "Measuring Public Corruption in the American States: A Survey of State House Reporters," *State
Politics & Policy Quarterly*, 3:420–438.

Bragues, George. 2012. "Portugal's Plight: The Role of Social Democracy,"
The Independent Review, 16:325–349, at www.independent.org/pdf/
tir/tir_16_03_1_bragues.pdf.

Browne, Matthew. 2014. "Italy's New 'Bulldozer' Prime Minister," at
www.americanprogress.org/issues/security/report/2014/03/26/86400/
italys-new-bulldozer-prime-minister/ (March 26).

Brunetti, Aymo and Beatrice Weder, 2003. "A Free Press is Bad for Corruption," *Journal of Public Economics*, 87:1801–1829.

Buenker, John D. 1998. *The History of Wisconsin: The Progressive Era,
1893–1914.* Volume 4. Madison: State Historical Society of Wisconsin, at http://ir.uiowa.edu/cgi/viewcontent.cgi?article=10328&context=
annals-of-iowa.

Bulgarian Properties. 2008. "History of Bulgarian Education," available at http://bulgarianproperties.info/history-of-bulgarian-education/.

Buquet, Daniel and Rafael Piñeiro. 2014. "Corruption and Government Improvement in Uruguay." Presented at the Annual Meeting of the American Political Science Association, Washington, DC, at http://papers.ssrn.com/sol3/papers.cfm?abstract_id=2479528.

Campbell, Craig. 2014. "Free, Compulsory and Secular Education Acts Australia, 1850–1910," *Dictionary of Educational History in Australia and New Zealand (DEHANZ)*, February 28. Available http://dehanz.net.auat http://dehanz.net.au/entries/free-compulsory-secular-education-acts/.

Campos, Jose Edgardo and Hilton L. Root. 1996. *The Key to the Asian Miracle: Making Shared Growth Credible*. Washington, DC: Brookings Institution.

Carstesen, Kai and Erich Gundlach. 2006. "The Primacy of Institutions Reconsidered: Direct Income Effects of Malaria Prevalence," *World Bank Economic Review*, 20:309–333.

Canadian Encyclopedia. n.d. a. "History of Education," at www.thecanadianencyclopedia.ca/en/article/history-of-education/.

Canadian Encyclopedia. n.d. b. "Property Law," at www.thecanadianencyclopedia.ca/en/article/property-law/.

Charron, Nicholas. 2015. "Do Corruption Measures Have a Perception Problem? Assessing the Relationship Between Experiences and Perceptions of Corruption among Citizens and Experts," *European Political Science Review*, DOI http://dx.doi.org/10.1017/S1755773914000447.

Charron, Nicholas, Victor Lapuente, and Bo Rothstein. 2013. *Quality of Government and Corruption from a European Perspective*. Cheltenham, UK: Edward Elgar.

Charton, Albert. 1970. "The Social Function of Education in French West Africa." in W. Bryant Mumford in consultation with Major G. St. J. Orde-Brown, eds, *Africans Learn to Be French*. New York: Negro Universities Press.

Chaudhary, Latika. 2007. "An Economic History of Education in Colonial India," at http://economics.ucr.edu/seminars_colloquia/2007/political_economy_development/LatikaChaudhary5-6-07.pdf.

2012. "Chapter 10: Caste, Colonialism and Schooling: Education in British India," at http://papers.ssrn.com/sol3/papers.cfm?abstract_id=2087140.

Chavez, Rebecca Bill. 2003. "The Construction of the Rule of Law in Argentina: A Tale of Two Provinces," *Comparative Politics*, 35:417–437.

Cherkasov, Aleksander. 2011. "All Russian Primary Education (1894–1917): Developmental Milestones," *Social Evolution and History*, 10:138–149, at www.socionauki.ru/journal/files/seh/2011_2/138–149.pdf.

Cinnirella, Francesco and Erik Hornung. 2011. "Landownership Concentration and the Expansion of Education," at http://papers.ssrn.com/sol3/papers.cfm?abstract_id=1939848.

Cizakca, Murat. n.d. "Economic Dimensions of Foundations in the Ottoman Era," in Davut Aydin, Ali Carkoglu, Murat Cizakca, and Afatos Goksen, *Philanthropy in Turkey: Citizens, Foundations, and the Pursuit of Social Justice*. Istanbul: TUSEV (Third Sector Foundation of Turkey), at www.tusev.org.tr/usrfiles/files/economic_dimensions_of_foundations_in_the_ottoman_era.pdf.

Clair, Matthew, Peter Blair Henry, and Sandile Hlatshwayo. 2013. "Two Tales of Entrepreneurship: Barbados, Jamaica, and the 1973 Oil Price Shock," *Proceedings of the American Philosophical Society*, 157:32–57, at https://amphilsoc.org/sites/default/files/proceedings/1570103.pdf.

Clark, Martin. 1984. *Modern Italy 1971–1982*. London: Longman.

Cochrane, Paul. 2016. "Revealed: Secret Details of Turkey's New Military Pact with Qatar," at www.middleeasteye.net/news/turkey-qatar-military-agreement-940298365.

Comin, Diego, William Easterly, and Erick Gong. 2010. "Was the Wealth of Nations Determined in 1000 BC?," *American Ecnomic Journal: Macroeconomics*, 2:65–97.

Commager, Henry Steele. 1950. *The American Mind*. New Haven: Yale University Press.

Coppedge, Michael, John Gerring, Staffan I. Lindberg, Svend-Erik Skaaning, Jan Teorell, David Altman, Michael Bernhard, M. Steven Fish, Adam Glynn, Allen Hicken, Carl Henrik Knutsen, Kyle Marquardt, Kelly McMann, Farhad Miri, Pamela Paxton, Daniel Pemstein, Jeffrey Staton, Eitan Tzelgov, Yi-ting Wang, and Brigitte Zimmerman. 2015. "V-Dem [Country-Year/Country-Date] Dataset v5." Varieties of Democracy (V-Dem) Project, at www.v-dem.net/en/data/.

Cornwell, Elmer E., Jr. 1964. "Bosses, Machines, and Ethnic Groups," *Annals of the American Academy of Political and Social Sciences*, 353:27–39.

Cremin, Lawrence A. 1976. *Traditions of American Education*. New York: Basic Books.

1980. *American Education: The National Experience 1783–1876*. New York: Harper and Row.

Cruz, Cesi and Philip Keefer. 2010. "Programmatic Political Parties and Public Sector Reform," at http://papers.ssrn.com/sol3/papers.cfm?abstract_id=1642962.

Cumming, Alan and Ian Cumming. 1977. "New Zealand's Education Act of 1877(1)," *Paedagogica Historica*, 17:305–314.

Cummings, William K. 1980. *Education and Equality in Japan*. Princeton, NJ: Princeton University Press.

Dahlström, Carl, Johannes Lindvall, and Bo Rothstein. 2013. "Corruption, Bureaucratic Failure and Social Policy Priorities." *Political Studies* 61:523–542.

Dahlström, Carl, Victor Lapuente, and Jan Teorell. 2012. "The Merit of Meritocratization: Politics, Bureaucracy, and the Institutional Deterrents of Corruption," *Political Research Quarterly* xx(x): 1–13.

Darden, Keith. 2013. *Resisting Occupation: Mass Literacy and the Creation of Durable National Loyalties*. New York: Cambridge University Press.

Davis, John A. 2015. "A Tale of Two Italys? The 'Southern Question' Past and Present." In Erik Jones and Gianfranco Pasquino (eds.), *The Oxford Handbook of Italian Politics*, Oxford Handbooks Online, DOI: 10.1093/oxfordhb/9780199669745.013.5.

Deininger, Klaus and Lyn Squire. 1996. "A New Data Set: Measuring Economic Income Inequality," *World Bank Economic Review*, 10: 565–592.

Della Porta, D. and A. Vannucci. 1999. *Corrupt Exchanges*. New York: Aldine.

Denmark. n.d. "Folk High Schools," at http://denmark.dk/en/practical-info/study-in-denmark/folk-high-schools/.

Dincer, Oguzhan and Michael Johnston. 2015. "Measuring Illegal and Legal Corruption in American States: Some Results from the Edmond J. Safra Center for Ethics Corruption in America Survey," Edmond J. Safra Working Papers, No. 58, at http://papers.ssrn.com/sol3/papers .cfm?abstract_id=2579300.

Di Scala. Spencer M. 2004. *Italy: From Revolution to Republic 1700 to the Present*. Boulder: Westview Press.

Dittmar, Jeremiah and Skipper Seabold. 2015 "Media, Markets and Institutional Change: Evidence from the Protestant Reformation," Centre for Economic Performance Discussion Paper 1367, at http://cep.lse.ac.uk/pubs/download/dp1367.pdf.

Dittmar, Jeremiah and Ralf R. Meisenzahl. 2016. "State Capacity and Public Goods: Institutional Change, Human Capital and Growth in Early

Modern Germany," Centre for Economic Performance Discussion Paper 1418, at http://cep.lse.ac.uk/pubs/download/dp1418.pdf.

Dittmar, Jeremiah and Skipper Seabold. 2015 "Media, Markets and Institutional Change: Evidence from the Protestant Reformation," Centre for Economic Performance Discussion Paper 1367, at http://cep.lse.ac.uk/pubs/download/dp1367.pdf.

Domke, Joan. 2011. *Education, Fascism, and the Catholic Church in Franco's Spain*. Dissertations. Paper 104. http://ecommons.luc.edu/luc_diss/104, Loyola University of Chicago.

Donadio, Rachel and Liz Alderman. 2012. "For Greece, Oligarchs Are Obstacle to Recovery," *New York Times* (December 5): A6, A14 available at www.nytimes.com/2012/12/06/world/europe/oligarchs-play-a-role-in-greeces-economic-troubles.html?_r=0.

Dore, R.P. 1964. "Education: Japan." In Robert E. Ward and Dankwart A. Rustow, eds., *Political Modernization in Japan and Turkey*. Princeton: Princeton University Press.

Dreier, Peter. 2012. "Why Has Milwaukee Forgotten Victor Berger?" (July 6) at www.huffingtonpost.com/peter-dreier/why-has-milwaukee-forgott_b_1491463.html.

Dutta, Indranil and Ajit Mishra. 2013. "Does Inequality Foster Corruption?," *Journal of Public Economic Theory*, 15:602–619.

Easterlin, Richard A. 1981. "Why Isn't the Whole World Developed?," *Journal of Economic History*, 41:1–19.

Easterly, William and Ross Levine. 2012. "The European Origins of Economic Development," at www.nyudri.org/wp-content/uploads/2013/10/European-Origins-Development-Nov2013.pdf.

Education, *Annual Report of the United States Commissioner of Education*; 1918–1956, U.S.

Office of Education, *Biennial Survey of Education in the United States*, Statistics of State School Systems, various issues; 1958–1996, U.S. Department of Education, *Digest of Education Statistics 1997*.

Education Bulgaria. ND, at http://countrystudies.us/bulgaria/30.htm.

Embassy of the United Arab Emirates, Cultural Division. n.d. "Education in UAE: K-12 Education," at http://uaecd.org/k-12-education.

Engerman, Stanley L. and Kenneth L. Sokoloff. 2012. *Economic Development in the Americas Since 1500*. New York: Cambridge University Press.

"Factor Endowments, Inequality, and Paths of Development Among New World Economies," National Bureau of Economic Research Working Paper 9259, at www.nber.org/papers/w9259.

n.d. "The Long-Term Persistence of Inequality in the Americas Since European Colonization." Unpublished paper.

Espuelas, Sergio. 2014. "The Inequality Trap. A Comparative Analysis of Social Spending Between 1880 and 1930," *Economic History Review*, doi: 10.1111/1468–0289.12062.

Estonia.org. 2016. "Public education as the basis of independent nationhood," March 29, at www.estonica.org/en/Education_and_science/The_history_of_Estonian_education_%E2%80%94_the_story_of_the_intellectual_liberation_of_a_nation/Public_education_as_the_basis_of_independent_nationhood/.

Estonia Public Broadcasting. 2013. "Estonia Scores High Marks in PISA Education Tests," December 3, at http://news.err.ee/v/news/politics/education/ab06c831-b8b0–4e00–8c38–48a9f1a806ba/estonia-scores-high-marks-in-pisa-education-tests.

European Commission. 2014. *Annex Estonia to the EU Anti-Corruption Report*, at http://ec.europa.eu/dgs/home-affairs/what-we-do/policies/organized-crime-and-human-trafficking/corruption/anti-corruption-report/docs/2014_acr_estonia_chapter_en.pdf.

Evans, Sterling. 1999. *The Green Republic: A Conservation History of Costa Rica*. Austin: University of Texas Press.

Färdigh, Mathias A. 2013. *What's the use of a free media? the role of media in curbing corruption and promoting quality of government (Diss)*. Göteborg: Department of Journalism Media and Communication University of Gothenburg.

Fehr, Ernst and Urs Fischbacher. 2005. "The Economics of Strong Reciprocity." Pp. 151–193 in *Moral Sentiments and Material Interests: The Foundations for Cooperation in Economic Life*, edited by H. Gintis, S. Bowles, R. Boyd, and E. Fehr. Cambridge, MA: The MIT Press.

Fenton, John H. 1966. *Midwest Politics*. New York: Holt, Rinehart, and Winston.

Ferguson, Niall. 2011. *Civilization: The West and the Rest*. London: Allen Lane.

Fernandez, Michael and Loh Kah Seng. 2008. "The Left-Wing Trade Unions in Singapore, 1945–1970." In Michael D. Barr and Carl A. Trocki, eds., *Paths Not Taken: Political Pluralism in Post-War Singapore*. Singapore: NUS Press.

Ferris, Lindsay. 2014. "Snap Shot Georgia: From Closed-door Corruption to Open Data," at https://sunlightfoundation.com/blog/2014/09/03/snap-shot-georgia-from-closed-door-corruption-to-open-data/.

Fisman, Raymond and Roberta Gatti 2002. "Decentralization and Corruption: Evidence Across Countries," *Journal of Public Economics*, 83:325–345. Washington, DC: The World Bank.

Fitchen, Edward D. 1974. "Primary Education in Colonial Cuba: Spanish Tool for Retaining 'La Isla Siempre Leal?'", *Caribbean Studies*, 14:105–120.

Flecha (Garcia), Consuela. 2011. "Education in Spain: Close-up of Its History in the 20th Century," *Analytical Reports in International Education*, 4:17–42, at www.researchgate.net/publication/266890862_ Education_in_Spain_Close-up_of_Its_History_in_the_20th_Century.

Flere, Sergej with Adnreja Barle Lakota, Jana Bezenšek, and Miran Lavriè. 2004. "Educational Equity and Inequity in Slovenia: Country Analytical Report," at www.oecd.org/education/school/38692842.pdf.

Foldvari, Péter and Bas van Leeuwen, 2011. "Should Less Inequality in Education Lead to a More Equal Income Distribution?," *Education Economics*, 19:537–554.

Folk School Alliance. ND. "A Brief History of Folk Schools," at www .peopleseducation.org/a-brief-history-of-folk-schools/.

Folke, Olle, Shigeo Hirano, and James M. Snyder, Jr. 2011 "Patronage and Elections in U.S. States," *American Political Science Review*. 105567–105585.

Fragoudaki, A. 2015. *Education and Social Reproduction in Post-War Greece*, at www.athenssocialatlas.gr/en/article/postwareducation/.

Frankel, Jeffrey A. 2010. "The Natural Resource Curse: A Survey." National Bureau of Economic Research Working Paper 15836, at www.nber.org/ papers/w15836.pdf.

Frankema, Ewout. 2009. "The Expansion of Mass Education in Twentieth Century Latin America: A Global Comparative Perspective," *Revista de Historia Económica*, 27:359–396.

2010. "The Colonial Roots of Land Inequality: Geography, Factor Endowments, or Institutions?" *Economic History Review*, 63:418–451.

2011. "Colonial Taxation and Government Spending in British Africa, 1880–1940: Maximizing Revenue or Minimizing Effort?," *Explorations in Economic History*, 48:136–149.

Frey, Frederick W. 1964. "Education: Turkey." In Robert E. Ward and Dankwart A. Rustow, eds., *Political Modernization in Japan and Turkey*. Princeton, NJ: Princeton University Press.

Frisk Jensen, Mette. 2008. *Korruption og embedsetik: Danske embedsmænds korruption i perioden 1800 til 1886 (Diss.)*. Aalborg: Aalborg Universitet.

Fukuyama, Francis. 2004. *State-Building: Governance and World Order in the Twenty-First Century*. Ithaca, NY: Cornell University Press.

Gabriè, Ales. "The Education System in Slovenia in the 20th Century," DR,16:7–23, at http://dk.fdv.uni-lj.si/dr/dr32–33gabric.PDF.

Galor, Oded, Omer Moav, Dietrich Vollrath. 2009. "Inequality in Landown-ership, the Emergence of Human-Capital Promoting Institutions, and the Great Divergence," *Review of Economic Studies* (76):143–179.

Gambetta, Diego. 1993. *The Italian Mafia: The Business of Private Protec-tion*. Cambridge, MA: Harvard University Press.

2002. "Corruption: An Analytical Map." In Stephen Kotkin and Andras Sajo, eds., *Political Corruption in Transition: A Skeptic's Handbook*. Budapest: CEU Press.

Garrouste, Christelle. 2010. "100 Years of Educational Reforms in Europe: A Contextual Database," European Commission Joint Research Centre, at http://publications.jrc.ec.europa.eu/repository/bitstream/JRC57357/reqno_jrc57357.pdf.

Gelman, Jorge. 2013. "Economic Inequalities in Nineteenth-Century Argentina," *Journal of European Economic History*, 42:48–86.

Gillard, Derek. 2011. "Education in England: A Brief History," at http://www.educationengland.org.uk/history/.

Glaeser, Edward L. and Claudia Goldin. 2006. "Corruption and Reform: Introduction." In Edward L. Glaeser and Claudia Goldin, eds., *Corrup-tion and Reform: Lessons from America's Economic History*. Chicago: University of Chicago Press.

Glaeser, Edward, Rafael La Porta, Florencio Lopez-De-Silanes and Andrei Shleifer. 2004. "Do Institutions Cause Growth?," *Journal of Economic Growth*, 9:271–303.

Glaeser, Edward, Giacomo A.M. Ponzetto, and Andrei Shleifer. 2007. "Why Does Democracy Need Education?," *Journal of Economic Growth*, 12:77–99.

Glaeser, Edward L., Jose Scheinkman, and Andrei Shleifer. 2003. "The Injus-tice of Inequality," *Journal of Monetary Economics*, 50:199–222.

Glaeser, Edward L. and Bryce A. Ward. 2006. "Myths and Realities of American Political Geography." Harvard Institute of Economic Research Discussion Paper 2100 at http://post.economics.harvard.edu/hier/2006papers/2006list.html.

Globalsecurity.org. n.d. "Bhutan–India Relations," at www.globalsecurity.org/military/world/bhutan/forrel-in.htm.

Go, Su and Peter Lindert. 2010. "The Uneven Rise of American Public Schools to 1850," *Journal of Economic History*, 70:1–26.

Göbel, Christian. 2015. "Anticorruption in Taiwan: Process Tracing Report," at http://ancorage-net.org/content/documents/pdp07–01.pdf.

Goldin, Claudia. 2006. "School Enrollment Rates, by Sex and Race: 1850–1994." In Susan B. Carter, Scott Sigmund Gartner, Michael R. Haines, Alan L. Olmstead, Richard Sutch, and Gavin Wright, eds., *Historical Statistics of the United States, Millennial Edition Online*. New York:

Cambridge University Press, at http://hsus.cambridge.org/HSUSWeb/toc/showChapter.do?id=Bc.

Goldin, Claudia and Lawrence F. Katz. 1999. "Human Capital and Social Capital: The Rise of Secondary Schooling in America, 1910–1940," *Journal of Interdisciplinary History*, 29:683–723.

2008. *The Race between Education and Technology*. Cambridge, MA: Belknap Press.

Graff, H. J. (1987) *The Labyrinths of Literacy. Reflections on Literacy Past and Present*. Pittsburgh: University of Pittsburgh Press.

Grant, Oliver. 2005, *Migration and Inequality in Germany 1870–1913*. Oxford: Clarendon Press.

Gray, Richard. 1986. "Christianity." In Andrew Roberts, ed., *The Colonial Moment in Africa*. Cambridge: Cambridge University Press.

Green, Andy. 1990. *Education and State Formation: The Rise of Education Systems in England, France and the USA*. New York: St. Martin's Press.

Griera, Mar. 2007. "The Education Battle: The Role of the Catholic Church in the Spanish Education System" in Gerald Grace and Joseph O'Keefe, S.J. eds.: *International Handbook of Catholic Education*. Berlin: Springer.

Grimes, Marcia and Lena Wangnerud. 2010. "Curbing Corruption Through Social Welfare Reform? The Effects of Mexico's Conditional Cash Transfer Program on Good Government," *American Review of Public Administration*, 40:671–690.

Guiliano, Paola, and Nathan Nunn. 2013. "The Transmission of Democracy: From the Village to the Nation-State," *American Economic Review*, 103 (3):86–92.

Gylfason, Thorvaldur and Gylfi Zoega. 2002. "Inequality and Economic Growth: Do Natural Resources Matter?" CESifo Working Paper, No. 712, at http://hdl.handle.net/10419/75958.

Hald, Ernhard. 1857. "On National Education in Denmark." Presented to the National Statistical Society, at http://books.google.com/books/about/On_National_Education_in_Denmark.html?id=WUnocQAACAAJ.

Hamoudi, Amar and Jeffrey D. Sachs. 1999. "The Changing Global Distribution of Malaria: A Review." CID Working Paper 2, at https://www.hks.harvard.edu/centers/cid/publications/faculty-working-papers/cid-working-paper no. 2.

Hanson, E. Mark. 1988. "Education, Dictatorship, and Democracy in Spain: An Analysis of Administrative Reform," at http://files.eric.ed.gov/fulltext/ED301929.pdf.

Hay, Simon I., Carlos A. Guerra, Andrew J. Tatem, Abdisalan M. Noor, and Robert W. Snow. 2004. "The Global Distribution and Population at

Risk of Malaria: Past, Present, and Future," *Lancet Infectious Diseases*, 4:327–336, at doi: 10.1016/S1473-3099(04)01043–6.

Hega, Gunther M. 2011. "The Political Functions of Education in Deeply-Divided Countries: Coming Together Apart: The Case of Switzerland." In Theodor Hanf (ed.): *The Political Function of Education in Deeply Divided Countries, Series on Ethnicity, Religion and Democracy*. Baden Baden, Germany: Nomos Verlag, at http://homepages.wmich.edu/ ̃hega/The%20Political%20Functions%20of%20Education%20in% 20Switzerland.pdf.

Heggoy, Alf Andrew. 1973. "Education in French Algeria: An Essay on Cultural Conflict," *Comparative Education Review*, 17:180–197.

Heldring, Leander and James A. Robinson. 2012. "Colonialism and Economic Development in Africa," National Bureau of Economic Research Working Paper 18566, www.nber.org/papers/w18566.

Hibbs, Douglas A., Jr. and Ola Olsson. 2004. "Geography, Biogeography, and Why Some Countries Are Rich and Others Poor," *PNAS*, 101 (March 9):3715–3720, at www.pnas.org_cgi_doi_10.1073_pnas .0305531101.

Hoffman, Nancy and Robert Schwartz. 2015. *Gold Standard: The Swiss Vocational Education and Training System*, at www.ncee.org/ wp-content/uploads/2015/03/SWISSVETMarch11.pdf.

Howe, Frederic C. 1912. *Wisconsin: An Experiment in Democracy*. New York: Charles Scribner's Sons.

Huber, Evelyne and John D. Stephens. 2005. "Successful Social Policy Regimes? Political Economy, Politics, and the Structure of Social Policy in Argentina, Chile, Uruguay, and Costa Rica," Conference on Democratic Governability Kellogg Institute, University of Notre Dame, October 7–8, 2005, at https://kellogg.nd.edu/faculty/research/pdfs/huber .pdf.

Huillery, Elise. 2014. "The Black Man's Burden: The Cost of Colonization of French West Africa," *Journal of Economic History*, 74:1–38.

Hyll-Larsen, Peter. 2013. "Free or Fee: Corruption in Primary School Admissions." In Transparency International, *Global Corruption Report: Education*. Oxon, UK, Routledge.

Ignacio, Jose and Garcia Hamilton. 2005. "Historical Reflections on the Splendor and Decline of Argentina," *Cato Journal*, 25:521–540.

Ihm, Chon Sum. 1995 "South Korea." In Paul Morris and Anthony Sweeting, eds., *Education .and Development in East Asia*. New York: Garland.

Iyer, Lakshmi. 2010. "Direct Versus Indirect Colonial Rule in India," *Review of Economics and Statistics*, 92:693–713.

Jing, Su. 2007. "Corruption by Design? A Comparative Study of Singapore, Hong Kong, and Mainland China." Crawford School of Economics and Government, Australian National University, at http://ancorage-net .org/content/documents/pdp07–01.pdf.

Johansson, Egil. 2009. "The History of Literacy in Sweden." In Harvey J. Graff, Alison Mackinnon, Bergt Sandin, and Ian Winchester, eds., *Understanding Literacy in its Historical Contexts. Socio-cultural history and the legacy of Egil Johansson*. Lund, Sweden: Nordic Academic Press.

Johnston, Michael. 2015. *Corruption Contention and Reform*. New York: Cambridge University Press.

Josephson, Matthew. 1938. *The Politicos*. New York: Harcourt, Brace, and World.

Kaestle, Carl F. and Maris A. Vinovskis. 1980. *Education and Social Change in Nineteenth-Century Massachusetts*. Cambridge: Cambridge University Press.

Kalniņš, Valts. 2015. "Process-Tracing Case Study Report on Estonia," German Institute of Global and Area Studies, at www.againstcorruption .eu/wp-content/uploads/2015/05/D3-Estonia_Kalni%C5%86%C5 %A1.pdf.

Kaufmann, Daniel, Aart Kraay, and Massimo Mastruzzi. 2007. "Growth and Governance: A Reply," *Journal of Politics*, 69:555–562.

Keefe, Patrick Rodden. 2015. "Corruption and Revolt," www.newyorker .com/magazine/2015/01/19/corruption-revolt.

Key, V.O. Jr. 1936. *The Techniques of Political Graft in the United States*. Chicago: University of Chicago Libraries.

Kilicap, Sevinc Sevda. 2009. *Exploring Politics of Philanthropy*. Unpublished thesis, Master of International Studies in Philanthropy, University of Bologna.

Kim, Gwang-Jo. 2002. "Education Policies and Reform in South Korea." In Africa Region, The World Bank, *Secondary Education in Africa: Strategies for Renewal*, available at http://siteresources.worldbank.org/ INTAFRREGTOPEDUCATION/Resources/444659–1220976732806/ Secondary_Education_Strategies_renewal.pdf.

Kim, Sunwoong and Ju-Ho Lee. 2003. "The Secondary School Equalization Policy in South Korea." Unpublished paper, University of Wisconsin-Milwaukee.

Kirby, David G. 2006. *A Concise History of Finland*. New York: Cambridge University Press.

Kramer, Andrew E. 2016. "Spooked by Russia, Tiny Estonia Trains a Nation of Insurgents," *New York Times* (October 31), at www.nytimes.com/ 2016/11/01/world/europe/spooked-by-russia-tiny-estonia-trains-a-nation-of-insurgents.html.

Krauss, Clifford. 1998. "The Welfare State Is Alive, if Besieged, in Uruguay," *New York Times*, (May 3), at www.nytimes.com/1998/05/03/world/the-welfare-state-is-alive-if-besieged-in-uruguay.html.

Kumlin, Staffan and Bo Rothstein. 2010. "Questioning the New Liberal Dilemma: Immigrants, Social Networks and Institutional Fairness," *Comparative Politics*, 41:63–87.

Knudsen, Tim. 1995. *Dansk statsbygning*. 1. København: Jurist-og Økonom-forbundets Forlag.

Kupatadze, Alexander. 2012. "Explaining Georgia's Anti-Corruption Drive," *European Security*, 21:16–36.

2015. "Georgia: Breaking Out of a Vicious Cycle?" at www.againstcorruption.eu/wp-content/uploads/2015/05/D3-Georgia_Kupatadze.pdf.

Kuran, Timur. 2014. "Institutional Roots of Authoritarian Rule in the Middle East: Civic Legacies of the Islamic Waqf." Economic Research Initiatives at Duke Working Paper 171 available at http://ssrn.com/abstract=2449569.

2013. "The Political Consequences of Islam's Economic Legacy," *Philosophy and Social Criticism*, 39:395–405.

2001. "The Provision of Public Goods under Islamic Law: Origins, Impact, and Limitations of the Waqf System," *Law and Society Review*, 35:841–898.

Lambsdorff, Johann Graf. 2005. "The Methodology of the 2005 Corruption Perceptions Index." Transparency International and the University of Passau (Germany), at ww1.transparency.org/cpi/2005/dnld/methodology.pdf.

Lee, Philip. 2003. "Had LKY Not Been Tough Then," *Straits Times* (Singapore), September 20:27.

Lee, Rance P.L. 1981. "The Folklore of Corruption in Hong Kong," *Asian Survey*, 21:355–368.

Leite, Carlos and Jens Weidmann. 1999. "Does Mother Nature Corrupt? Natural Resources, Corruption, and Economic Growth?," Washington: International Monetary Fund Working Paper WP, at www.imf.org/external/pubs/ft/wp/1999/wp9985.pdf.

Lindmark, D. 2009 "Universalism in the Swedish History of Literacy," In Harvey J. Graff, Alison Mackinnon, Bergt Sandin, and Ian Winchester, eds., *Understanding Literacy in its Historical Contexts. Socio-cultural history and the legacy of Egil Johansson*. Lund, Sweden: Nordic Academic Press.

Lijphart, Arend. 1968. *The Politics of Accommodation*. Berkeley: University of California Press.

Lindert, Peter. 2004. *Growing Public: Social Spending and Economic Growth Since the Eighteenth Century*, 2 vols. New York: Cambridge University Press.

2008. "Kenneth Sokoloff on Inequality in the Americas." In Dora L. Costa and Naomi R. Lamoreaux, eds., *Understanding Long-Run Economic Growth: Geography, Institutions, and the Knowledge Economy.* Chicago: University of Chicago Press.

Lindert, Peter H. and Jeffrey G. Williamson. 2011. "American Incomes Before and after the Revolution." National Bureau of Economic Research Working Paper 17211, available at www.nber.org/papers/w17211.

Lipset, Seymour Martin. 1959. "Some Social Requisites of Democracy: Economic Development and Political Legitimacy," *American Political Science Review*, 53:69–105.

1996. *American Exceptionalism: A Double-Edged Sword.* New York: W.W. Norton

Lo, Jack M.K. 2001. "Controlling Corruption in Hong Kong: From Colony to Special Administrative Region," *Journal of Contingencies and Crisis Management*, 9:21–28.

Look4. N .d. "1877 Education Made Compulsory and Free," at http://schools.look4.net.nz/history/new_zealand/time_line2/free_education.

Loving, Katherine (ed.), "The Wisconsin Idea: The Vision that Made Wisconsin Famous," available at www.ls.wisc.edu/documents/wi-idea-history-intro-summary-essay.pdf.

Maddison, Angus. 1971. "The Economic and Social Impact of Colonial Rule in India." In Angus Maddison, *Class Structure and Economic Growth: India & Pakistan since the Moghuls*, available at www.ggdc.net/maddison/articles/moghul_3.pdf.

2003. *The World Economy: Historical Statistics.* Paris: OECD, at www.oecd.org/dev/asia-pacific/developmentcentrestudiestheworldeconomy-historicalstatistics.htm.

Majid, Harun Abdul. 2007. *Rebellion in Brunei: The 1962 Revolt, Imperialism, Confrontation and Oil.* London: I.B. Tauris and Company, at https://tengkudhaniiqbal.files.wordpress.com/2014/11/abdul-harun-majid-rebellion-in-brunei-the-1962-revolt-imperialism-confrontation-and-oil-2007.pdf.

Malinowski, Bronislaw. 1943. "The Pan-African Problem of Culture Contact," *American Journal of Sociology*, 48:649–665.

Management Systems International. 2005. *Causes of the Rose Revolution: Lessons for Democracy Assistance.* Prepared for the USAID Workshop on Democratic Breakthroughs in Serbia, Georgia, and Ukraine, at http://csis.org/files/media/csis/pubs/ci.causesroserevolution.03.05.pdf.

Manion, Melanie. 2004. "Lessons for Mainland China from Anti-Corruption Reform in Hong Kong," *The China Review*, 4:81–97.

Mantena, Rama Sundari. 2010. "Imperial Ideology and the Uses of Rome in Discourses on Britain's Indian Empire." In Mark Bradley, ed., *Classics and Imperialism in the British Empire*. Oxford: Oxford University Press, available at http://ramamantena.files.wordpress.com/2011/03/rama-mantena-contribution-to-classics-and-imperialism-volume1.pdf.

Massey, Douglas S. 2007. *Categorically Unequal: The American Stratification System*. New York: Russell Sage Foundation.

Mathien, Julie. 2001. *Children, Families, and Institutions on Late 19th and Early 20th Century Ontario*. M.A. Thesis, Department of Theory and Policy Studies, Ontario Institute for Studies in Education of the University of Toronto, at https://tspace.library.utoronto.ca/bitstream/1807/15580/1/MQ58891.pdf.

Mauro, Paolo 1998. "Corruption and the Composition of Government Expenditure," *Journal of Public Economics*, 69:263–279.

2002. "The Effects of Corruption on Growth and Public Expenditure." In Arnold Heidenheimer and Michael Johnston, eds. *Political Corruption*, third ed. New Brunswick, NJ: Transaction.

Mayhew, David R. 1986. *Placing Parties in American Politics*. Princeton: Princeton University Press.

McCord, Gordon C. and Jeffrey D. Sachs. 2013. "Development, Structure, and Transformation: Some Evidence on Comparative Economic Growth." National Bureau of Economic Research Working Paper 19512, at www.nber.org/papers/w19512.

McCarthy, Charles. 1912. *The Wisconsin Idea*. New York: Macmillan.

McCreadie, Marion. 2006. "The Evolution of Education in Australia," *History Australia*, at www.historyaustralia.org.au/ifhaa/schools/evelutio.htm.

Meier, Kenneth J. and Thomas M. Holbrook. 1992. "'I Seen My Opportunities and I Took 'Em:' Political Corruption in the United States." *Journal of Politics* 54 (February):135–155.

Meinander, Henrik and Tom Geddes. 2011. *A History of Finland*. London: Hurst.

Menes, Rebecca. 2006. "Limiting the Reach of the Grabbing Hand. Graft and Growth in American Cities, 1880 to 1930," In Edward L. Glaeser and Claudia Goldin, eds., *Corruption and Reform: Lessons from America's Economic History*. Chicago: University of Chicago Press, available at www.nber.org/chapters/c9978.pdf.

Merton, Robert K. 1968. *Social Theory and Social Structure*, enlarged edition. Glencoe, IL: Free Press.

Meyer, John W., Francisco O. Ramirez, and Yasemin Nuhoglu Soysal. 1992. "World Expansion of Mass Education, 1870–1980," *Sociology of Education*, 65:128–149.

Ministry of Education and Culture (Hungary). 2008. *Education in Hungary: Past, Present, and Future, An Overview*. Available at www.nefmi.gov .hu/letolt/english/education_in_hungary_080805.pdf.

Morrison, Christian and Fabrice Murtin. 2009. "The Century of Education," *Journal of Human Capital*, 3:1–42, available at www.fabricemurtin .com.

Mpka, M. N.d. "Overview of Educational Development: Pre-colonial to Present Day," available at http://onlinenigeria.com/education/? blurb=534.

Mungiu-Pippidi, Alina. 2015. *The Quest for Good Governance*. Cambridge: Cambridge University Press.

  2011. "Contextual Choices in Fighting Corruption: Lessons Learned." Hertie School of Governance: Report commissioned by the Norwegian Agency for Development Cooperation, Berlin.

  2006. "Corruption: Diagnosis and Treatment," *Journal of Democracy*, 17:86–99.

Murdoch, John.... *The Women of India and What Can Be Done for Them*. 2nd ed. Madras: The Christian Vernacular Education Society, 1891. *Nineteenth Century Collections Online*. Web. 19 Sept. 2013, at http:// tinyurl.galegroup.com/tinyurl/8yZw0.

Murtin, Fabrice. n.d. "On the Demographic Transition," available at www .fabricemurtin.com.

Murtin, Fabrice and Romain Wacziarg. 2010. "The Demographic Transition 1870–2000," available at www.fabricemurtin.com.

National Commission. 1972. "Compulsory Education in New Zealand," at http://unesdoc.unesco.org/images/0000/000010/001035eo.pdf.

New Zealand Legislation. 1988. "Protection of Personal and Property Rights Act 1988," at www.legislation.govt.nz/act/public/1988/0004/ latest/DLM126528.html.

New Zealand Parliament Hansard. 2005. "New Zealand Bill of Rights (Private Property Rights) Amendment Bill – First Reading," at www .parliament.nz/en-nz/pb/debates/debates/47HansD_20050511_ 00001261/new-zealand-bill-of-rights-private-property-rights-amendment.

North, Douglas C. 1990. *Institutions, Institutional Change, and Economic Performance*. New York: Cambridge University Press.

North, Douglass, John Joseph Wallis, and Barry R. Weingast, eds. 2009. *Violence and Social Orders: A Conceptual Framework for Interpreting Recorded History*. New York: Cambridge University Press.

Novais, Andréa. 2012. "Types of Corruption in Brazil," at http:// thebrazilbusiness.com/article/types-of-corruption-in-brazil.

Nugent, Jeffrey B. and James A. Robinson. 2010. "Are Factor Endowments Fate?," *Revista de Historia Económica /Journal of Iberian and Latin American Economic History*, 28:45–82.

Nunes, Ana Bela. "Education and Economic Growth in Portugal: A Simple Regression Approach," at www.repository.utl.pt/bitstream/10400.5/ 1013/1/EDUCATION%20AND%20ECONOMIC%20GROWTH .pdf.

Nunn, Nathan. 2007. "Slavery, Inequality, and Economic Development: An Examination of the Engerman–Sokoloff Hypothesis," at http://scholar .harvard.edu/files/nunn/files/domestic_slavery.pdf.

Nunn, Nathan and Leonard Wantchekon. 2011. "The Slave Trade and the Origins of Mistrust in Africa," *American Economic Review*, 101 (December):3221–3252.

OECD (Organization for Economic Cooperation and Development). 1999. *Denmark*, at www.oecd.org/edu/innovation-education/1908360.pdf.

2006. *Mauritius*, at www.oecd.org/dev/36741476.pdf.

2013. *Country Note: Education at a Glance 2013 Estonia*, at www.oecd .org/edu/Estonia_EAG2013%20Country%20Note.pdf.

2014. "Education Policy Outlook: Portugal," atwww.oecd.org/edu/ EDUCATION%20POLICY%20OUTLOOK_PORTUGAL_EN.pdf.

Okano, Kaori and Motonori Tsuchiya. 1999. *Education in Contemporary Japan: Inequality and Diversity*. Cambridge: Cambridge University Press.

Olken, Benjamin A. and Rohini Pande. 2012. "Corruption in Developing Countries," *Annual Review of Economics*, 4:479–505.

Olson, Mancur. 1993. "Dictatorship, Democracy, and Development," *American Political Science Review*, 87:567–576.

Olsson, Ola and Douglas A. Hibbs, Jr. 2005. "Biogeography and Long-run Economic Development," *European Economic Review*, 49:909–938.

Oslo Times. n.d. "History of Education in Norway," at http://theoslotimes .com/article/history-of-education-in-norway.

Owsiak, Stanislaw. 2003. "The Ethics of Tax Collection," *Finance and Common Good*, 13/14:65–77.

Pahud de Motranges, Rene. ND. "Religion and the Secular State in Switzerland," at www.iclrs.org/content/blurb/files/Switzerland.1.pdf.

Palma, Nuno and Jaoime Reis. 2012. "A Tale of Two Regimes: Educational Achievement and Institutions in Portugal, 1910–1950," at www.lse.ac.uk/economicHistory/seminars/ModernAndComparative/ papers2011–12/A-tale-of-two-regimes.pdf.

Papava, Vladimer. 2006. "The Political Economy of Georgia's Rose Revolution," *East European Democratization*, 657–667.

Pereirinha, Jose. 1995. "Poverty and Social Exclusion in Portugal: A General Overview of Situations, Processes, and Policies," *Druzhoslovne*

Rezprave, 11:169–182, at www3.mruni.eu/ojs/social-work/article/view/1900/1717.

Persson, Torsten, Guido Tabellini, and Francesco Trebbi. 2003. "Electoral Rules and Corruption," *Journal of the European Economic Association*, 1:958–989.

Peterson, Brenton D. 2016. "Kikuyu or Kenyan? Government Service Provision and the Salience of Ethnic Identities," at http://papers.ssrn.com/sol3/papers.cfm?abstract_id=2773896.

Pingtjin, Thum. 2013. "The Fundamental Issue is Anti-Colonialism, Not Merger: Singapore's 'Progressive Left', Operation Coldstore, and the Creation of Malaysia," Asia Research Institute Working Paper Series No. 211, at www.ari.nus.edu.sg/wps/wps13_211.pdf.

Portugal–Education, at http://countrystudies.us/portugal/61.htm.

Premo, Bianca. 2005. *Children of the Father King: Youth, Authority, and Legal Minority in Colonial Lima*. Chapel Hill, NC: University of North Carolina Press.

Putnam, Robert. 1993. *Making Democracy Work: Civic Traditions in Modern Italy*. Princeton: Princeton University Press.

Putterman, Louis. 2008. "Agriculture, Diffusion, and Development: Ripple Effects of the Neolithic Revolution," *Economica*, 75:729–748.

Qatar – Educational System – Overview. n.d. at http://education.stateuniversity.com/pages/1244/Qatar-EDUCATIONAL-SYSTEM-OVERVIEW.html.

Quah, Jon S.T. 2001. "Singapore: Meritocratic City-State." In John Funston, ed., *Government and Politics in Southeast Asia*. Singapore: Institute of Southeast Asia Studies.

2013. "Curbing Corruption and Enhancing Trust in Government." In Jianhong Liu, Bill Hebenton, and Susyan Jou, eds., *Handbook of Asian Criminology*. New York: Springer.

Radio Australia. 2012. "Brunei – 50 years Under Emergency Rule," at www.radioaustralia.net.au/international/radio/program/connect-asia/brunei-50-years-under-emergency-rule/1060346.

Ramirez, Francisco O. and Boli, John 1987. "The Political Construction of Mass Schooling: European Origins and Worldwide Institutionalization," *Sociology of Education*, 60:2–17.

Rankin, Monica. 2012. *The History of Costa Rica*. Santa Barbara. CA: Grenwood Press.

Robertson, Claire C. 1977. "The Nature and Effects of Differential Access to Education in Ga Society," *Africa: Journal of the International African Institute*, 47:208–219.

Rolwing, Kevin F. 1997. "Spanish Education Reshaped by Political Changes, Economic Realities," *World Education News and Reviews*, 10:19–23, at www.wes.org/ewenr/02july/piaddition.pdf.

Romero, Simon. 2016. "How Web of Corruption Ensnared Brazil," *New York Times* (April 4):A1, A6.

Rothstein, Bo. 2017. "The Relevance of Comparative Politics." In Daniele Caramani, ed., *Comparative Politics*. Oxford: Oxford University Press.

2015. "The Moral, Economic, and Political Logic of the Swedish Welfare State." In Jon Pierre, ed., *The Oxford Handbook of Swedish Politics*, 69–86. Oxford: Oxford University Press.

2011. *The Quality of Government: Corruption, Social Trust and Inequality in a Comparative Perspective*. Chicago: The University of Chicago Press.

2005. *Social Traps and the Problem of Trust*. Cambridge: Cambridge University Press.

Rothstein, Bo, Marcus Samanni, and Jan Teorell. 2012. "Explaining the Welfare State: Power Resources vs. the Quality of Government," *European Political Science Review*, 4 (1):1–28. doi: 10.1017/s1755773911000051.

Rothstein, Bo and Jan Teorell. 2015. "Getting to Sweden, Part II: Breaking with Corruption in the Nineteenth Century." *Scandinavian Political Studies*, 38(3):238–254

2012. "Defining and Measuring Quality of Government." Pp. 6–26 in *Good Government: The Relevance of Political Science*, edited by S. Holmberg and B. Rothstein. Cheltenham: Edward Elgar.

Rothstein, Bo and Eric M. Uslaner. 2005. "All for All: Equality, Corruption, and Social Trust," *World Politics*, 58:41–72.

Rueschemeyer, Dietrich, Evelyne Huber Stephens, and John D. Stephens. 1992. *Capitalist Development and Democracy*. Chicago: University of Chicago Press.

Ruhil, Anirudh V.S. and Pedro J. Camoes. 2003. "What Lies Beneath: The Political Roots of State Merit Systems," *Journal of Public Administration Research and Theory*, 13:27–42.

Sachs, Jeffrey D. 2012. "Reply to Acemoglu and Robinson's Response to My Book Review," at http://jeffsachs.org/2012/12/reply-to-acemoglu-and-robinsons-response-to-my-book-review/.

Sachs, Jeffrey D. and Pia Malaney. "The Economic and Social Burden of Malaria," *Nature*, 415 (February 7):680–685.

Sachs, Jeffrey D. and Andrew M. Warner. 1997. "Natural Resource Abundance and Economic Growth," Center for International Development, Harvard University, at www.cid.harvard.edu/ciddata/warner_files/natresf5.pdf.

Saez, Emmanuel and Gabriel Zucman. 2014. "Wealth Inequality in the United States Since 1913: Evidence from Capitalized Income Tax Data," National Bureau of Economic Research Working Paper, at www.nber.org/papers/w20625.

Sahlberg, Pasi. 2007. "Education Policies for Raising Student Learning: the Finnish Approach," *Journal of Education Policy*, 22:147–171.

	2011. "The Professional Educator: Lessons from Finland," *American Educator* (Summer):34–38.

Sainsbury, Maree. 2003. *Moral Rights and Their Application in Australia*. Leichhardt, NSW: Federation Press.

Salvatore, Fillippo. 2011. "History of Italy (From 1945 to the present): Part 4 of 4," at: www.panoramitalia.com/en/arts-culture/history/history-italy-1945-present/385/#sthash.UWaiwaU0.dpuf.

Schilling, Heinz. 1983. "The Reformation in the Hanseatic Cities," *The Sixteenth Century Journal*, 14:443–456.

Schwartzman, Simon. 2003. "The Challenges of Education in Brazil," available at www.drclas.harvard.edu/files/Simon-Schwartzman-Challenges-of-Education-in-Brazil.pdf.

Scott, James C. 1972. *Comparative Political Corruption*. Englewood Cliffs, NJ: Prentice-Hall.

Sen, Amartya. 2011. "Quality of Life: India vs. China." *New York Review of Books* LVIII(2011:25):44–47.

Shepherd, Jessica. 2010. "World Education Rankings: Which Country Does Best at Reading, Maths and Science?," at www.theguardian.com/news/datablog/2010/dec/07/world-education-rankings-maths-science-reading.

Slade, Gavin. 2012. "Georgia's War on Crime: Creating Security in a Post-Revolutionary Context," *European Security*, 21:37–56.

Smith, D.M. 1997. *Modern Italy. A Political History*. New Haven: Yale University Press.

Sokoloff, Kenneth L. and Stanley L. Engerman. 2002. "Factor Endowments, Inequality, and Paths of Development among New World Economies," National Bureau of Economic Research Working Paper 9259, at www.nber.org/papers/w9259.

	2000. "History Lessons: Institutions, Factor Endowments, and Paths of Development in the New World,' *Journal of Economic Perspectives*, 14:217–232.

Solt, Frederick. 2009. "Standardizing the World Income Inequality Database," *Social Science Quarterly*, 90:231–242.

Sombart, Werner. 1976. *Why Is There No Socialism in the United States?* White Plains: M.E. Sharpe.

Spain Exchange Country Guide. ND. "Religious Beliefs in Belgium," at www.studycountry.com/guide/BE-religion.htm.

Spolaore, Enrico and Romain Wacziarg. 2013. "Long-Term Barriers to Economic Development," National Bureau of Economic Research Working Paper 19361 www.nber.org/papers/w19361.

StateUniversity.com. n.d. "Denmark – History and Background," at http://education.stateuniversity.com/pages/368/Denmark-HISTORY-BACKGROUND.html.

Steffens, Lincoln. 1931. *The Autobiography of Lincoln Steffens*. New York: Literary Guild.

Stenquist, Bjarne. 2009. *Den vita segerns svarta skugga: Finland och inbördeskriget 1918*. Stockholm: Atlantis.

"Story: Country Schooling." n.d. www.teara.govt.nz/en/country-schooling/page-1.

Strauss, Gerald. 1988. "The Social Function of Schools in the Lutheran Reformation in Germany," *History of Education Quarterly*, 28: 191–206.

Sustainable Governance Indicators. 2014. "Portugal," at www.sgi-network .org/2014/Portugal/Social_Policies.

Svallfors, Stefan. 2013. "Government Quality, Egalitarianism, and Attitudes to Taxes and Social Spending: a European Comparison," *European Political Science Review*, 5:363–380.

Szyliowicz, Joseph S. 1969. "Education and Political Development in Turkey, Egypt, and Iran," *Comparative Education Review*, 13:150–166.

"Switzerland in the 19th Century." n.d. at www.eda.admin.ch/content/dam/PRS-Web/en/dokumente/der-bundesstaat-im-19-jahrhundert_EN.pdf.

Taylor, Mark Zachary. 2016. *The Politics of Innovation*. New York: Oxford University Press.

Ting, Michael M., James M. Snyder Jr., Shigeo Hirano, and Olle Folke. 2013. "Elections and Reform: The Adoption of Civil Service Systems in the U.S. States," *Journal of Theoretical Politics*, 25:365–387.

Tingsten, Herbert. 1969. *Gud och fosterlandet: studier i hundra års skolpropaganda*. Stockholm: Norstedt.

Teorell, Jan, and Bo Rothstein. 2015. "Getting to Sweden, Part I: War and Malfeasance, 1720–1850," *Scandinavian Political Studies* 38(3):217–237.

Transparency International. 2014. "Transparency International Corruption Perceptions Index 2014," at www.ey.com/Publication/vwLUAssets/EY-transparency-international-corruption-perceptions-index-2014/$FILE/EY-transparency-international-corruption-perceptions-index-2014.pdf.

Treisman, Daniel. 2007. "What Have We Learned About the Causes of Corruption from Ten Years of Cross-National Empirical Research?," *Annual Review of Political Science*, 10:211–244 DOI: 10.1146/annurev.polisci.10.081205.095418

UNESCO. 2006. *World Data on Education: Barbados*, 6th edition, at www .ibe.unesco.org/sites/default/files/Barbados.pdf.

2008. *World Data on Education: Mauritius*, 6th edition, at www
.ibe.unesco.org/Countries/WDE/2006/SUB-SAHARAN_AFRICA/
Mauritius/Mauritius.pdf.

2010/11. *World Data on Education: Bhutan*, at www.ibe.unesco.org/
fileadmin/user_upload/Publications/WDE/2010/pdf-versions/Bhutan
.pdf.

University of Chicago Chronicle. 1997. "New Look at Evolution of Education," 16 (June 12), at http://chronicle.uchicago.edu/970612/education
.shtml.

Uslaner, Eric M. 2002. *The Moral Foundations of Trust*. New York: Cambridge University Press.

2006. "Tax Evasion, Trust, and the Strong Arm of the Law." In Nicholas
Hayoz and Simon Hug, eds., *Trust, Institutions, and State Capacities: A
Comparative Study*. Bern: Peter Lang AG, available at www.bsos.umd
.edu/gvpt/uslaner/uslanerstgallen.pdf.

2008. *Corruption, Inequality, and the Rule of Law*. New York: Cambridge
University Press.

Uslaner, Eric M. and Mitchell Brown. 2005. "Inequality, Trust, and Civic
Engagement," *American Politics Research*, 33:868–894.

Vanhanen, Tatu. 1997. *Prospects of Democracy: A Study of 172 Countries*.
London: Routledge.

Van Zandem, Jan Luiten, Joerg Baten, Peter Foldvari, and Bas van Leeuwen.
2011. "The Changing Shape of Global Inequality 1820–2000: Exploring a New Dataset," Center for Global Economic History, University of
Utrecht, at www.cgeh.nl/working-paper-series/.

van de Walle, Francine. 1980. "Education and the Demographic Transition
in Switzerland," *Population and Development Review*, 63:463–472.

Vick, Malcolm. 1992. "Community, State and the Provision of Schools
in Mid-Nineteenth Century Australia," *Australian Historical Studies*,
25:51.

Voigtländer, Nico and Hans-Joachim Voth. 2011. "Persecution Perpetu-
ated: The Medieval Origins of Anti-Semitic Violence in Nazi Germany."
National Bureau of Economic Research, NBER Working Paper 17113,
Cambridge, MA.

Volansky, Ami. 2007. "The Israeli Education System," prepared for the *International Encyclopedia of Education*, at www.tau.ac.il/~danib/israel/
SNR2009-Education(English).pdf.

Wallis, John Joseph. 2006. "The Concept of Systemic Corruption in American History." In Edward L. Glaeser and Claudia Goldin, eds., *Corruption and Reform: Lessons from America's Economic History*. Chicago:
University of Chicago Press.

Walker, Francis A. Superintendent of Census. 1872. *The Statistics of the Population of the United States*. Washington: Government Printing Office.

Wängnerud, Lena. 2012. "Why Women Are Less Corrupt than Men." Pp. 212–232 in *Good Government: The Relevance of Political Science*, edited by S. Holmberg and B. Rothstein. Cheltenham: Edward Elgar.

Weber, Eugen. 1976. *Peasants into Frenchmen: The Modernization of Rural France 1870–1914*. Stanford, CA: Stanford University Press.

Welzel, Christian. 2013. *Freedom Rising*. New York: Cambridge University Press.

West, Edwin. 1996. "The Spread of Education Before Compulsion: Britain and America in the Nineteenth Century," at https://fee.org/articles/the-spread-of-education-before-compulsion-britain-and-america-in-the-nineteenth-century/.

Wiebe, Robert H. 1967. *The Search for Order*. New York: Hill and Wang.

Wietzke, Frank-Borge. In press. "Long-term Consequences of Colonial Institutions and Human Capital Investments: Sub-national Evidence from Madagascar," *World Development*.

Williamson, Jeffrey G. 2010. "Five Centuries of Latin American Income Inequality," *Revista de Historia Económica /Journal of Iberian and Latin American Economic History*, 28:227–252.

  2015. "Latin American Inequality: Colonial Origins, Commodity Booms, or a Missed 20th Century Leveling?" National Bureau of Economic Research Working Paper 20915, available at www.nber.org/papers/w20915.

Witte, Els, Jan Craeybeckx, and Alain Meynen. 2009. *Political History of Belgium: From 1830 Onwards*. Brussels, Belgium: ASP-Academic and Scientific Publishers.

Wolfinger, Raymond E. 1972. "Why Political Machines Have Not Withered Away and Other Revisionist Thoughts," *Journal of Politics*, 34:365–398.

Woodberry, Robert D. 2012. "The Missionary Roots of Liberal Democracy," *American Political Science Review*, 106:244–274.

World Bank. 2012. *Fighting Corruption in Public Services: Chronicling Georgia's Reforms*, at www-wds.worldbank.org/external/default/WDSContentServer/WDSP/IB/2012/01/20/000356161_20120120010932/Rendered/PDF/664490PUB0EPI0065774B09780821394755.pdf.

  n.d. "Implementation of Education Reforms in Mauritius," at http://siteresources.worldbank.org/INTAFRREGTOPEDUCATION/Resources/444659–1232743000972/Implementation_Education_Reform_Mauritius.pdf.

World Economic Forum. 2014. *The Global Competitiveness Report 2013–2014*, at http://www3.weforum.org/docs/WEF_GlobalCompetitivenessReport_2013–14.pdf.

Wright, Gavin. 2003. "Slavery and American Agricultural History," *Agricultural History*, 77:527–552.

Ylikangas, Heikki. *1995. Vägen till Tammerfors. striden mellan röda och vita i finska inbördeskriget 1918.* Stockholm: Atlantis.

You, Jong-sung. 2005. *A Comparative Study of Income Inequality, Corruption, and Social Trust: How Inequality and Corruption Reinforce Each Other and Erode Social Trust*, Unpublished Ph.D. dissertation (draft), Department of Government, Harvard University.

2008. "Inequality and Corruption: The Role of Land Reform in Korea, Taiwan, and the Philippines." Presented at the Annual Conference of the Association for Asian Studies, Atlanta, April, available at http://irps.ucsd.edu/assets/001/503066.pdf.

2013. "The Origins of the Developmental State in South Korea: A Reexamination of the Park Chung-hee Myth." Presented at the Annual Meeting of the International Studies Association, San Francisco, CA, April.

2015. *Democracy, Inequality, and Corruption.* New York: Cambridge University Press.

n.d. "1nequality and Corruption: The Role of Land Reform in Korea, Taiwan, and the Philippines." Unpublished paper, University of California–San\sDiego, available at http://irps.ucsd.edu/assets/001/503066.pdf.

You, Jong-sung and Sanjeev Khagram. 2005. "A Comparative Study of Inequality and Corruption," *American Sociological Review*, 70:136–157.

Young, Cristobal. 2009. "Religion and Economic Growth in Western Europe: 1500–2000," at http://web.stanford.edu/~cy10/public/Religion_and_Economic%20Growth_Western_Europe.pdf.

Yu, Wenxuan. 2015. "Anti-Corruption Strategies in Singapore: Demystifying the Singapore Model." In Yahong Zhang and Cecilia Lavena, eds., *Government Anti-Corruption Strategies: A Cross-Cultural Perspective.* Boca Raton, FL: CRC Press.

Zanganeh, Lila Azam. 2013. "Has the Great Library of Timbuktu Been Lost?," *The New Yorker* (January 29) available at www.newyorker.com/news/news-desk/has-the-great-library-of-timbuktu-been-lost.

Ziegler, Rolf. 1998. "Trust and the Reliability of Expectations," *Rationality and Society*, 10:427–450.

Index